GRE® Vocabulary

In Practice

Erica L. Meltzer

◤THE CRITICAL READER
New York

ISBN-13: 978-0-9975178-3-5
ISBN-10: 0997517832

ALSO BY ERICA MELTZER

The Ultimate Guide to SAT® Grammar & Workbook

SAT® Vocabulary: A New Approach (with Larry Krieger)

The Critical Reader: The Complete Guide to SAT® Reading

The Critical Reader: AP® English Language and Composition Edition

The Complete Guide to ACT® English

The Complete Guide to ACT® Reading

The Complete GMAT® Sentence Correction Guide

Table of Contents

. . . .

Introduction

Just as I was wrapping the first draft of this book, I had a couple of chance encounters that made me reconsider some of my assumptions about how students go about prepping for the revised GRE®. The first encounter occurred in, of all places, a clothing store. The clerk was young man in his early 20s; he was unusually outgoing and friendly, and he seemed determined to strike up a conversation. We exchanged pleasantries, and he asked me what I did for work. To my surprise, when I mentioned that I wrote test-prep books, his face lit up. "Ever write anything for the GRE?" he asked. Needles to say, that got my attention. As it turned out, he was planning to apply for his master's in Engineering. I told him about my almost-finished manuscript of this book. In turn, he told me about the vocabulary app he was using. I hadn't done much research on GRE apps, so I asked him whether his had been updated for the post-2012 test – that is, whether it was just designed to teach vocabulary, or whether it also covered the various types of applications. At this, he looked a bit puzzled, so I explained the ways in which vocabulary was tested on the current GRE as opposed to the pre-2012 version. What followed was a lively conversation about the state of standardized testing and the attempts of various testing organizations to make their exams more "relevant." He struck me as very bright and curious, so I was surprised that he was unaware of the changes that had been made to the test. At the time, I assumed his situation was merely an anomaly.

Several weeks later, however, I had yet another encounter with a prospective graduate student, this one applying for Nursing. She had already taken the test but, like the previous student, she had prepared for the vocabulary section with an app. Although she had found the study process enjoyable, her verbal score had been middling.

Given that those two separate conversations had occurred by chance, at separate times, and with complete strangers, I started to wonder how many other students were studying for the GRE in a way that did not fully prepare them for the demands of the test. Ironically, it was only then, *after* I had finished writing hundreds of practice GRE vocabulary question, that I became fully aware of the need for a book devoted to strategy and practice, as opposed to a traditional vocabulary book with long lists of words and definitions.

To be clear, I am in no way denying the importance of studying vocabulary. If vocabulary is not your strong suit, or if you are not a native English speaker, then you may in fact need to spend a significant amount of time learning new words. The problem is that just memorizing dozens, or hundreds, or even thousands of definitions is probably not sufficient to ace to the fill-in-the-blank vocabulary portion of the current exam. A colleague of mine used to describe the Math section of the pre-2016 SAT as a "math-flavored test," and I think it's equally appropriate to describe the GRE as a vocabulary-flavored one. (It's no coincidence that both tests were produced by ETS.)

So although a strong knowledge of challenging vocabulary is still necessary to excel on the GRE, the words themselves are only half the story. Text Completions and Sentence Equivalences are essentially miniature logic puzzles designed to test how well you can apply your vocabulary knowledge. The focus is much less on how many esoteric definitions you have learned (and, to be fair, some of the words on the old GRE were pretty esoteric) than on how well you can use definitions and relationships between ideas to draw logical inferences about intended meanings. *As a result, the most challenging questions may sometimes not contain particularly difficult words at all.* To be properly prepared for these questions, you must become comfortable with a wide range of strategies, including reading forwards and backwards; navigating double negatives; distinguishing between positive/negative ideas and positive/negative words; identifying subtle context cues in the absence of clear transitions; working through blanks out of order; and resisting the tendency to make assumptions based on incomplete information. These are hardly things that can be learned from conventional vocabulary books.

The other reason that learning to work with Text Completions and Sentence Equivalences is so potentially valuable is that many sentences/passages essentially function as condensed versions of the types of arguments you will encounter on the passage-based reading: one scholar believes x, whereas other scholars believe y; scientist x went against the conventional wisdom and no one believed her, but now her views are becoming mainstream; new research shows that a once-controversial theory may in fact be correct, so people are beginning to take it seriously. Learning to identify the underlying structure and characteristics of these common argument "templates" can help you decipher longer, more complex passages more effectively elsewhere on the GRE. Not coincidentally, these correspond to the types of arguments you are likely to encounter on a regular basis in graduate school, regardless of your field of study. In that regard, it seems fair to call the GRE a relevant test.

~Erica Meltzer

Part 1

....

Question Types and Strategies

In this section:

- Introduction to vocabulary question types
- General rules for working through questions
- Key transitional words and phrases
- Playing positive and negative
- Using prefixes and roots
- Guided practice questions
- High-frequency word lists

Overview of GRE Vocabulary Questions

There are two types of GRE fill-in-the blank vocabulary questions: Text Completions and Sentence Equivalences.

1) Text completions

Text Completions range from single sentences to short paragraphs and contain one, two, or three blanks. Answers can consist of either single words or short phrases.

When a sentence contains only one blank, you will be given five answer choices. When a sentence contains two or three blanks, you will be given six or nine choices respectively – three options for each blank.

While all of the answers must work together to produce a logical sentence or paragraph, each individual answer can be selected independently.

The city of Genoa (i) _____ rapidly after its defeat at the battle of Chioggia in 1380, eventually losing its (ii) _____ and falling under foreign rule.

Blank (i)	Blank (ii)
(A) thrived	(D) autonomy
(B) declined	(E) uniqueness
(C) persevered	(F) urbanity

In the sentence above, choice (B), *declined*, is the only word consistent with the idea of defeat, so (B) is the logical answer for Blank (i). The selection of (B) does not, however, influence the letter of the correct answer for Blank (ii). Choices (D), (E), and (F) must be considered separately.

For Blank (ii), the phrase *falling under foreign rule* indicates that Genoa was no longer independent, so the correct answer must mean something like independence. That is the definition of *autonomy*, so (D) is correct.

2) Sentence Equivalences

Sentence Equivalences consist of a single sentence with one blank and are accompanied by six answer choices. These questions ask you to identify two words that fit logically in the blank, and that produce the same meaning when plugged into the sentence.

Although the correct words are usually synonyms, they can also have markedly different meanings. In case of the latter, you must make sure to focus on the overall meaning that results when the words are plugged in, rather than on the independent meanings of the words themselves.

It's a subtle distinction, and it can take a bit of wrangling to wrap your head around, so let's look at an example of each scenario.

> Mostly known for his depictions of bustling London streets, Dickens was equally inspired by the far more _____ mountains of the Swiss countryside.
>
> [A] expansive
> [B] tranquil
> [C] lucid
> [D] serene
> [E] provincial
> [F] uncouth

The sentence sets up a contrast between the *bustling London streets* and *the far more _____ mountains of the Swiss countryside*. Logically, the blank must be filled with words indicating that the Swiss mountains were the opposite of the bustling city – something like calm or peaceful. *Tranquil* and *serene* are a close pair of synonyms meaning just that, so [B] and [D] are correct. Straightforward, right?

Now, however, consider this version of the question.

> Mostly known for his depictions of bustling London streets, Dickens was equally inspired by the far more _____ mountains of the Swiss countryside.
>
> [A] expansive
> [B] tranquil
> [C] lucid
> [D] bucolic
> [E] provincial
> [F] uncouth

This time, the answer choices include one option meaning calm/peaceful, but there is no longer a synonym for that word. As a result, the focus must shift to which other option creates the same basic meaning when it is plugged into the sentence. In this case, that word is *bucolic*, which means rustic, or related to country living. Although it does not have the exact same meaning as *tranquil*, it accurately conveys the idea that the Swiss mountains were the opposite of the bustling (busy and energetic) city. *Expansive* (large), *lucid* (clear), *provincial* (small-minded), and *uncouth* (rude, unrefined) all do not fit.

How to Work Through Vocabulary Questions

Although text completions and sentence equivalences do require slightly different approaches, there are nevertheless some basic strategies that apply to both question types and that you can use to reduce your chances of overlooking crucial information or making careless errors.

Note that these steps are useful even if you are a champion reader with a stellar vocabulary. To reiterate: GRE vocabulary questions, particularly two- and three-blank text completions, are also designed to test logical reasoning skills. As a result, sentences/passages can sometimes be quite confusing. It is likely that you will encounter questions in which you understand every single word but cannot seem to wrap your head around what the sentence or passage is actually *saying*. Working systematically ensures you do not inadvertently overlook key information, especially as questions become more challenging and you grow more fatigued. It also ensures you do not become overly dependent on the answer choices, which can sometimes mislead you.

To be sure, you will not always need to follow these steps strictly. When you are able to identify correct answers immediately and securely, there is absolutely no reason to spend time working meticulously through each aspect of the question. But that said, it is advisable to practice working through the steps even on easier questions, simply to get yourself into the habit of doing so. If you are accustomed to working by instinct and are suddenly confronted with a question you cannot answer that way, you are likely to freeze, or guess, or read the question repeatedly without really grasping what it's saying or how to begin answering it. If, on the other hand, you have already internalized a clear process for working through dense material, you are much less likely to fall into these sorts of traps on the actual exam.

1) Read the entire sentence or passage, from start to finish

This may sound like a very obvious piece of advice, but it's not nearly as obvious as you might imagine. It is very tempting to jump to plug in words as you read through the sentence, and in many cases you will in fact be given sufficient information to perform that step accurately.

In some instances, however, you may simply not have enough information to judge the meaning of a given word. Sometimes, a particular assumption may initially seem reasonable but will then be contradicted by information later on. If you've already started thinking in a particular direction, it is usually very difficult to stop and re-work through the question from scratch.

Moreover, without the full context, you are likely to overlook correct answers because you are trying to ascribe an inaccurate meaning to the sentence or passage. When you take the time to understand everything upfront, these errors typically decrease.

2) Identify key words or phrases

Sentences will always contain built-in clues to either the definition of the blank(s), or to the relationship(s) between them. It is important that you identify these clues before plugging in your own words or consulting the answer choices.

Note that as questions become more challenging, key words and phrases tend to become less obvious. While easy questions often contain clear transitions such as *because* and *although*, which clearly indicate relationships between parts of the sentence, hard questions may sometimes contain no transition words at all. In such cases, you will need to infer meanings and relationships based on a variety of subtler clues.

3) Plug in your own words, and jot them down

If one of the words you plugged in, or a close synonym, appears as an answer choice, you can pick that option confidently and ignore the other answers. Make sure to refer back to your notes, though! You do not want to spend time working carefully through a question, only to get sidetracked by plausible-sounding wrong answer.

Note that when a text completion contains multiple blanks, it may be easier to start with the second or third blank and work backwards. In some cases, you may not have enough information to answer the first blank upfront and will have no choice but to work from one or both of the later blanks.

Ideally, you should spend **no more than a couple of seconds** on this step. It doesn't matter if you scribble down an approximate definition or a very simple word. The point is to save time by getting a general idea of what belongs in the blanks, not to come up with the exact answers. If nothing comes to mind, jump to Step 4.

4) Play positive/negative

If you can't think up your own word, try to determine whether the words in the blanks are positive or negative, and jot that information on your scratch paper. **If a blank is positive, draw a (+), e.g., B1+; if it's negative, draw a (–), e.g., B2 –. Do not try to rely on your memory.**

Working this way simplifies the process and prevents you from getting tangled up in nuances and connotations before it is necessary to do so.

Important: If you are unsure whether an answer could fit, keep it. Correct answers may involve words that sound odd to you, or that you would not think to use on your own. Likewise, you should never choose a word only because you know what it means, or eliminate a word because you do not know what it means (or sort of have a vague idea of what it maybe might kind of mean). Your knowledge of a word and your liking of how it sounds in context have zero bearing on whether that word is right or wrong. Zero.

5) Check the answers, in order

Unless you spot the correct answer immediately, in which case you can simply choose it and move on, you should initially consider the choices in order. Working this way keeps you thinking logically and systematically, whereas skipping around increases the chances that you'll miss important information.

If you are unsure of the meaning of a word, try to use roots to determine its meaning or "charge" – that is, whether it is positive or negative. (For a discussion of roots, see p. 21.)

6) Reread the question with the words plugged in

Even if you're certain about your answers, you should take the time to confirm that the words you've chosen truly do make sense in context. When you answer complicated questions, it is all too easy to become confused and select a word that does not really fit. Plugging your choices back into the sentence or paragraph allows you to notice problems you didn't notice the first time around. In addition, you should double-check that your answers to Sentence Equivalences do in fact produce the same meaning when plugged in, especially when they are not exact synonyms.

And remember: what you don't know might not matter.

One of the challenges of GRE vocabulary questions is that despite their relative compactness, they can contain a considerable amount of information – some of which is relevant and some of which is not. It is of course true that in some cases, you will need to know the definitions of challenging words within the sentence or passage itself in order to answer determine the answer(s). Other times, however, the question may provide sufficient information for you to make very reasonable assumptions, even if you do not know the exact definition of every word.

For example:

> Scott Turow's courtroom thrillers are famed for their **visceral** appeal:
> their thrilling and suspenseful plots often _____ intense emotions.

If you don't know what *visceral* means, your first reaction upon reading the sentence might be to pause and turn the word over in your mind, searching for a definition and worrying that you are missing something important.

While this is an understandable reaction, it is also one that will cost you precious time and prevent you from focusing on what you do know. In this case, the phrase *thrilling and suspenseful plots* is more than enough to tell you that the blank must be filled with a word meaning something like provoke or stimulate. The meaning of *visceral* is irrelevant.

In the following pages, we're going to look at a variety of strategies for further breaking down questions and working through them as effectively as possible.

Using Transition Words to Predict Meanings

Whenever you read a sentence or passage, you should always be on the lookout for **transition words**: words that indicate logical relationships between parts of a sentence.

Transitions fall into three main categories: continuers, cause-and-effect words, and contradictors.

1) Continuers are words that indicate an idea is continuing in the direction it began.

Common examples include *and, also, in addition, furthermore, moreover,* and *likewise.*

When continuers appear, the correct answer will most likely express the same idea as another key word or phrase in the sentence/passage. In some cases, it may be a synonym for the key word or phrase, while in others it may be a more extreme form.

For example:

> One of the (i) _____ types of grain, sorghum can withstand harsh conditions and is particularly important in regions where <u>soil is poor</u> **and** resources are (ii) _____.

Let's just focus on the second blank. The fact that the continuer *and* links the blank to the phrase *soil is poor* tells us that the correct word must be consistent with the idea of harsh conditions and poor soil. We might plug in something like *scarce*.

2) Cause, effect, and **explanation** words indicate that someone or something is causing a particular result, or explain why an action is occurring.

Common examples includes *so, therefore, thus, hence, because, as a result,* and *consequently.*

In addition, **colons** and **dashes** are also commonly used to signal explanations.

For example:

> The first astronauts were required to undergo <u>mental</u> evaluation before their flight **because** the _____ danger inherent in space travel was judged to be as important as the physiological one.

The transition *because* indicates that the blank must be filled with a word related to the idea of mental evaluation – it must mean something like psychological.

3) Contradictors introduce opposing or contradictory information.

Common examples include *but, yet, however, nevertheless, although,* and *despite.*

When these words appear, you need to look for **antonyms** for other key words in the sentence, or for words that contrast with other key words in the sentence.

For example:

> **Although** the southern part of Tunisia is covered by the <u>Sahara Desert</u>, the remaining areas of the country contain exceptionally _____ soil and hundreds of miles of coastline.

The contradictor *although* indicates that the two parts of the sentence contain opposite ideas, and *Sahara Desert* tells us that the word in the blank must mean the opposite of dry or barren. We might plug in *healthy* or *good.*

The chart on the following page provides an extensive list of the key transitional words and phrases you are likely to encounter in both Text Completions and Sentence Equivalences.

Common Transitional Words and Phrases

Continuers	Cause-and-Effect	Contradictors
Add Information Also And Furthermore In addition Moreover **Give Example** For example For instance **Define** That is **Emphasize** Even In fact Indeed Not only…but also **Compare** Just as Likewise Similarly	Accordingly As a result As such Because Consequently Hence Since So Therefore Thus	Alternately Alternatively (Al)though But Despite Even so Even though For all* However In contrast In spite of Instead Meanwhile Nevertheless On the contrary On the other hand Otherwise Rather Still Whereas While Yet

*Note that *for all* is a commonly misunderstood transitional phrases. It means despite, not for everything.

You should also be aware that the phrase *all but* means essentially, not everything except.

Parallel Structure

Parallel structure involves the repetition of a particular grammatical structure within a sentence or series of sentences. It is typically used to indicate that particular elements are of equal importance.

When vocabulary questions involve parallelism, the structure of the sentence indicates the definitions of the words in the blanks.

For example:

> The new translation is both (i) _____ and (ii) _____: it captures the <u>clarity</u> of the original without sacrificing any of its <u>subtlety or complexity</u>.

The colon indicates that the second half of the sentence explains the first half. The two blanks linked by *and* in the first half of the sentence must mirror the two ideas in the second half. Blank (i) = clarity, Blank (ii) = subtlety and complexity.

Alternately, the sentence could be phrased in this way:

> Because it captures the clarity of the original without sacrificing any of its subtlety or complexity, the new translation has been praised not only for its (i) _____ but also for its (ii) _____.

In this case, the structure is reversed, but the logic is the same. Because the first half of the sentence presents the ideas of clarity and subtlety, in that order, the two blanks in the second half must follow the same structure.

Double Negatives

One common point of confusion in determining the charges of blanks involves double negatives. When a negative word, e.g., *impossible*, is paired with an additional negation, e.g., *not*, a **positive idea** is created. For example, not impossible = possible.

In such cases, you must be able to keep track of the distinction between the charge of the words themselves and the idea that they convey.

For example:

> Although the logistical challenges and colossal amounts of capital involved in introducing cleaner forms of energy can make such transitions slow and difficult to implement, these factors are **unlikely to preclude** next-generation technologies from playing a _____ role in the United States economy before 2050.

The first half of the sentence indicates that using clean energy is very difficult and expensive. That's a negative idea.

Now, the contradictor *although* indicates that the second half of the sentence must contain a positive idea. That is extremely important to keep in mind because the information immediately before the blank contains a double negative: <u>un</u>likely to preclude.

Preclude = prevent, so *unlikely to preclude* = unlikely to prevent.

In other words, the sentence is talking about a situation that IS likely to occur: clean energy will probably play an in important role in the US economy by the year 2050. As a result, Blank (i) must be filled with a positive word meaning something like important. Although the words used to indicate that meaning are negative, the idea itself is positive.

Second Meanings

One other factor you should keep in mind as you look at answer choices is that you are likely to encounter a variety of common words used in their second or third meaning, e.g., *bent* used to mean inclination, or *table* to mean discontinue.

While these words may or may not be correct when they appear as answer choices, you should not be too quick to discount them. If a word seems too simple to appear on the GRE, chances are it's being used in an alternate definition.

Remember that the goal of the GRE is not primarily to test complicated and obscure vocabulary. On the contrary, ETS deliberately aims to test a variety of types of words, some of which do not conform to the stereotype of a "GRE word" and are unlikely to be found on most traditional vocabulary lists.

For an extensive list of common words with alternate meanings, see p. 70.

Using Roots to Make Educated Guesses

In some cases, a familiarity with roots can allow you to make educated guesses about the meanings of words, and to quickly identify answers likely to be correct. In fact, learning how to take words apart in order to make reasonable assumptions about their meanings is just as important as learning a lot of vocabulary words. If you've simply memorized dozens of definitions, you'll have no way of figuring out whether unfamiliar words fit or not, and will be less certain about some of the answers you choose. Knowing how the components of a word can reveal its meaning gives you much more flexibility and control, which in turn can boost your confidence.

If you've studied a Romance language to a high level, you will be at a significant advantage because many of the words on the GRE have Latin and Greek roots. English words that would be considered fairly esoteric by most people are often similar to extremely common French and Spanish and Italian words. For example, English-speakers generally don't go around using words like *arboreal*, but if you know that *arbre*, *arbòl*, or *albero* means tree, you can probably figure out that *arboreal* has something to do with trees.

Likewise, the definition of a word like *concatenation* is essentially the sum of its parts: the prefix CON- means with, and *catena* means chain in Italian. So *concatenation* literally means with a chain. And indeed, a concatenation is a series of linked things or events.

The charts beginning on p. 58 provide an extensive list of common roots that you are likely to encounter on the GRE.

Let's look at an example:

> Because he has authored numerous books that draw upon a wide range of fields, including many that he has never formally studied, Jared Diamond has earned a reputation as _____.

| (A) an autodidact |
| (B) a pedant |
| (C) a polymath |
| (D) an iconoclast |
| (E) a pioneer |

It's relatively easy to figure out that the word in the blank goes along with the idea of doing a lot of different things: Diamond has written books in a *wide range of fields*, including *many that he has never formally studied*.

If you know that the root POLY- means many, you can make a very educated guess that (C) is correct, even if you do not know the meanings of the other answers. The question is essentially testing your ability to make a reasonable assumption based on an understanding of how words are constructed.

One more:

In his paintings, Edvard Munch (i) _____ outside influences with his own original visions, blurring the line between originality and (ii) _____.

Blank (i)	Blank (ii)
(A) synthesized	(D) verisimilitude
(B) defiled	(E) iconoclasm
(C) acclimated	(F) mimesis

The key phrase *blurring the line* indicates that Munch's work integrated or blended outside works with his own original visions, so Blank (i) must be a synonym for one of those terms. That points directly to (A).

For Blank (ii), however, things are less straightforward. The correct word must mean the opposite of originality, something like copying, but the answers are more challenging. This is where roots are useful.

VER- means truth, which is exactly the opposite of what you want. *Iconoclasm* (attacking accepted norms) may be associated with artists, but it does not fit in context. This answer plays on associative interference, a phenomenon in which the mind creates an unsupported connection between two loosely related ideas. *Mimesis*, however, contains the root MIM-, which is like *mimic* or *mime*. That fits, so (F) is correct.

One potential **difficulty** that can arise when working with roots involves linguistic "drift:" words that have evolved to mean something different from what their components would suggest.

For every straightforward relationship between a word and its subparts, e.g., *implacable* (unforgiving, unappeasable: IM-, not + PLAC-, peace), there is a word whose definition is more than the sum of its components, e.g., *obdurate* (stubborn: OB-, against + DUR-, hard). Furthermore, two roots may be written identically but have different meanings, e.g., PED- can mean either child or foot.

Roots thus tend to be more reliable for playing positive/negative than for determining actual meanings. For example, the jump from *obdurate* to *stubborn* might be too large, but the prefix OB- clearly points to a negative word. Sometimes, just knowing a word's charge may be enough to get you to the answer.

For example, let's try the following exercise:

> Vita Sackville-West's youthful literary output was _____: by the age of eighteen, she had completed eight historical novels, five plays, and a large number of poems.

(A) ob-
(B) ambi-
(C) re-
(D) pro-
(E) de-

The sentence indicates that Sackville-West's output was extensive, so a positive word is required. PRO- is positive, so you can make an educated guess that (D) is correct.

Prefixes Can Also Be Misleading

Even when they are considered in terms of positive/negative, roots and (especially) prefixes can occasionally be deceptive. Words that would seem to be negative can sometimes be positive (e.g., *discretion*), and words that would seem to be positive can be negative (e.g., *profligate*).

For example:

> Though seemingly _____ and even attractive in appearance, nightshade has long been recognized as one of the most poisonous plants grown in the western hemisphere.

> [A] innocuous
> [B] ephemeral
> [C] toxic
> [D] disquieting
> [E] harmless
> [F] duplicitous

The phrase *and even attractive in appearance*, tells us that the word we're looking for must be positive. *Toxic* is clearly wrong, but after that you might be uncertain.

If you just go by the fact that IN- and DIS- are usually negative, you'll end up crossing out the right answer. Although words that begin with those prefixes are generally negative, in this case, *innocuous* is actually negating a negative: IN-, not + NOC-, harm = **not** harmful, which is positive and fits.

Unfortunately, aside from actually knowing what certain words mean, there's no trick to recognizing these exceptions. In general, your best bet is to simply use the rules you know: the exceptions are relatively few, and roots can be important tools. Worrying about the exceptions can hurt you a lot more than it can help.

Putting it Together: Text Completions

While the steps detailed in the previous pages might seem like a lot of information to keep in mind while you are taking the test, it is important to stress that they need not be time-consuming. Ideally, they should be completed in no more than a few seconds, allowing you to work through questions more quickly and confidently. In the initial stages, however, it is likely that you will need to proceed more deliberately than you are accustomed to doing – and possibly more slowly than will feel comfortable.

But to reiterate: when you are confronted with the most challenging text completions, which can be long and quite complex, this type of systematic approach represents your best chance of avoiding the many pitfalls you could encounter.

Let's look at how these steps apply in practice. We're going to start with something straightforward and then work through progressively more challenging material.

Text Completion #1

Some butterfly species are regarded as **pests** <u>because</u> in their larval stages they can (i) _____ crops or trees; <u>however</u>, other species play a more (ii) _____ role because their caterpillars consume harmful insects.

Blank (i)	Blank (ii)
(A) damage	(D) conspicuous
(B) fertilize	(E) nefarious
(C) relinquish	(F) beneficial

The key words *pest* and *because* indicate that Blank (i) must be filled with a negative word meaning harm. (B), *fertilize*, is positive and can thus be eliminated immediately. *Damage* and *relinquish* are both negative, but *relinquish* (give something up) doesn't make sense in context. Only (A) fits with the context of crops and insects.

For Blank (ii), the contradictor *however* sets up a contrast with the first half of the sentence and indicates that the blank must be filled with a positive word meaning something like helpful. (F), *beneficial*, fits perfectly. *Conspicuous* (standing out) can sometimes be positive, but this word does not make sense at all here. Don't get distracted by *nefarious* (cruel). Even if you don't know what that word means, *beneficial* works so well that *nefarious* is irrelevant. But if you feel compelled to consider it anyway, the prefix NE- (not) strongly suggests that *nefarious* is negative.

Important: As a rule, you should always work from what you do know to what you don't know. If a word you know fits perfectly, you should choose it and move on. Worrying about unfamiliar vocabulary will only slow you down and cause you to second-guess yourself.

As text completions increase in difficulty, challenges can manifest themselves in a variety of ways. Most obviously, the overall level of the vocabulary and syntax becomes more sophisticated. While the easiest text completions are written at a level appropriate for a general college-level audience, the most difficult ones are written at the level of an academic article or advanced textbook, and may make use of academic jargon.

As the questions progress, you may also find that you need to read further into a sentence or paragraph for key information. For example, a blank that appears at the beginning of a sentence may not be defined until several lines later. You may also need to determine the meaning of Blank (ii) or Blank (iii) in order to determine the meaning of Blank (i).

Finally, vocabulary words other than those in the answer choices may be indirectly tested – that is, you may need to know the definitions of other challenging words in the sentence in order to determine the meaning of the word(s) in one or more of the blanks.

Let's look at a more challenging example.

Text Completion #2

Some countries fail spectacularly, with a total (i) _____ of all state institutions; others collapse by being utterly unable to (ii) _____ their societies' enormous potential for growth.

Blank (i)	Blank (ii)
(A) abhorrence	(D) forestall
(B) disintegration	(E) venerate
(C) indulgence	(F) tap

This question still gives us a fair amount of information to work with. For Blank (i), the phrase *fail spectacularly* indicates that we're looking for extremely negative word meaning breakdown. *Disintegration* corresponds clearly to the idea of failing spectacularly, and if you stay focused on that fact, you should be fine.

Make sure not to get distracted by (A). *Abhorrence* is also an extremely negative word, but it means loathing, which doesn't fit. Logically, countries fail because they collapse, not because they loathe state institutions. *Indulgence* is positive and does not fit at all.

Now for Blank (ii), which is where things might start to get a little hairy.

Collapse and *utterly unable* are clearly intended to convey a negative idea, but the negation *unable* requires that a positive word be inserted in the blank. Logically, this word must mean something like fulfill: a society that could not fulfill its potential for growth would be at risk for collapse.

If you are not well-versed in the ways of ETS, your first instinct might to wonder what a ridiculous answer like *tap* is doing in a sentence about failing countries. If you know something about how the test works, however, the presence of such a word should be a signal that you need to pay extra-close attention to that option. In fact, *tap* means not only knock lightly but also gain access to, i.e. *tap into*.

That makes sense: countries fail because their resources can't be gotten ahold of or used effectively. *Forestall* (prevent) makes no sense, and *venerate* (greatly respect) does not fit, even though it is positive. (F) is thus the answer to Blank (ii).

Note that it is very difficult to answer this question correctly without either knowing *forestall* and *venerate*, or recognizing the alternate meaning of *tap*.

Now let's try a three-blank example.

Text Completion #3

According to Virginia Woolf, the works of Charlotte and Emily Brontë were _____ by their authors' social and economic disadvantages. This view, however, is disputed by some critics, who argue that the Brontës _____ their position with remarkable deftness. Forced into the marketplace of female labor, they returned home as quickly as they could, and in their retreat from society found the autonomy to _____ their most original work.

Blank (i)	Blank (ii)	Blank (iii)
(A) constrained	(D) undermined	(G) implicate
(B) mitigated	(E) incentivized	(H) ratify
(C) enthralled	(F) exploited	(J) cultivate

The word *disadvantages* strongly suggests that Blank (i) is negative, but you cannot know for certain until you read to the end of the second sentence and consider Blank (ii).

The phrase *remarkable deftness* indicates that Blank (ii) is positive; even if you don't know what *deft* (skillful) means, you can still use the word *remarkable* to make an educated guess that a positive word is required.

The word *however* at the beginning of the second sentence indicates a contrast between that sentence and the previous sentence, telling you that Blank (i) is indeed negative and must mean something like held back or disadvantaged. (When you're plugging in, it's fine to use words that already appear in the sentence.) The only word that fully fits that definition is *constrained*, so the answer to Blank (i) is (A). *Mitigated* means lessened, but it's used in the context of lessening something bad, like pain. It doesn't quite work here. *Enthralled* means fascinated, which doesn't make sense at all.

To plug in your own word for Blank (ii), think about what the two sentences must logically be saying. Basically, Woolf thought that the Brontë sisters' works were hurt by the Brontës poverty, but other people believe that the Brontës used their position to their advantage. As a result, Blank (ii) must mean something like took advantage of. That is the definition of *exploited*, so (F) is correct. *Undermined* (subverted) is negative, and *incentivized* makes no sense whatsoever. Note that *exploit* often has a negative connotation but that the word can be used in a positive/neutral sense as well, as is the case here.

Now for Blank (iii). The phrase *most original work* indicates that this blank must be positive, and that it should mean something like produce. The word that most closely captures that meaning is *cultivate*, making (J) the answer. *Implicate* has a negative connotation. For example, it is common to say that a suspect is implicated in a crime. *Ratify* (formally approve) is positive, but it's something a person does to a document or an agreement – authors cannot ratify their work.

While questions based on longer texts with multiple blanks tend to be more challenging, hard text completions are not necessarily long. They may, for example, consist of only one blank but with multiple answer choices consisting of very challenging words or uncommon alternate meanings. Alternately, they might include answer choices that are not particularly challenging, but in the context of sentences that have very challenging key words or that require a substantial amount of deciphering.

If the sentence itself is straightforward and the answer choices difficult, there is nothing you can do other than study vocabulary and roots; the particular set of words you get is a matter of chance. If the sentence is hard and the answers easy, however, you are must work very carefully to ensure you understand just what the sentence or passage is actually saying. If you jump to plug in the answer choices without doing the groundwork first, you are likely to become confused.

Text Completion #4

The field of tap dance has seldom _____ astonishing solo dancers; it is exceptional tap choreographers that are rare.

(A) scoffed at
(B) wavered about
(C) inquired about
(D) tended toward
(E) wanted for

This question may be short, but it is not exactly straightforward. There's no transition to indicate the relationship between the two parts of the sentence, so figuring out what sort of word belongs in the blank requires a bit more thought upfront than might otherwise be necessary.

The information before the semicolon doesn't provide any real clues about the meaning of the word in the blank, so if you made a quick assumption and plugged in something like *produced*, you'd get nowhere fast. Instead, you must work from the second half of the sentence, the information after the semicolon.

What do we learn there? Exceptional tap *choreographers* are rare.

The first half of the sentence discusses astonishing solo *tap dancers*. That's a different group of artists, so we can reasonably assume that the two sides are presenting contrasting information.

Logically, if the second half of the sentence is saying that exceptional tap choreographers are rare, then the first half must be saying that astonishing tap dancers are *not* rare, i.e. that they are common.

Now we need to be careful again. The first half of the sentence contains a negation, *seldom*. Because that part of the sentence indicates that astonishing tap dancers are common, then the word in the blank must mean something like *lacked*. If something is common, then it is seldom <u>not</u> present, or <u>not</u> lacking.

The correct word must therefore be a synonym for *lacking*.

Scoffed at (looked down on), *wavered about* (went back and forth between), *inquired about*, and *tended toward* all do not fit. And if you're only thinking in terms of first definitions, neither does *wanted for*. Used in its second meaning, however, *wanted for* can indeed mean lacked, so the answer is (E). The sentence is essentially saying that there have traditionally been many exceptional tap dancers, but that exceptional tap choreographers are much harder to find.

Practice Set #1: Identifying Key Information and Plugging In

Now we're going to try an exercise. The following questions are presented without answer choices, in order to remove any temptation to start by looking at the options provided. You are responsible only for identifying the key words and phrases, and for plugging in your own words. (Suggested answers are on p. 32.)

1. In Ancient Egyptian art, human figures are consistently depicted in a rigid and _____ manner; in contrast, animals are often well-observed and lifelike.

    Circle or underline key words

    Definition or (+/-): _____

2. The outwardly _____ appearance of the Afar Triangle, one of the world's most geologically active regions, belies the presence of fiery pools of lava lying just beneath its surface.

    Circle or underline key words

    Definition or (+/-): _____

3. We are generally encouraged to think of movies as common property. Even the term "popular culture" implies a degree of democratic _____ between consumers and producers.

    Circle or underline key words

    Definition or (+/-): _____

4. All of the factors that allowed the Great Barrier Reef to (i) _____ are changing at unprecedented rates and may cause it to (ii) _____ below a crucial threshold from which it cannot recover.

    Circle or underline key words

    Blank (i) definition or (+/-) _____

    Blank (ii) definition or (+/-) _____

5. Sara's ability to mimic her friends is (i) _____ ; her impressions are so convincing that one cannot help but be (ii) _____ while watching them.

    Circle or underline key words

    Blank (i) definition or (+/-) _____

    Blank (ii) definition or (+/-) _____

6. Matisse was both (i) _____ and (ii) _____: he belonged to no officially recognized school of artists and was known for his undeniably odd behavior.

    Circle or underline key words

    Blank (i) definition or (+/-) _____

    Blank (ii) definition or (+/-) _____

7. While most leaf forms are structured to maximize the absorption of sunlight, a minority have adapted to (i) _____ the amount of light they absorb and (ii) _____ exposure to excessive heat.

    Circle or underline key words

    Blank (i) definition or (+/-) _____

    Blank (ii) definition or (+/-) _____

8. Some critics have suggested that the author's study of anthropology (i) _____ his literary style, and indeed, anthropological references often (ii) _____ his works.

    Circle or underline key words

    Blank (i) definition or (+/-) _____

    Blank (ii) definition or (+/-) _____

9. A systemic illness, of which demanding hours and a busy workflow are mere symptoms, (i) _____ the culture of medicine. As is true for any disease, treating the symptoms without (ii) _____ the underlying cause is unlikely to result in a (iii) _____ long-term prognosis.

   Circle or underline key words

   Blank (i) definition or (+/-) _____

   Blank (ii) definition or (+/-) _____

   Blank (iii) definition or (+/-) _____

10. Although antibiotics are designed to (i) _____ dangerous bacteria, there are always a few inherently hardy microbes that survive and (ii) _____, passing on their genes – and grit – to their offspring. As subsequent generations of these microbial gladiators endure further onslaughts of drugs, they evolve even greater (iii) _____, improving their defenses and sometimes spreading their adaptations throughout the microbial universe.

    Circle or underline key words

    Blank (i) definition or (+/-) _____

    Blank (ii) definition or (+/-) _____

    Blank (iii) definition or (+/-) _____

Answers: Text Completion Plug-Ins

1. Key words/phrases: rigid, in contrast
    Blank: negative; fake, artificial

2. Key words/phrases: outwardly, belies, fiery pools of lava
    Blank: positive; calm, peaceful, serene, tranquil

3. Key words/phrases: common property
    Blank: positive; collaboration, collusion

4. Key words/phrases: changing, below, cannot recover
    Blank (i): positive; flourish, thrive
    Blank (ii): negative; drop, decline

5. Key words/phrases: so convincing that
    Blank (i): positive; amazing, extraordinary
    Blank (ii): positive; amazed, impressed

6. Key words/phrases: no officially recognized school of artists, odd behavior
    Blank (i): neutral/positive; independent, a loner
    Blank (ii): negative; strange, odd, eccentric

7. Key words/phrases: while, maximize, excessive heat
    Blank (i): negative; reduce, minimize
    Blank (ii): negative; reduce, minimize

8. Key words/phrases: indeed
    Blank (i): positive; influence
    Blank (ii): positive; appear in

9. Key words/phrases: illness, symptoms, underlying cause, unlikely to result
    Blank (i): negative; afflict, harm, plague
    Blank (ii): positive; understanding
    Blank (iii): positive; good, positive, welcome

10. Key words/phrases: Although antibiotics, dangerous bacteria, survive, improving
    Blank (i): negative; destroy, obliterate, decimate
    Blank (ii): positive; reproduce
    Blank (iii): positive; grit, resilience, toughness

Practice Set #2: Multiple-Choice Text Completions

Now try a multiple-choice set of Text Completions. Make sure to break down each question, the way you did in the previous exercise. If necessary, cover the answer choices until you are ready to look at them. (Answers p. 37)

1. The company's leaders have a poor record of keeping their promises, suggesting that they will be unable to meet the _____ set out by union officials in the new contract.

   Circle or underline key words

   Definition or (+/-): _____

(A) allowances
(B) benefits
(C) stipulations
(D) evaluations
(E) delegations

2. Because music plays a key role in facilitating social functions, researchers are beginning to question whether it truly is as _____ an invention as they once believed it to be.

   Circle or underline key words

   Definition or (+/-): _____

(A) expressive
(B) harmonious
(C) demanding
(D) creative
(E) frivolous

3. The English botanist James Edward Smith demonstrated (i) _____ interest in science, exhibiting an intense (ii) _____ the natural world from the earliest years of his childhood.

Circle or underline key words

Blank (i) definition or (+/-) _____

Blank (ii) definition or (+/-) _____

Blank (i)	Blank (ii)
(A) a halting	(D) distaste for
(B) an inexplicable	(E) curiosity about
(C) a precocious	(F) foundation in

4. Rabindrinath Tagore, who succeeded in modernizing Bengali art, did so largely by (i) _____ the hidebound classical forms whose pervasive influence had (ii) _____ previous attempts at innovation.

Circle or underline key words

Blank (i) definition or (+/-) _____

Blank (ii) definition or (+/-) _____

Blank (i)	Blank (ii)
(A) jettisoning	(D) stymied
(B) perpetuating	(E) fostered
(C) disseminating	(F) chastised

5. Although the two authors disagree about almost everything, they share one stunning feature: both write with an air of absolute moral (i) _____, each convinced that his or her position is (ii) _____.

Circle or underline key words

Blank (i) definition or (+/-) _____

Blank (ii) definition or (+/-) _____

Blank (i)	Blank (ii)
(A) rectitude	(D) cutting edge
(B) authenticity	(E) devoid of merit
(C) outrage	(F) beyond reproach

6. Companies in many industries today must (i) _____ rapid change and rising uncertainty. In such conditions, even well-established brands cannot take their (ii) _____ for granted; there is pressure to keep learning what's new and (iii) _____ what's next.

Circle or underline key words

Blank (i) definition or (+/-) _____

Blank (ii) definition or (+/-) _____

Blank (iii) definition or (+/-) _____

Blank (i)	Blank (ii)	Blank (iii)
(A) linger over	(D) dominance	(G) extricating
(B) advocate for	(E) fallibility	(H) reiterating
(C) contend with	(F) determination	(J) anticipating

7. For centuries, (i) _____ have questioned the authorship of Shakespeare's plays. In fact, the names of no fewer than 50 candidates, including those of Francis Bacon, Christopher Marlowe, and Queen Elizabeth I, have been (ii) _____ as the true writer of the Bard's works. Despite the (iii) _____ of alternatives, scholars have as yet found no evidence to corroborate the idea that Shakespeare's plays should be attributed to anyone other than Shakespeare.

Circle or underline key words

Blank (i) definition or (+/-) _____

Blank (ii) definition or (+/-) _____

Blank (iii) definition or (+/-) _____

Blank (i)	Blank (ii)	Blank (iii)
(A) skeptics	(D) set up	(G) plethora
(B) zealots	(E) put forth	(H) rejection
(C) prognosticators	(F) reined in	(J) paucity

8. In his 1798 "Principle of Population," Malthus argued that populations left (i) _____ expand so far beyond the limits of their resources that a crisis inevitably reduces them to a more (ii) _____ size. The basis of this theory has been fundamentally discredited, primarily as a result of advances in agricultural techniques and reductions in human fertility. Nevertheless, modern proponents believe that population growth will eventually outstrip natural resources, (iii) _____ the notion that Malthus's ideas were pessimistic and inhumane.

Circle or underline key words

Blank (i) definition or (+/-) _____

Blank (ii) definition or (+/-) _____

Blank (iii) definition or (+/-) _____

Blank (i)	Blank (ii)	Blank (iii)
(A) vacant	(D) substantial	(G) investigating
(B) exposed	(E) ungainly	(H) rebuffing
(C) unchecked	(F) modest	(J) traversing

Explanations: Multiple-Choice Text Completions

1. C

Key words/phrases: promises, contract
Blank: positive

The reference to promises suggests that these are things company leaders have difficulty keeping. Logically, those leaders will be unable to meet the ones laid out in the new contract. The blank must therefore be filled with a neutral/positive word conveying the idea of promises or requirements. Although none of the words can be eliminated because it is explicitly negative, only *stipulations* fits the context of the sentence: this word refers specifically to requirements set out by a contract, making (C) correct.

2. E

Key words/phrases: key role, question, once
Blank: negative; unimportant

The fact that music *plays a key role in facilitating social functions* indicates that it is a very important invention. The sentence, however, indicates that researchers are beginning to question how they *once* perceived music. The implication is that they used to believe music was not a particularly important invention but that they now believe it is quite significant. Because the blank must describe how researchers used to view music, the correct word must be negative and mean something like unimportant or trivial. *Expressive, harmonious,* and *creative* are all positive, and *demanding* does not make sense. That leaves *frivolous,* which is a logical choice to describe something unimportant. (E) is thus correct.

3. C, E

Key words/phrases: botanist, earliest years
Blank (i): positive; early, advanced
Blank (ii): positive; interest in, fascination with, love of

The word *botanist* strongly implies that Smith had a positive attitude toward science, and that both blanks will be positive. In addition, Blank (i) must describe a person who was interested in science *from the earliest years of his childhood. Halting* and *inexplicable* are both somewhat negative, whereas *precocious* is both positive and directly consistent with the idea of someone who has an intense interest in a subject at a young age. (C) is thus the answer to Blank (i).

For Blank (ii), *distaste* is negative and can be eliminated. (F) does not make logical sense: a person can really only have a foundation in a subject, not in the natural world. It makes much more sense that a child with a precocious interest in science would exhibit *curiosity about* the natural world. (E) is thus the answer to Blank (ii).

4. A, D

Key words/phrases: hidebound, previous attempts
Blank (i): negative; rejecting
Blank (ii): negative, prevented

The fact that Tagore *succeeded in modernizing Bengali art* implies that he rejected *hidebound classical forms*. Blank (i) must therefore be filled with a negative word that means rejecting. *Jettisoning* is the only option to fit the required definition, so (C) is the answer to Blank (i).

For Blank (ii), if the classical forms were both *hidebound* (rigid, outdated) and *pervasive* (widespread), then it is reasonable to assume that those forms would have prevented previous attempts at innovation. Blank (ii) must therefore be filled with a word meaning something like prevented. *Fostered* implies exactly the opposite, and it is not possible for an art form to *chastise* (scold) anyone or anything – only a person can do that. That leaves *stymied* (blocked), which fits perfectly, making (D) the answer to Blank (ii).

5. A, F

Key words/phrases: convinced, position
Blank (i): positive; certainty, authority, correctness
Blank (ii): positive; correct, perfect

Because the sentence provides more information about Blank (ii), the easiest way to answer this question is to work from Blank (ii) back to Blank (i). Logically, each author would be *convinced that his or her position* was absolutely right, so Blank (ii) must be filled with a strongly positive phrase meaning something like correct or perfect. Something *devoid of merit* (lacking merit) would be the opposite of correct, and *cutting edge* makes no sense at all. Only *beyond reproach* (beyond criticism) logically describes how someone would regard a cherished view. (F) is thus the answer to Blank (ii).

Because the information after the comma explains Blank (i), that blank must be filled with a word consistent with the idea of being beyond reproach – something strong like *authority* or *conviction*. A position defined by moral *authenticity* would not necessarily be above criticism. In fact, it could easily expose weaknesses or shortcomings. *Outrage* is a very strong word, but a position characterized by anger would not necessarily be one that was perfect. In contrast, a person who possessed moral *rectitude* (rightness) would logically believe that his or her position was immune to criticism. (A) is thus the answer to Blank (i).

6. C, D, J

Key words/phrases: uncertainty, well-established, what's next
Blank (i): confront, deal with
Blank (ii): success
Blank (iii): keeping up with, predicting

For Blank (i), the key phrase *rising uncertainty* suggests that the blank should be filled with a negative word implying that companies must learn to manage a changing or unstable environment. *Linger over* makes no sense, and it is highly doubtful that companies would *advocate for* uncertainty, but *contend with* correctly connotes the challenge that companies must face. (C) is thus the answer to Blank (i).

The reference to *well-established brands* suggests that Blank (ii) must take something very positive, e.g., success, for granted. A *fallibility* is a weakness, which is negative and means exactly the opposite of the required word. *Determination* is positive but does not make sense in context. *Dominance* logically describes the position that a well-established brand might occupy in the market, making (D) the answer to Blank (ii).

For Blank (iii), the key phrase *what's next* suggests that the blank must mean something like predicting. *Anticipating* is the only word to match that definition. *Extricating* (disentangling) and *reiterating* (reinforcing) do not make sense at all. (J) is thus the answer to Blank (iii).

7. A, E, G

Key words/phrases: questioned, no fewer than 50 candidates
Blank (i): doubters, skeptics
Blank (ii): suggested
Blank (iii): numerous

Blank (i) must be filled with a word referring to people who *have questioned the authorship of Shakespeare's plays*. By definition, these people must be *skeptics* (doubters), not *zealots* (fanatics) or *prognosticators* (fortune-tellers). (A) is thus the answer to Blank (i). Note that it does not matter if you know the definitions of (B) and (C) as long as you know (A).

Blank (ii) must be filled with a word describing something done to the names of the many possible alternative candidates, in regard to Shakespeare's works. Try plugging in something like *suggested* or *proposed*. The only match is *put forth*, making (E) the answer to Blank (ii).

The key phrase *no fewer than 50 candidates* provides an important clue to Blank (iii). That is a very large number, and the correct answer must describe that fact. *Paucity* (lack) implies exactly the opposite, and *rejection* does not make sense – the contradictor *despite* indicates that the two halves of the sentence must present contrasting ideas, and the second half of the sentence states that scholars *have* thus far rejected the idea of an alternate author. *Plethora* (multitude, excess) logically refers back to the fact that so many alternate candidates have been proposed, making (G) the answer to Blank (iii).

8. C, F, H

Key words/phrases: expand, reduces, proponents
Blank (i): negative; alone, uncontrolled
Blank (ii): positive; smaller, manageable
Blank (iii): negative; rejecting

The key phrase *expand so far beyond the limits of their resources* suggests that the populations in question must be experiencing uncontrolled growth. Blank (i) must convey that idea. It does not make sense to speak of a *vacant* population, and a population left *exposed* would be vulnerable and thus likely to decrease rather than increase. *Check* means kept under control, so something that is *unchecked* is uncontrolled. (C) is thus the answer to Blank (i).

For Blank (ii), if the populations are *reduced*, then their size must be smaller and less out-of-control. *Substantial* and *ungainly* imply exactly the opposite, whereas *modest* accurately describes something of reasonable size. (F) is thus the answer to Blank (ii).

Blank (iii) must be filled with a word indicating the relationship between *modern proponents [of Malthus]* and *the notion that Malthus's ideas were pessimistic and inhumane.* Even though those are very negative qualities, *proponents* would by definition have a positive view of Malthus. Logically, they would reject the idea that Malthus's ideas were pessimistic and inhumane, so Blank (iii) must mean something like rejecting. The only option corresponding to that definition is *rebuffing*, making (H) the answer to Blank (iii).

Putting it Together: Sentence Equivalences

Sentence Equivalences can be both easier and harder than Text Completions: easier because you will never be asked to deal with more than one blank, but harder because you will need to identify not only one correct answer but two. In addition, you must ensure that both answers not only fit the sentence but produce the same meaning.

While that may sound fairly straightforward in principle, the GRE unsurprisingly has a number of tricks up its sleeve. In addition to the true pair of synonyms (or almost-synonyms) that logically fit the sentence, you are also likely to encounter the following:

- Words that are similar to the correct pair of words but that do not produce the same meaning as the correct pair.

- Words that logically fit the sentence but that do not have a close synonym among the answer choices.

- Pairs of words that have the same meaning, or very similar meanings, but that do not logically fit the sentence.

In addition, correct answers may come in the form of "**easy synonym, hard synonym.**" One half of the pair will be a common, everyday word (e.g., *rowdy*), whereas the other half of the pair will be a more exotic synonym (e.g., *obstreperous*).

You may be able to determine the definition of the word in the blank and identify the "easy" synonym without too much trouble, but if the remaining answers contain multiple unfamiliar words, things can get tricky.

Sentence Equivalence #1

The Seri people, indigenous inhabitants of the Mexican state of Sonora, have traditionally had no fixed settlements, choosing to maintain a _____ lifestyle.

[A] delectable
[B] vigorous
[C] peripatetic
[D] tranquil
[E] nomadic
[F] defensive

The key phrase *no fixed settlements* points directly to *nomadic*, so [E] is clearly correct.

But what about the other answer? If you know what *delectable*, *vigorous*, *tranquil*, and *defensive* mean, you can recognize that all of them clearly don't fit. That leaves [C] which must be correct by default.

What would happen, however, if you encountered this version of the question?

> The Seri people, indigenous inhabitants of the Mexican state of Sonora, have traditionally had no fixed settlements, choosing to maintain _____ lifestyle.
>
> [A] a captious
> [B] a sybaritic
> [C] a peripatetic
> [D] a subversive
> [E] a nomadic
> [F] an unorthodox

Now you can get to *nomadic* just as easily, but what about the second word? While you probably know *subversive* and *unorthodox*, there's a smaller chance that you'll know *captious, sybaritic,* and *peripatetic* well enough to either identify the correct answer directly or determine it through process of elimination.

So here we have a problem. *Unorthodox* sort of fits because people who don't live in fixed settlements certainly live an untraditional lifestyle, but that word isn't a synonym for *nomadic.* So one of the remaining choices must be correct. The question is which one.

If you know that the prefix PERI- means around, you might be able to make the connection between *peripatetic* and wandering around, but that's a fairly big leap. Otherwise, you have no choice but to take a wild guess or skip the question entirely.

Still worse, the question could be accompanied by this set of answer choices:

> The Seri people, indigenous inhabitants of the Mexican state of Sonora, have traditionally lacked fixed settlements, choosing to maintain _____ lifestyle.
>
> [A] a captious
> [B] a sybaritic
> [C] a peripatetic
> [D] a subversive
> [E] an itinerant
> [F] an unorthodox

Even if you plug in *nomadic,* you'll immediately get stuck when you look at the answers unless you know what *itinerant* (wandering) means. Furthermore, if you don't know *itinerant,* you're even more likely to get sidetracked by *unorthodox.*

When all else fails, most people's first instinct is to glom onto the words they're most familiar with and "twist" them to make them fit. A key part of studying for the vocabulary portion of the GRE often involves learning to resist this tendency and avoid choosing words that do not truly make sense just for the sake of choosing an answer.

Sentence Equivalences: Working Backwards

If you have an excellent vocabulary as well as a good understanding of how the GRE works, you may also find it useful to work backwards through sentence equivalences, using the choices themselves to spot the likely answers.

Consider this: if two words make up the only pair of synonyms among the answer choices, then they must be correct by default. While you should always plug your answers back into the sentence to be safe, it is sometimes possible to determine the correct answers almost instantaneously, without reading the sentence at all.

Sentence Equivalence #2

In the decades after moveable type was invented, many booksellers _____ machine-printed books because they considered handmade books to be of higher quality.

[A] recommended
[B] rejected
[C] embellished
[D] salvaged
[E] accumulated
[F] eschewed

If you wanted to work meticulously through this question, identifying key words and plugging in definitions, you could probably arrive at the correct answers without too much trouble.

A much faster way of answering the question, however, is to recognize that *rejected* and *eschewed* are the only two words with the same meaning and that they are therefore the only possible answers. The sentence is irrelevant.

Notice that you can still answer the question even without knowing the definition of *eschewed*, provided that you do know (A)-(E) and can recognize that none of those words is a synonym for *rejected*.

Think of it this way: the phrase *because they considered handmade books to be of higher quality* tells us the blank must indicate that booksellers viewed machined-printed books negatively. Looking only at (A)-(E), *rejected* is the only option that clearly fits. As a result, the other correct answer must be (F).

Remember, however, that sentence equivalences may contain, in addition to the correct pair of words, a second <u>incorrect</u> pair – words that have the same meaning but that do not logically complete the sentence. If you jump to pick the first set of synonyms you see, you could get the question wrong.

For example, what if the question was accompanied by this set of answer choices?

> In the decades after moveable type was invented, many booksellers
> _____ machine printed books because they considered handmade
> books to be of higher quality.
>
> [A] compiled
> [B] rejected
> [C] embellished
> [D] salvaged
> [E] accumulated
> [F] eschewed

Although *compiled* and *accumulated* have very similar meanings, neither word logically completes the sentence. If you jumped to pick them without taking the time to plug them back in, you would get the question wrong. Only *rejected* and *eschewed* fit. And the fact that *eschewed* is a less common word than the others is precisely the point.

Exercise: Easy Synonym, Hard Synonym

For each of the words below, select the correct synonym from choices (A)-(E).

1. Liking:

   [A] proclivity
   [B] corollary
   [C] impetus
   [D] acumen
   [E] candor

2. Brief:

   [A] cavalier
   [B] expedient
   [C] pungent
   [D] perfunctory
   [E] sybaritic

3. Brave:

   [A] recondite
   [B] intrepid
   [C] onerous
   [D] judicious
   [E] torpid

4. Essence:

   [A] iteration
   [B] cavalcade
   [C] aspersion
   [D] epitome
   [E] edification

5. Generous

   [A] baleful
   [B] demure
   [C] magnanimous
   [D] voluble
   [E] acquiescent

6. Block:

   [A] fulminate
   [B] exhort
   [C] vituperate
   [D] renounce
   [E] occlude

7. Predict:

   [A] prognosticate
   [B] eulogize
   [C] capitulate
   [D] equivocate
   [E] extol

8. Poor:

   [A] impecunious
   [B] sycophantic
   [C] irate
   [D] petulant
   [E] impetuous

9. Lie:

   [A] commiserate
   [B] disseminate
   [C] prevaricate
   [D] exonerate
   [E] vindicate

10. Sentimental:

   [A] eclectic
   [B] mawkish
   [C] obsequious
   [D] caustic
   [E] whimsical

11. Enlighten

[A] edify
[B] impugn
[C] rectify
[D] tout
[E] adulate

12. Praise:

[A] compunction
[B] panegyric
[C] succor
[D] euphony
[E] imprecation

13. Fake:

[A] arduous
[B] florid
[C] nominal
[D] factitious
[E] sybaritic

14. Stubborn:

[A] exultant
[B] facetious
[C] stilted
[D] imperious
[E] intractable

15. Talkative:

[A] ruminative
[B] derisive
[C] loquacious
[D] expeditious
[E] voracious

16. Severe:

[A] succinct
[B] reticent
[C] soporific
[D] austere
[E] indignant

17. Scold:

[A] obstreperous
[B] acquiescent
[C] admonish
[D] diffident
[E] penurious

18. Unimportant:

[A] trivial
[B] vindicate
[C] scrutinize
[D] eschew
[E] disseminate

19. Clever:

[A] prosaic
[B] ingenious
[C] mirthful
[D] garrulous
[E] benevolent

20. Relevant:

[A] pugnacious
[B] indelible
[C] quotidian
[D] germane
[E] cursory

Exercise: Identifying Synonyms

For each set of answers, circle the pair or pairs of synonyms (maximum of two pairs).

1. [A] tenacious
   [B] secretive
   [C] mundane
   [D] surreptitious
   [E] adroit
   [F] disquieting

2. [A] harsh
   [B] incredulous
   [C] wistful
   [D] capricious
   [E] abrasive
   [F] nostalgic

3. [A] eclectic
   [B] defensive
   [C] plastic
   [D] laudatory
   [E] pliable
   [F] diffident

4. [A] perplexing
   [B] cordial
   [C] divisive
   [D] enigmatic
   [E] voluble
   [F] garrulous

5. [A] didactic
   [B] convivial
   [C] immense
   [D] pensive
   [E] mirthful
   [F] profound

6. [A] reject
   [B] allay
   [C] scrap
   [D] defy
   [E] expound
   [F] prolong

7. [A] onerous
   [B] liminal
   [C] curious
   [D] extant
   [E] odd
   [F] ambivalent

8. [A] undermine
   [B] beseech
   [C] repudiate
   [D] abate
   [E] exhort
   [F] prevaricate

9. [A] rebuke
   [B] surround
   [C] forestall
   [D] tamper
   [E] woo
   [F] preclude

10. [A] pedestrian
    [B] reminiscent
    [C] fulsome
    [D] banal
    [E] redolent
    [F] illusory

11. [A] defiant
    [B] abstemious
    [C] portentous
    [D] irrelevant
    [E] abrupt
    [F] picayune

12. [A] sheepish
    [B] captious
    [C] maudlin
    [D] judicious
    [E] fractious
    [F] dispassionate

13. [A] spurious
    [B] volatile
    [C] erudite
    [D] mercurial
    [E] inept
    [F] specious

14. [A] perspicacious
    [B] laconic
    [C] cavalier
    [D] utilitarian
    [E] taciturn
    [F] prurient

15. [A] congenial
    [B] prolific
    [C] ephemeral
    [D] astute
    [E] cursory
    [F] dormant

16. [A] intransigent
    [B] contemptuous
    [C] jingoistic
    [D] recalcitrant
    [E] diffident
    [F] effete

17. [A] esoteric
    [B] anomalous
    [C] evocative
    [D] weighty
    [E] pendulous
    [F] abstruse

18. [A] benign
    [B] eclectic
    [C] ineffable
    [D] heretical
    [E] insipid
    [F] multifarious

19. [A] separate
    [B] candid
    [C] bucolic
    [D] meticulous
    [E] discrete
    [F] inscrutable

20. [A] miser
    [B] contrarian
    [C] amateur
    [D] dilettante
    [E] misanthrope
    [F] zealot

(Answers on p. 53, after the exercise beginning on the next page.)

Now, try some multiple-choice practice questions. (Answers p. 54)

1. Paradoxically, the attainment of creative success in any field nearly always requires individuals to _____ a cherished ideal or familiar way of working.

    Circle or underline key words

    Definition or (+/-) _____

    [A] deflect
    [B] renounce
    [C] imbibe
    [D] abandon
    [E] probe
    [F] adhere to

2. Icebergs, strong winds, and large waves make the waters around Cape Horn extremely perilous; only the most _____ sailors attempt to brave them.

    Circle or underline key words

    Definition or (+/-) _____

    [A] resourceful
    [B] intrepid
    [C] headstrong
    [D] experienced
    [E] steadfast
    [F] daring

3. Although scholars initially suspected that the nearly 200 year-old manuscript, ostensibly written by a fugitive female slave, was a fraud, the author's identity was eventually _____ by experts.

    Circle or underline key words

    Definition or (+/-) _____

    [A] authenticated
    [B] defended
    [C] interrogated
    [D] substantiated
    [E] remonstrated
    [F] decried

4. Grapefruit juice interacts dangerously with many common medications; only a few sips can transform a _____ dose into one that is highly toxic.

Circle or underline key words

Definition or (+/-) _____

[A] routine
[B] trivial
[C] therapeutic
[D] benign
[E] soporific
[F] curative

5. Urban zones are traditionally defined by energy and innovation, whereas rural areas have long been associated with the process of growing older and embracing a more _____ set of habits.

Circle or underline key words

Definition or (+/-) _____

[A] subdued
[B] intractable
[C] reactionary
[D] advantageous
[E] mellow
[F] perfidious

6. Because scoring in gymnastics is almost entirely subjective, its structure profoundly shapes the sport's shifting values – whether originality or technical perfection is currently in _____.

Circle or underline key words

Definition or (+/-) _____

[A] retreat
[B] fashion
[C] excess
[D] vain
[E] charge
[F] vogue

7. While many cultures view sharks as rapacious beasts, civilizations that live in close association with the sea tend to regard these creatures with respect, even _____.

   Circle or underline key words

   Definition or (+/-) _____

   [A] indulgence
   [B] wistfulness
   [C] ambivalence
   [D] contempt
   [E] reverence
   [F] veneration

8. Profoundly respectful of the past, the nineteenth century painter Dominique Ingres assumed responsibility for guarding academic _____ against the encroaching popularity of the new Romantic style.

   Circle or underline key words

   Definition or (+/-) _____

   [A] convention
   [B] compliance
   [C] orthodoxy
   [D] innovation
   [E] obstinacy
   [F] introspection

9. Spanish culture _____ during the reign of Phillip II, initiating the Golden Age that left a lasting legacy in literature, music, and the visual arts.

   Circle or underline key words

   Definition or (+/-) _____

   [A] flourished
   [B] dissipated
   [C] stagnated
   [D] genuflected
   [E] blossomed
   [F] triumphed

10. Believing she was no longer suited for the role, the actress gave little thought to rejecting it; however, she later reconsidered, worried that she had acted too _____.

Circle or underline key words

Definition or (+/-) _____

[A] zealously
[B] rashly
[C] subversively
[D] uncouthly
[E] stoically
[F] precipitously

Answers: Easy Synonym, Hard Synonym

1. A
2. D
3. B
4. D
5. C
6. E
7. A
8. A
9. C
10. B
11. A
12. B
13. D
14. E
15. C
16. D
17. C
18. A
19. B
20. D

Answers: Identifying Synonyms

1. B, D
2. A, E; C, F
3. C, E
4. A, D; E, F
5. B, E
6. A, C
7. C, E
8. B, E
9. C, F
10. A, D; B, E
11. D, F
12. B, E
13. A, F; B, D
14. B, E
15. C, E
16. A, D
17. A, F; D, E
18. B, F
19. A, E
20. C, D

Explanations: Practice Sentence Equivalences

1. B, D

Key words/phrases: paradoxically, attainment
Blank: negative; give up, let go of, reject

The key word *paradoxically* sets up a contrast between *the attainment of creative success* and the blank. It suggests that in order to achieve success, the opposite – giving something up – must occur as well. The blank must therefore be filled with negative words conveying that meaning. *Imbibe* (ingest) and *probe* do not fit, and *adhere to* means exactly the opposite of the required words. *Deflect* is negative but does not quite have the right connotation; the issue is that something must be given up, not diverted. In addition, this word lacks a close synonym among the other choices. *Renounce* and *abandon* both convey the idea that people must give up their ideals in order to achieve success, making [B] and [D] correct.

2. B, F

Key words/phrases: Icebergs, strong winds, large waves, perilous
Blank: positive OR negative; skillful, daring; crazy

The sentence indicates that the waters around Cape Horn are *extremely perilous* (dangerous), so logically, the blank must be filled with words indicating that the sailors who try to navigate them are either very brave, very skillful, or very foolish. *Resourceful*, *headstrong* (stubborn, reckless), and *experienced* all fit, but don't get too tempted by them – none of these words has a close synonym among the other choices. *Steadfast* (loyal) does not make sense at all. *Intrepid* and *daring* fit perfectly and are a classic "easy word/hard word" pair. If you can spot them upfront, you can avoid getting distracted by the single answers that fit.

3. A, D

Key words/phrases: Although, suspected, fraud
Blank: positive; confirmed

The contradictor *although* indicates a contrast between the two halves of the sentence. The first half states that scholars *initially* suspected that the manuscript was fraud, so the second half must provide an opposing idea – namely that the manuscript was not a fraud. The blank must therefore be filled with positive words conveying that idea. *Interrogated* and *decried* are both negative, and *remonstrated* (pleaded) does not make sense at all. *Defended* could plausibly fit, but this word lacks a close synonym among the other choices. *Authenticated* and *substantiated* both indicate that experts proved the author was indeed a fugitive female slave, providing an appropriate contrast to the doubt described earlier in the sentence.

4. C, F

Key words/phrases: dangerously, highly toxic
Blank: positive; helpful, effective, safe

The fact that grapefruit juice *interacts dangerously with many common medications* suggests that it can turn a safe or normal dose of a medicine into a toxic one. *Routine*, *trivial* (negligible), and *benign* (harmless) all make sense in context, but none of these words has a close synonym among the other choices. *Soporific* (sleep-inducing) does not make sense at all. *Therapeutic* and *curative* have very similar meanings, and both accurately convey the idea that a normally helpful amount of a medication can become dangerous when mixed with grapefruit juice.

5. A, E

Key words/phrases: energy, innovation, whereas, growing older
Blank: neutral/very slightly negative; quiet, conventional

The contradictor *whereas* sets up a contrast between the energy and innovation associated with cities and some quality of rural areas. The blank must therefore be filled with words meaning the opposite of energetic or innovative. *Intractable* (stubborn) and *perfidious* (disloyal) are far too negative and do not make sense at all. *Advantageous* is far too positive, and there is nothing in the sentence to indicate that energy and innovation are not good things. *Reactionary* contrasts with *innovation*, but this word lacks a close synonym among the other choices. That leaves *subdued* and *mellow*, which are both consistent with the idea of a quiet, unexciting lifestyle. [A] and [E] are thus correct.

6. B, F

Key words/phrases: subjective, shifting values
Blank: positive; valued, emphasized

The fact that gymnastics scoring is *subjective*, and that its values are *shifting*, indicates that the types of moves most likely to earn athletes points are variable. The blank must be filled with positive words reflecting that fact – they must mean something like valued. *Retreat*, *excess*, and *vain* are all negative, and it does not make sense to say that originality or technical perfection can be *in charge*. In contrast, the statement that these two qualities are *in fashion* or *in vogue* accurately reflects the idea of shifting values. [B] and [F] are thus correct.

7. E, F

Key words/phrases: While, respect, even
Blank: positive; love, admiration

The contradictor *while* sets up a contrast between the prevailing negative view of sharks and the more positive view held by cultures that *live in close association with the sea*. In addition, the word *even* indicates that the blank must be filled with a stronger form of *respect*. *Ambivalence* and *contempt* are negative, and *wistfulness* (longing) does not make sense. *Indulgence* fits, but this word lacks a close synonym among the other choices. That leaves *reverence* and *veneration*, both of which indicate profound respect and logically complete the sentence. [E] and [F] are thus correct.

8. A, C

Key words/phrases: Profoundly respect of the past, new Romantic style
Blank: neutral; tradition, convention

Don't get distracted by the specifics of the sentence: it does not matter if you know anything about Ingres or nineteenth century painting as long as you clue into the theme of tradition (*profoundly respectful of the past*) vs. innovation (<u>*new Romantic style*</u>). The sentence implies that Ingres considered himself responsible for upholding the past, i.e. *tradition*. [A] is thus the first answer. *Compliance, obstinacy,* and *introspection* do not fit, and *innovation* is exactly the opposite of what is required. That leaves *orthodoxy*. Although this word is not an exact synonym for *tradition*, it conveys the same meaning: Ingres was deeply attached to the accepted way of doing things. [C] is thus the second answer.

9. A, E

Key words/phrases: Golden Age, lasting legacy
Blank: positive; grew, matured, did really well

The key phrases *Golden Age* and *lasting legacy* indicate that the blank must be filled with positive words. *Dissipated* and *stagnated* are both negative and can be eliminated. It does not make any sense to say that Spanish culture *genuflected* (bowed down) during the reign of Phillip II, so [D] can be crossed out as well. Be careful with [F]: *triumphed* makes sense in context, but this word lacks a close synonym among the other choices. In contrast, *flourished* and *blossomed* are synonyms that both imply a flowering of culture, an idea consistent with the idea of a golden age. [A] and [E] are thus correct.

10. B, F

Key words/phrases: gave little thought to, second thoughts
Blank: negative; quickly, thoughtlessly

The fact that the actress *gave little thought* to rejecting the role, and that she later had second thoughts, suggests that she believed she had decided too quickly or hastily. The blank must be filled with somewhat negative words consistent with that idea. *Zealously* (enthusiastically) does not quite fit with the idea of rejecting something, and in any case, this word lacks a close synonym among the other choices. *Subversively* and *uncouthly* (rudely) are both negative, but neither conveys the idea of excessive haste. The same is true of *stoically* (unemotionally). That leaves *rashly* and *precipitously*, which are synonyms that logically describe an action undertaken without forethought or with excessive haste. [B] and [F] are thus correct.

Prefixes and Roots

Positive

Ama – Love
amiable = easy to get along with

Amic – Friend
amicable = friendly

Ana – Not, Without
anarchy = without rule

Bene – Good
beneficial = helpful, good
(bene- + fic = do)

Dom – Mastery
indomitable = unable to be conquered
(in-, not + dom = cannot be mastered)

Eu – Happy
euphonic = pleasant sounding
(eu- + phon, sound)

Fid – Loyal
perfidy = disloyal
(per-, through, beyond, + fid = beyond
loyalty)

Lev – Light (weight)
alleviate = to relieve from pain,
literally to make lighter

Luc, Lux – Light (absence of dark)
lucid = clear

Macro – Large
Macrocosm – world, universe

Magna – Large
magnanimous = very generous
(magna- + anim, soul)

Moll – Soft
emollient = substance that softens

Multi – Many
multifarious = complex, having many
different aspects

Pac, Plac – Peace
placate = to soothe, make peaceful

Poly – Many
polymath = person knowledgeable about
or accomplished in many different areas

Pro – In favor of
prolong = make longer

Sym, Syn – together
synthesize = bring together

Val – Value
Valid = true, literally having value

Vener – Worship, Love
venerate = hold in high regard

Ver – True
verisimilitude = appearance of truth
(ver + simil, similar = similar to the truth)

Vig – Energy
invigorate = energize

Vinc – Win
vindicate = be proven correct

Negative

A – Not, Without
anomalous = unusual, exceptional
(a- + nom, name = without a name)

Amic – Friend
amicable = friendly

Ana – Not, Without
anarchy = without rule

Anti – Against
antipathy = dislike
(anti- + path, feeling)

Bell – War
belligerent, bellicose = threatening,
violent

Contra – Against
contradict = dispute
(contra- + dict, say = say against)

Culp – Guilt
exculpate = free from guilt
(ex-, from + culp)

De – Not
deride = insult

Deb – Weak
debilitate = to make weak, cripple

Dis, Dys – Not
disparage = to put down, insult

Err – Wrong
erroneous = wrong

Fall – Wrong
fallacious = false

Fict – False
fictitious = fake, false

Im, In – Not
ineffable = inexpressible

Ira – Anger
irate = angry

Mal – Bad
malicious = cruel, evil

Micro – Tiny
Microscope = instrument for viewing tiny
objects

Mis – Not, Wrong
misnomer = incorrectly named
(mis- + nom, name = wrong name")

Ne – Not, Wrong
nefarious = cruel
(ne- + far, do = wrongdoer)

Ob – Against
obdurate, obstinate = stubborn

Pej – Bad
pejorative = insulting

Pug – Violent
pugnacious = violent, looking for a fight

Umbr – Dark
umbrage = offense

Un – Not
Unsubstantiated = baseless, not proven

Vac – Empty OR Waver
vacuous = empty, meaningless

Volut – Twist
convoluted = twisted
(con-, with + volut)

Neutral or Positive/Negative

Ambi – Both
ambivalent = having mixed feelings
(ambi- + val, value)

Ante – Before
antebellum = before the war
(ante- + bell, war)

Anthro – Human
misanthrope = one who hates people

Auto – Self
autonomous = independent

Bi – Two
Bifurcate = split down the middle

Chron – Time
chronic – constant, literally all the time

Circum – Around
circumspect = careful, cautious
(circum- + spect, look)

Co, Con – With
condescending = looking down on

Cog – Think
cognition = thought

Corp – Body
corporeal = having a body

Cosmo – World
cosmopolitan = worldly, sophisticated

Di – Two
dichotomy = contradictory, separated
into two seemingly mutually exclusive
groups

Dia – Through
dialect = regional or local form of a language
(dia- + lect, read = read through)

Dict – Say
dictum = saying, cliché

Dur – Hard, Lasting
durable = long-lasting

E, Ex – From
extemporaneous = done without
preparation
(ex + temp, time = away from time)

Equi – Equal, Same
equivocal = using ambiguous language,
sometimes with the intention to mislead
(equi- + voc, voice = literally equal voice)

Fac, Fic – Make, do
facile = easy (literally doable)

Gen – Knowledge, Innate, Type
ingenuous = naive
(in-, not + gen = not having knowledge)

Grav – Weight, Serious
gravity = seriousness

Hetero – Different
heterogeneous = varied, multifaceted
(hetero- + gen = different types)

Homo – Same
homogeneous = same
(homo- + gen = same type)

Inter – Between
interrupt = come between
(inter- + rupt = burst)

Lib – Free OR Book
liberate = to set free

Loc, Loq – Words, Speech
loquacious = talkative

Ment – Mind
mentality = mindset

Morph – Shape
amorphous = shapeless
(a-, not + morph = no shape)

Mut – Change
immutable = fixed, unchanging
(im-, not + mut)

Nerv – boldness, courage
enervate – to sap of energy
(e-, from + nerv = take away courage)

Nom – Name
nominal = superficially, in name only

Os – Bone
ossify = become hard, like bone

Para – Alongside, Contrary to
Paradox = seemingly contradictory
ideas

Path – Feeling OR Disease
pathos = feeling of compassion
pathology = the science of disease

Ped – Child
pedestrian = boring, unoriginal
(literally, childish)

Pend – Hang
pendulous = hanging, heavy

Per – Through
perspicacious = perceptive
(per- + spic, look = look through)

Peri – Around
periphery = border

Phon – Sound
euphony = pleasing sounds
(eu-, happy + phon)

Port – Carry
portentous = significant
(literally carrying a lot of weight)

Re – Again
revive = bring back to life
(re- + viv, live = make live again)

Scrut – Look, Examine
Scrutinize = look very closely

Sens, Sent – Feel
sentimental = emotional, displaying or
appealing to tender feelings

Seq – Follow
obsequious = servile follower, toady

Spec/Spect – Look
spectator = one who watches

Stat – Stand
static = unmoving, literally in a state of
standing still

Sub – Below
substantiate = support, prove
(sub- + sta, stand = stand below)

Super – Above
supercilious = condescending (looking
down on)

Tac – Silence
taciturn = silent, not talkative

Tact – Touch
tactile = related to touch

Temp – Time
temporize = procrastinate, delay

Ten – Hold
tenacious = stubborn, holding on

Terr – Earth
Terrestrial = related to the earth

Tract – Move
intractable = stubborn
(in-, not + tract, move = not moving)

Trans – Beyond, Through
intransigent = stubborn, unmovable
(in- + trans = not going through)

Urb – City
urbane = sophisticated

Vap – Air, Steam
evaporate = to become air

Ven – Come
advent = beginning, literally coming of

Vid, Vis – See
invisible = unable to be seen

Vit, Viv – Life
convivial = merry, lively
(con-, with + viv = with life)

Voc, Vox – Voice
vociferous = loud

Vol – Desire, Fly (v.), Volume
volatile = unstable, literally ready
to fly)

Volut – Turn, Twist
convoluted = extremely complex
(con-, with + volut = with turns)

Words by Category

Smart, Original

Adept
Acumen
Adroit
Astute
Canny
Ingenious
Innovative
Perspicacious
Perspicuous
Savvy
Shrewd

Unoriginal

Banal
Cliché
Derivative
Hackneyed
Mundane
Pedestrian
Prosaic
Quotidian
Trite
Vacuous
Vapid

Dull, Unintelligent

Fatuous
Obtuse

Friendly, Easygoing

Affable
Amiable
Amicable
Complaisant
Congenial
Docile
Tractable

Flexible

Malleable
Plastic

Give In

Acquiesce
Capitulate
Indulge

Stubborn

Intractable
Intransigent
Obdurate
Obstinate
Recalcitrant
Tenacious

Happy

Ebullient
Elated
Exultant
Jovial
Jubilant
Mirthful
Sanguine

Unhappy

Dejected
Despondent
Lugubrious
Melancholy

Angry/Violent

Bellicose
Belligerent
Captious
Fractious
Intemperate
Irascible/Irate
Pugnacious
Rancor(ous)
Salvo
Truculent

Cruel/Evil

Callous
Malevolent
Nefarious

Destroy

Decimate
Eradicate
Extirpate
Obliterate

Liking For

Bent
Penchant
Predilection
Proclivity

Dislike for

Abhor(rent)
Animosity
Antipathy
Enmity
Inimical
Repugnant

Praise, Admiration

Acclaim
Accolades
Adulate
Encomium
Eulogize/Eulogy
Extol
Laud
Lionize
Panegyric
Plaudits
Revere
Tout
Venerate

Manipulate

Cajole
Coerce

Criticize

Abase
Assail
Debase
Deride
Disdain
Disparage
Excoriate
Impugn
Malign
Revile
Vituperate

Scold, Punish

Admonish
Censure
Chastise
Rebuke

Free from Blame

Exculpate
Exonerate
Penitent
Repentant

Hardworking

Assiduous
Diligent
Prolific (productive)
Sedulous

Careful, Examine Closely

Circumspect
Fastidious
Meticulous
Peruse
Punctilious
Scrupulous
Scrutinize

Lazy, Careless

Apathetic
Desultory
Haphazard
Indifferent
Indolent
Lackadaisical
Slapdash

Dishonest

Charlatan
Chicanery
Disingenuous
Dissemble
Dupe
Feign
Mendacious
Prevaricate
Specious
Spurious

Soothe

Alleviate
Ameliorate
Appease
Assuage
Mitigate
Mollify
Palliate
Placate

Make Worse

Aggravate
Exacerbate

High Point

Zenith
Apex

Low Point

Nadir

Large, Excessive Amount

Bevy
Copious
Myriad
Plethora
Surfeit

Small Amount

Circumscribed
Dearth
Paucity

Diverse

Eclectic
Heterogeneous
Motley
Multifarious

Sophisticated

Cosmopolitan
Urbane

Narrow-Minded

Insular
Parochial
Provincial

Polite

Cordial
Decorum/Decorous
Discreet

Impolite, Crude

Boor(ish)
Philistine

Practical

Pragmatic
Prudent
Utilitarian

Suspicious

Chary
Incredulous
Skeptical
Wary

Naïve, Impractical

Callow
Credulous
Gullible
Ingenuous
Quixotic

Clear, Direct

Candid
(Pel)lucid
Unequivocal

Unclear, Incomprehensible

Ambiguous
Inscrutable
Nebulous
Obfuscate
Opaque

Indecisive, Uncertain

Ambivalent
Equivocate/Equivocal
Vacillate
Waver

Wordy, Complicated

Byzantine
Convoluted
Florid
Prolix
Verbose

Plain, Using Few Words

Austere
Economical
Laconic
Perfunctory
Severe
Spare
Tacit(urn)
Terse

Secretive

Furtive
Surreptitious

Outgoing, Talkative

Garrulous
Gregarious
Loquacious
Voluble

Shy, Standoffish

Aloof
Bashful
Diffident
Reserved
Timid
Timorous

Passionate

Ardent/Ardor
Fervid
Fervent

Inflated, Overblown

Bombastic
Histrionic
Turgid

Nervous

Apprehensive
Flustered
Nonplussed

Noisy, Rowdy

Boisterous
Obstreperous

Calm, Quiet

Phlegmatic
Quiescent
Sedate
Serene
Stoic
Tranquil
Unflappable
Unruffled

False, Fake

Ersatz
Factitious
Fallacious
Sophistry
Specious
Spurious

Generous

Altruistic
Magnanimous
Munificent
Philanthropic

Greedy

Avaricious
Cupidity

Stingy

Miserly
Parsimonious

Fixed, Long-Lasting

Immutable
Steadfast

Inconsistent

Capricious
Erratic
Fickle
Impetuous
Mercurial
Sporadic
Volatile
Whimsical

Unfaithful

Fickle
Treacherous

Short-Lived

Cursory
Ephemeral
Fleeting
Transitory

Well-Known

Acclaimed
Exalted
Illustrious
Lofty
(Pre)eminent

Essence, Standard-Bearer

Crux
Epitome
Paradigm
Paragon

Relevant

Germane

Unimportant

Ancillary
Inconsequential
Marginal(ize)
Peripheral
Picayune
Trivial(ize)

Obscure

Abstruse
Arcane
Esoteric
Recondite

Spread, Promote

Disperse
Disseminate
Perpetuate
Propagate

Ease

Facilitate
Streamline

Support

Bolster
Corroborate

Contradict

Belie
Gainsay

Prevent, Block

Forestall
Hinder
Obviate
Occlude
Preclude
Stymie
Thwart
Undermine

Reject, Break

Abjure
Abrogate
Eschew
Jettison

Modest, Humble

Deferential
Demure
Self-abnegating
Self-effacing

Arrogant

Condescending
Contemptuous
Disdain(ful)
Officious
Pompous
Supercilious

Sentimental

Cloying
Maudlin
Mawkish
Treacly

Harsh, Burning

Acerbic
Caustic
Vitriolic

Sarcastic, Dry Humor

Facetious
Flippant
Sardonic
Wry

Luxurious, Showing Off

Fulsome
Opulent
Ostentatious
Sybarite/Sybaritic

Poor, Rejecting Luxury

Abstemious
Ascetic
Austere
Impecunious
Indigent
Penurious

Brave/Bold

Audacious
Intrepid

Nervous

Apprehensive
Trepidation

Cowardly

Craven
Pusillanimous

Speed, Enthusiasm

Alacrity
Dispatch
Galvanize
Zeal

Lacking Energy

Enervate
Lethargic
Soporific
Torpid/Torpor
Vitiate

Revolutionary, Rebel

Apostate
Heretic
Iconoclast
Maverick
Seditious

Wild, Wasteful

Degenerate
Depraved
Licentious
Prodigal
Profligate
Wanton

Extremist

Zealot

Traditional, Rigid

Hidebound
Orthodox
Ossified
Staid

Changeable

Malleable
Mutable
Plastic
Protean

Wandering

Itinerant
Peripatetic

Odd

Curious
Eccentric
Idiosyncratic
Peculiar
Quirky

Healthful

Salubrious
Salutary

Harm, Disease

Affliction
Malignant
Noisome
Noxious
Pestilence
Scourge

Harmless

Benign
Innocuous

Coming Together

Amalgam
Coalesce
Conciliate
Confluence
Propitiate
Reconcile

Flattering

Obsequious
Sycophant(ic)

Occurring By Chance

Fortuitous
Providential
Serendipitous

Teaching, Learning

Didactic
Edify
Erudite
Pedantic

Additional Words to Know

Abate – Decrease, diminish

Abdicate – Step down (e.g., a monarch)

Abscond – Steal away

Abeyance – Cessation

Abstain – Refrain from

Aesthetic – Related to beauty

Amorphous – Formless, lacking shape

Ample – Large

Anachronism – Associated with the wrong historical period

Analogous – Comparable

Anodyne – Bland, inoffensive

Arbitrary – According to chance; not done according to any particular criteria

Arduous – Extremely difficult, challenging

Auspicious – Boding well

Bane – Source of unhappiness

Belie – Contradict

Blight – Ruin, affliction

Blithe – Carefree

Buoyant – Light, airy

Cacophony – Noisy racket

Calumny – Slander

Caveat – Warning

Clairvoyant – Psychic

Cogent – Logical, well-constructed (argument)

Comprehensive – All-encompassing

Concatenation – Chain of linked events

Demagogue – Political agitator

Devoid – Lacking

Diaphanous – Filmy, sheer

Diatribe – Rant

Dichotomy – Divided into two opposing sides that cannot be reconciled

Dictum – Saying

Dilettante – Amateur

Dirge – Song of mourning

Discrete –Separate, distinct

Disparate – Different, contrasting

Efficacy, Efficacious – Effective(ness)

Effigy – Model, likeness

Emollient – Substance that makes things softer

Endemic – Native

Euphemism – Nice way of expressing something negative

Euphony – Pleasant sounds

Excavate – Dig up, unearth

Expedite – Speed up (e.g., a process)

Expurgate – Purge

Extant – Existent

Foment – Incite

Fungible – Replaceable, exchangeable

Glib – Superficial

Hegemony – Overwhelming dominance of a single group

Homogeneous – Same

Hyperbole – Exaggeration

Imbue – Saturate with

Impervious – Immune

Implacable – Unable to be calmed

(Im)pregnable – Thoroughly protected

Inchoate – Undeveloped, unformed

Incorrigible – Bad beyond reform

Ineffable – Inexpressible, beyond words

Infamous – Famous for a negative reason

Insidious – intended to secretly undermine

Insinuate – Suggest slyly

Inundate – Flood

Jingoism – Extreme nationalism

Ludicrous – Absurd, ridiculous

Lugubrious – Mournful

Luminous – Filled with light

Malfeasance – Wrongdoing

Malinger – Person who pretends to be ill

Mar – Damage

Misanthrope – Person who dislikes people

Obtrude – Stick out

Ostracize – Make someone an outcast

Paradox – Apparent contradiction

Partisan – Factional, adhering strongly to one side

Pendulous – Hanging heavily

Pensive – Lost in thought

Ponderous – Weighty

Potent – Powerful

Preclude – Prevent

Pristine – Pure, undefiled

Prognosticate – Predict

Redolent – Reminiscent

Reductive – Overly simplified

Remonstrate – To plead with or beg in protest

Rue – Regret

Salient – Striking

Sate/Satiate – Satisfy

Tyro – Novice

Unadulterated – Pure, undiluted

Veracious/Veracity – Truth

Vex – Annoy

Vulnerable – Capable of being hurt

Warp – Distort

Watershed – Turning/tipping point

Winnow – Filter out, remove unwanted elements

Woo – Charm, seduce

Common Second Meanings

Afford, v. – To grant (e.g., an opportunity)

Appreciate, v. – To take into account, recognize the merits of, OR to increase in value

Arrest, v. – To stop (not just put handcuffs on a criminal)

Assume, v. – To take on responsibility for, acquire (e.g., to assume a new position)

August, adj. – Revered

Austerity, n. – Financial policy to reduce excess spending on luxury or non-essential items

Badger, v. – To pester or annoy (e.g., reporters repeatedly *badgered* the candidate)

Bent, n. – Liking for

Biting, adj. – Sharp, harsh (humor or criticism)

Capacity, n. – Ability

Chance, v. – To attempt

Check, v. – To restrain, control, or reduce (e.g., the vaccine checked the spread of the disease)

Coin, v. – To invent (e.g., coin a phrase)

Commute, v. – To reduce or eliminate a penalty (e.g., to commute a prison sentence)

Composed, adj. – Calm, unaffected

Compound, v. – To augment, make more extreme

Compromise, v. – To endanger or make vulnerable (e.g., to compromise one's beliefs)

Constitution, n. – Build (e.g., a football player has a solid constitution)

Consummate, adj. – Total, absolute (e.g., a consummate professional)

Contest, v. – To dispute

Conviction, n. – Certainty, determination (noun form of *convinced*)

Couch, v. – To hide

Cow, v. – To intimidate

Curious, adj. – Strange

Discriminating, adj. – Able to make fine distinctions (e.g., a *discriminating* palate).

Dispatch, n. – Speed, efficiency (e.g., she completed the project promptly and with great *dispatch*)

Doctor, v. – To alter or tamper with

Economy, n. – Thrift (e.g., a writer who has an *economical* style is one who uses few words)

Embroider, v. – To falsify, make up stories about

Entertain, v. – To consider

Exact, v. – To take (by force) or demand, e.g., to exact a toll = to cause difficulty or suffering

Exploit, v. – To make use of (note: does not carry a negative connotation)

Execute, v. – To carry out

Facility, n. – Ability to do something easily (e.g., a facility for learning languages)

Fluid, adj. – Shifting, not fixed

Foil, v., n. – To get in the way of, put a stop to (e.g., to foil a robbery); OR a secondary, often comedic character in a play or novel, used to emphasize the good qualities of the hero.

Grave, adj./Gravity, n. – Serious(ness)

Grill, v. – To question intensely and repeatedly (e.g., the police *grilled* the suspect thoroughly)

Hamper, v. – To get in the way of, hinder

Harbor, v. – To possess, hold (a belief); to hide (a criminal or wrongdoer)

Hedge, v. – To equivocate, not give a clear answer

Hobble, v. – To prevent, impede

Mint, v. – To produce money; adj., perfect, like new (e.g., the car was in *mint* condition)

Novel, adj. – New

Pepper, v. – To sprinkle, spread (e.g., the paper was *peppered* with the professor's comment's)

Provoke, v. – To elicit (e.g., a reaction)

Qualify, v. – To provide more information about or a more nuanced understanding of

Realize, v. – To achieve (a goal)

Reconcile, v. – To bring together opposing or contradictory ideas

Relate, v. – To tell, recount

Relay, v. – To pass on to someone else (e.g., to relay information)

Reservations, n. – Misgivings

Reserve, v. – To hold off on, delay (e.g., to reserve judgment)

Route, v. – To send by a particular path

Ruffled, adj. – Flustered, nonplussed

Sap, v. – To drain of energy

Scrap, v. – To eliminate

Shelve/Table, v. – To reject or discard (an idea or proposal)

Sober, adj. – Serious, formal

Solvent, adj. – Able to pay all debts (usually used in a business context)

Sound, adj. – Reliable, valid (e.g., a sound argument)

Spare, Severe, adj. – Unadorned, very plain

Static, adj. – Unchanging

Sustain, v. – To withstand

Tap, v. – To gain access to

Temper, v. – To moderate, make less severe

Unchecked, adj. – Rampant

Uniform, adj. – Constant, unvarying

Unqualified, adj. – Absolute

Upset, v. – To interfere with an expected outcome

Part 2

....

Questions by Level

In this section:

- Easy Text Completions and Sentence Equivalences

- Medium Text Completions and Sentence Equivalences

- Hard Text Completions and Sentence Equivalences

Text Completions: Easy

. . . .

1. One of the most educated women of her era, Queen Elizabeth I was a noted
    _____: she spoke French, Italian, and Spanish, as well as Welsh and
    Cornish.

    | (A) monarchist |
    | (B) patron |
    | (C) misanthrope |
    | (D) polyglot |
    | (E) sovereign |

2. For nearly a decade, Olympic figure-skating champion Michelle Kwan enjoyed
    _____ levels of publicity; no skater before her had received such extensive
    media coverage.

    | (A) inexplicable |
    | (B) trivial |
    | (C) unprecedented |
    | (D) unsustainable |
    | (E) recurrent |

3. Writers in the magical realist tradition often use characters with _____
    powers such as levitation, flight, and ESP in order to subtly comment on
    contemporary social issues.

    | (A) fantastical |
    | (B) malevolent |
    | (C) creative |
    | (D) unpredictable |
    | (E) illusory |

4. The Arco lamp's _____ appearance is the result of its eclectic design: the juxtaposition of forms and materials creates an impression that is entirely unique.

(A) luminous
(B) mundane
(C) distinctive
(D) robust
(E) sophisticated

5. Because female hyenas remain within their clan and inherit their mother's rank, sisters must compete with one another in order to avoid being relegated to a_____ position in the hierarchy.

(A) relative
(B) subordinate
(C) biological
(D) familial
(E) perceptible

6. Though technically accomplished and expressive, Van Gogh's early drawings never succeed in approaching the level of _____ that marks his most celebrated works.

(A) mediocrity
(B) instability
(C) tranquility
(D) infamy
(E) virtuosity

7. First described by Ibn Al-Haytham in his treatise *Optics* in 1021, the camera obscura was perhaps the earliest known imaging device, _____ of the modern-day photographic camera.

(A) a descendant
(B) a forerunner
(C) a relic
(D) a paragon
(E) an heir

8. Crucial to the internationalization of science has been the emergence of English as the undisputed world language, but this linguistic _____ presents challenges for both native and non-native speakers.

(A) juxtaposition
(B) dichotomy
(C) parochialism
(D) dominance
(E) vernacular

9. The sorry state of the city's historic quarter has prompted members of the local residents' association as well as professional conservationists to _____ its restoration.

(A) set off
(B) settle down
(C) point out
(D) stumble upon
(E) rally for

10. As a provider of nourishment and natural materials, the coconut tree is _____ resource: a single tree produces up to 6,000 fruits that can be used in hundreds of foods and other essential items.

(A) a hardy
(B) an organic
(C) a specialized
(D) a limited
(E) an invaluable

11. Decades of physiology research have produced a consensus that exercise is (i) _____ to health in most people. Nevertheless, several recent studies suggest that an excess of physical exertion can actually have (ii) _____ effects on the body.

Blank (i)	Blank (ii)
(A) detrimental	(D) lasting
(B) exclusive	(E) deleterious
(C) conducive	(F) unanticipated

12. One of the most popular stock characters in classical theater was the fool, whose puns allowed playwrights to (i) _____ their superiors without directly (ii) _____ the established social order.

Blank (i)	Blank (ii)
(A) come to terms with	(D) subverting
(B) make light of	(E) contemplating
(C) comply with	(F) solidifying

13. When it was published in 1966, Truman Capote's *In Cold Blood* was marketed as a work of non-fiction; however, in recent years, literary sleuths have turned up numerous instances of Capote's journalistic sins, ranging from minor (i) _____ to outright (ii) _____.

Blank (i)	Blank (ii)
(A) revelations	(D) abstraction
(B) platitudes	(E) defamation
(C) inaccuracies	(F) fabrication

14. Research suggests that the brain is not organized as a (i) _____ with a clear chain of command. Rather, it is a tumultuous (ii) _____ of surprisingly independent cells and neurons.

Blank (i)	Blank (ii)
(A) hierarchy	(D) amalgam
(B) regimen	(E) extraction
(C) mandate	(F) classification

15. Nineteenth century Romantic writers (i) _____ the revision process, insisting that the best literature flowed from spontaneous and (ii) _____ creative acts.

Blank (i)	Blank (ii)
(A) spurned	(D) organic
(B) embodied	(E) cultivated
(C) obscured	(F) controversial

16. Carbon has an importance that is (i) _____ to its (ii) _____: it is the key constituent of precious materials from diamonds to oil, yet it makes up less than 0.1 percent of the Earth's bulk.

Blank (i)	Blank (ii)
(A) unbecoming	(D) density
(B) irrelevant	(E) sparseness
(C) disproportionate	(F) appearance

17. The essence of jazz is (i) _____; no other genre of music relies so extensively on the art of composing (ii) _____.

Blank (i)	Blank (ii)
(A) improvisation	(D) in the moment
(B) speculation	(E) from the heart
(C) repetition	(F) without relief

18. The city's financial struggles are particularly (i) _____ because they were not the result of a single cause but rather developed from (ii) _____.

Blank (i)	Blank (ii)
(A) complex	(D) a revision of estimates
(B) puzzling	(E) a confluence of factors
(C) distinctive	(F) a scattershot approach

19. Although the book was well-received and has even been the recipient of several awards, the (i) _____ of its scope does occasionally (ii) _____ the author's central argument.

Blank (i)	Blank (ii)
(A) narrowness	(D) apply pressure to
(B) breadth	(E) undermine the validity of
(C) consistency	(F) detract from the focus of

20. The suppression of low-intensity forest fires inevitably leads to the occurrence of more dangerous fires. (i) _____ materials that would otherwise be destroyed are allowed to (ii) _____, creating conditions in which large-scale blazes can easily erupt.

Blank (i)	Blank (ii)
(A) Insoluble	(D) accumulate
(B) Terrestrial	(E) dissipate
(C) Combustible	(F) entangle

21. Experimental research suggests that (i) _____ fearful memories while people are asleep may paradoxically (ii) _____ the memories' effects, diminishing their intrusion into waking life. Activity changes in the amygdala, a region of the brain involved in emotion and fear, suggest that this treatment does not actually erase the fearful memories, but rather that it creates new, more (iii) _____.

Blank (i)	Blank (ii)	Blank (iii)
(A) disturbing	(D) mitigate	(G) adaptive responses
(B) evoking	(E) aggravate	(H) powerful associations
(C) soothing	(F) spread	(J) comprehensive analyses

22. In addition to founding the Barnum & Bailey circus, the showman P.T. Barnum sought to (i) _____ public attitudes about the theater, which in the nineteenth century was widely considered (ii) _____ and dissolute. By building the city's largest and most modern auditorium and naming it the "Moral Lecture Room," Barnum sought to reposition theaters as palaces of (iii) _____ middle-class entertainment and thus win the approval of New York City's moral crusaders.

Blank (i)	Blank (ii)	Blank (iii)
(A) transform	(D) seedy	(G) affordable
(B) reveal	(E) radical	(H) successful
(C) uphold	(F) humiliating	(J) respectable

23. Weather in the Grand Canyon (i) _____ according to (ii) _____: the forested rim is high enough to receive winter snowfall, but temperatures in the low-lying Inner Gorge can on occasion exceed 100 degrees Fahrenheit. Visitors are often surprised by these (iii) _____, which can lead to unpleasant side effects ranging from sunburn to hypothermia.

Blank (i)	Blank (ii)	Blank (iii)
(A) declines	(D) habitat	(G) stunning sights
(B) fluctuates	(E) elevation	(H) unpredictable results
(C) develops	(F) ecosystem	(J) extreme conditions

24. In spite of its shortcomings, the biography of Duke Ellington is (i) _____ by several major factors, including the author's (ii) _____ his subject and his well-supported (iii) _____ that Ellington is a world-class composer.

Blank (i)	Blank (ii)	Blank (iii)
(A) redeemed	(D) potential for	(G) conviction
(B) defined	(E) exuberance for	(H) warning
(C) foreshadowed	(F) defense of	(J) hunch

25. Grotte-Chauvet cave, which contains the world's earliest-known figure drawings, was closed off by a rockslide around 20,000 BCE and remained sealed until it was (i) _____ by archaeologists in 1994. Conditions in the interior of the cave were thus exceptionally (ii) _____ for millennia, and in the absence of natural damaging processes, the condition of the drawings remained (iii) _____.

Blank (i)	Blank (ii)	Blank (iii)
(A) disclosed	(D) stable	(G) primitive
(B) penetrated	(E) frigid	(H) pristine
(C) maintained	(F) stifling	(J) ancient

26. The government's recently instituted policy of fiscal (i) _____ is increasingly unpalatable to a wide cross-section of voters, who (ii) _____ the elimination of services that they have come to (iii) _____.

Blank (i)	Blank (ii)	Blank (iii)
(A) austerity	(D) exploit	(G) take for granted
(B) emancipation	(E) resent	(H) consider superfluous
(C) indulgence	(F) defend	(J) regard dubiously

27. Polygraphs, popularly known as lie detector tests, have failed to gain (i) _____ among scientists because the devices are easily (ii) _____ by people experienced at controlling their emotions. These tests are designed to gauge subjects' physiological reactions as they answer a series of questions; however, research indicates that there is no physiological reaction that is consistently associated with lying, making it difficult to (iii) _____ liars and truth-tellers.

Blank (i)	Blank (ii)	Blank (iii)
(A) permission	(D) imitated	(G) confide in
(B) currency	(E) distracted	(H) distinguish between
(C) momentum	(F) duped	(J) contend with

28. The same forces that drive individuals to consume more resources can also nudge them toward more (i) _____ practices: when people see their neighbors adopt habits conducive to (ii) _____ energy, they tend to become more environmentally (iii) _____.

Blank (i)	Blank (ii)	Blank (iii)
(A) feasible	(D) conserving	(G) credible
(B) delinquent	(E) squandering	(H) conscious
(C) sustainable	(F) obtaining	(J) unsound

29. The country's water problems stem in part from the fact that water is
(i) _____ so unevenly among different sectors. Agriculture (ii) _____
for over 90 percent of total water use but is responsible for less than 20 percent
of the country's GDP. Cities are thus often hobbled in their (iii) _____,
even as the economy shifts toward fields such as electronics manufacturing and
information technology.

Blank (i)	Blank (ii)	Blank (iii)
(A) commingled	(D) accounts	(G) efforts to modernize
(B) allocated	(E) prepares	(H) demands for justice
(C) amassed	(F) arranges	(J) desire for transparency

30. Internet reviews reveal the power of popular opinion: the more people review
a product positively or negatively, the more others are primed to respond
(i) _____. Nevertheless, opinion has its limits. The more popular a product
becomes, the more likely that its overall rating will (ii) _____. An excess of
positive opinion can lead to disappointment among the types of audiences for
whom it was never (iii) _____.

Blank (i)	Blank (ii)	Blank (iii)
(A) up front	(D) decline	(G) intended
(B) in kind	(E) vary	(H) required
(C) on the side	(F) improve	(J) permitted

Explanations: Easy Text Completions

1. D

Make sure to follow the key words instead of getting waylaid by things that are true about Queen Elizabeth but not good fits for the sentence. The key phrase – the list after the colon – talks about how many languages she spoke. In (D), the root POLY-, many, gives you a clue: a polyglot is someone who speaks many different languages, so (D) is correct. Connecting the idea of speaking many languages to the root POLY- allows you to spot the probable answer almost immediately. Don't get tempted by *monarchist* or *sovereign*; they might describe a queen, but they have nothing to do with languages. A *patron* is someone who supports another person, usually an artist. This word is also irrelevant. For *misanthrope*, break the word down into MIS-, against, and ANTHRO-, human: this word describes someone who dislikes other people, so (C) can be eliminated as well.

2. C

The information after the semicolon tells you that the correct answer will be related to the idea that *no* ice skater had *ever* received such extensive media coverage. *Unprecedented* fits because it means never been done before (UN-, not + PRE-, before). *Inexplicable* (mysterious), *trivial* (unimportant), *unsustainable* (unable to be maintained), and *recurrent* (occurring repeatedly) all do not fit.

3. A

The key words *levitation*, *flight*, and *ESP* indicate that the correct answer must mean something like supernatural. That is the definition of *fantastical*, so (A) is correct. *Malevolent* (evil: MAL-, bad + VOL-, will, intention), *creative*, *unpredictable*, and *illusory* are all things that may characterize magical powers, but they do not fit the context of the sentence.

4. C

Don't get thrown off by the references to the Arco lamp's *eclectic design* and to the *juxtaposition of forms*. Although those phrasings are potentially confusing, you do not need to know what either *eclectic* or *juxtaposition* means in order to answer this question. In reality, the key phrase is *entirely unique*. An object with that quality is by definition *distinctive*, so (C) is correct. Don't get distracted by (A): *luminous* means light-filled, which is consistent with the idea of a lamp but unrelated to the clues in the sentence. A lamp that is *entirely unique* is the opposite of one that is *mundane* (ordinary), so (B) can be eliminated. *Robust* (sturdy) does not fit at all, eliminating (D). And although the lamp may be *sophisticated*, that word is not directly indicated by the sentence, eliminating (E) as well.

5. B

The sentence indicates that the hyenas must compete with each other in order to *avoid being relegated* to the word in the blank. Logically, they would want to avoid being relegated to something bad, so the blank must be filled with a negative word. Furthermore, the key word *hierarchy* (ranking system) indicates that the blank will have something to do with status. *Relative* fits with the idea of a position; however, the correct word must describe a bad position, and a relative position can be either good or bad. *Perceptible* has the same problem because that type of position could be either high or low. A *subordinate* position, however, would clearly be undesirable. Logically, it is something to which an animal could be relegated. Although both *biological* and *familial* are consistent with the focus on wild animals and the concept of a clan, neither word is related to the idea of a low position within a hierarchy, so (C) and (E) do not fit.

6. E

The contradictor *though* indicates a contrast between the two halves of the sentence. The first half of the sentence focuses on positive traits of Van Gogh's early drawings (*technically accomplished and expressive*), so the second half must convey a negative idea. The sentence is essentially saying that Van Gogh's early work wasn't nearly as good as his later work. Be careful, though: the use of the negation *never* means that a positive word is required to fill the blank. Furthermore, the word must logically describe works of art and be a more extreme version of *accomplished* or *expressive*. *Mediocrity*, *instability*, and *infamy* are all negative, eliminating (A), (B), and (D). *Tranquility* (calm) is positive, but it does not fit the context: calm is not a more extreme version of technical accomplishment. Only (E) makes sense: *virtuosity* would logically be a characteristic of artistic masterpieces.

7. B

The key phrase *earliest known* indicates that the camera obscura existed long before the modern camera was invented. The blank must therefore be filled with a word that means something like predecessor. *Forerunner* is a synonym for those terms, so (B) is correct. *Descendant* and *heir* convey the opposite: both refer to things that come after. A very old object could be described as a *relic*, but it could exist either before or after another object. A *paragon* is a model of excellence, a definition that does not fit at all in the blank.

8. D

The blank refers to a quality possessed by the English language; logically, that quality must be related to the idea of an *undisputed world language*. *Dominant* would exactly describe a language holding that position, making (D) correct. *Juxtaposition* and *dichotomy* both imply a relationship between two separate entities, but the sentence focuses only on English and does not directly mention any other language. *Vernacular* (common speech) is a word often associated with languages, but it is used primarily to distinguish everyday speech from more formal or classical language. Don't be distracted by *parochialism*. Speaking only one language could be construed as parochial (unsophisticated, narrow-minded), but that is not at all what the sentence is saying. The focus is on the global preeminence of English, and *dominance* is a much more precise fit.

9. E

If the city's historic quarter is in *a sorry state* (i.e. a state of disrepair), then logically residents and conservationists would be in favor of its restoration. The word in the blank must therefore be positive and mean something like promote. The only option that makes sense is *rally for*, meaning lobby in favor of a cause. None of the other options makes sense in context. The answer is therefore (E).

10. E

The information after the colon illustrates the extraordinary range of products derived from the coconut tree, and the key phrase *other essential items* indicates that the tree is an important resource. An extremely positive word is thus required. *Hardy* (tough) is positive but not directly consistent with the idea of producing many essential items, and there is nothing in the sentence to indicate that the coconut tree is able to withstand difficult conditions. *Organic* is likewise inconsistent with the definition required by the sentence. *Specialized* and *limited* both directly contradict the fact that the coconut tree can be used in *hundreds of foods*. That leaves (E), which is correct. Don't be fooled by the prefix IN-. *Invaluable* is a positive word meaning extraordinarily important.

11. C, E

The contradictor *nevertheless* indicates that the two blanks must have opposite meanings. Logically, exercise would have a positive effect on people's health, so you can make a reasonable assumption that Blank (i) should be filled with a positive word. That eliminates *detrimental*, and *exclusive* does not make sense in context. *Conducive to* is both positive and logical (exercise is conducive to health), making (C) the answer to Blank (i). Blank (ii) must therefore be filled with a negative word meaning bad or harmful. *Lasting* and *unanticipated* both describe effects that exercise could have on a person's health, but neither is necessarily negative. Only *deleterious* (harmful) is clearly negative, making (E) the answer to Blank (ii).

12. B, D

The key words *fool* and *puns* indicate that Blank (i) must have something to do with mockery or making fun of. *Make light of* is the only option consistent with that idea, so (B) is the answer to Blank (i). *Comply with* implies the opposite of the required word – a fool who mocked social superiors would be defying them, not complying with them. *Come to terms with* makes no sense in context. Logically, then, Blank (ii) must mean something like threatening. If fools are mocking the social order, then they must be undermining it in some way. The only answer that fits is *subverting*, which is consistent with the idea of threatening. (D) is thus the answer to Blank (ii). Although *contemplating* the social order might be something a fool would do, *subverting* is much more directly consistent with the idea of mockery. *Solidifying* implies exactly the opposite of the required word because to solidify the social order would be to reinforce it.

13. C, F

The key phrase *journalistic sins* indicates that both blanks must be negative. In addition, the construction *ranging from _____ to outright _____* indicates that Blank (ii) must be filled with a stronger version of the word in Blank (i). *Revelations* is a neutral word that is inconsistent with the idea of sin, so (A) can be eliminated. *Platitudes* (clichés) is negative and could theoretically work, but there is no option for Blank (ii) that is a more extreme version of this word. Only *inaccuracies* makes sense and describes a less serious version of an option for Blank (ii): in the context of journalism, *inaccuracies* would be a sin, and *fabrication* (making things up) is an extreme form of inaccuracy. Although *defamation* (slander) is also negative, it is unrelated to accuracy, and *abstraction* does not make sense at all. (C) is thus the answer to Blank (i), and (F) is the answer to Blank (ii).

14. A, D

The contradictor *rather* indicates that the two blanks must have opposite meanings. For Blank (i), the key phrase *clear chain of command* is most directly consistent only with the idea of hierarchy, making (A) the answer. (Don't confuse *regimen* with *regiment*, which would also have a chain of command!) Blank (ii) must therefore mean the opposite of *hierarchy* and imply something disorganized and chaotic. *Extraction* has no such implication, and *classification* implies organization, leaving *amalgam*, which carries the correct connotation of something thrown together randomly. That makes (D) the answer to Blank (ii).

15. A, D

If the writers in question *insist[ed] that literature flowed from spontaneous...acts*, then they would logically be opposed to *the revision process*. Blank (i) must therefore be a negative word conveying the idea of opposition. The choice most consistent with that idea is *spurned* (rejected), making (A) the answer to Blank (i). Work that *embodied* the revision process would by definition be positive toward that process, so (B) does not fit. Although *obscured* is negative, this word does not carry the correct connotation: writers who obscured the revision process would simply seek to hide it, whereas the sentence suggests that the writers rejected the revision process entirely. (C) can therefore be eliminated as well.

Blank (ii) is paired with *spontaneous*, indicating that the correct answer must be similar to that word. *Organic* is most directly consistent with that idea – it implies that literature arises naturally and does not need to be revised. (E) does not fit because *cultivated* is the opposite of spontaneous. (F) does not make sense either because there is nothing in the sentence to indicate that Romantic writers believed the best literature was *controversial*. (D) is thus the answer to Blank (ii).

16. C, E

The information before the colon provides no hints as to what sorts of words might belong in the blank. As a result, it is necessary to rely on the information after the colon and work backwards. What does the second half of the sentence indicate? That carbon is not a common mineral, yet it is a key component of *precious materials*. The colon signals that the second half of the sentence serves to explain the first half, so the blanks must be filled with words that express similar ideas. In addition, the word *its* implies that the second blank must be filled with a word that describes a characteristic of carbon – a characteristic described in the second half of the sentence. For Blank (ii), the only answer consistent with the information after the colon is *sparseness* (rarity), which corresponds to the statement that carbon makes up *less than 0.1 percent of the Earth's bulk*. *Density* conveys exactly the opposite, and the sentence does not discuss carbon's *appearance* at all. (E) is thus the answer to Blank (ii).

Working from that information, the most logical answer for Blank (i) is *disproportionate*. When plugged in, it creates a meaning that corresponds to the information after the colon: carbon isn't very common, but it is very important. That's another way of saying that carbon is much more important than its relative scarcity would indicate. *Unbecoming* (unfitting) does not make sense in context, and *irrelevant* would imply that carbon is not important – a meaning directly contradicted by the phrase *key constituent of precious metals*.

17. A, D

If you know something about jazz, then you can probably make the safe assumption that *improvisation* is the answer to Blank (i) because jazz is famous for emphasizing that skill. For Blank (ii), the only answer consistent with (A) is (D); to improvise is, by definition, to compose *in the moment*. Otherwise, you must rely on the structure of the sentence for clues. The information after the semicolon expands on what is meant by *the essence of jazz*, so logically, Blank (ii) must be similar in meaning to Blank (i). Again, the only pair of words with similar meanings are (A) and (D).

18. A, E

The easiest way to approach this question is to start with Blank (ii) because you have more information about it. The key phrase *not the result of a single cause* tells you that Blank (ii) must be filled with a phrase meaning multiple causes. The only option that makes sense is *a confluence* (coming together) *of factors*. (E) is therefore the answer to Blank (ii). Based on that information, the answer to Blank (i) must be *complex*. If the city's financial struggles are the result of many factors, then they would logically be complicated. There is nothing in the sentence to support the idea that the financial struggles are either *puzzling* or *distinctive*. (A) is thus the answer to Blank (i).

19. B, F

The contradictor *although* indicates that the two halves of the sentence express opposing ideas. The first half describes the book's positive qualities (it was *well received* and has won *several awards*), so the second half of the sentence must convey a negative idea. In addition, Blank (ii) must convey the logical result of Blank (i). The only pair that makes sense is *breadth* for Blank (i) and *detract from the focus of* for Blank (ii). If the book is very large in scope, then it could easily be viewed as lacking in focus. That makes (B) the answer to Blank (i) and (F) the answer to Blank (ii).

20. C, D

Look to the first sentence for clues to the blanks. That sentence indicates that the prevention of low-intensity forest fires creates the conditions for high-intensity forest-fires to occur. Logically, the second sentence must elaborate on that idea. For Blank (i), the only option consistent with the idea of forest fires is *combustible* (flammable), making (C) the answer. Neither *insoluble* (unable to be dissolved) or *terrestrial* (found on Earth) fits. The sentence indicates that these materials are not destroyed, so Blank (ii) must mean something like build up. More combustible materials = bigger fires. *Accumulate* most directly fits the required definition, making (D) the answer to Blank (ii). *Dissipate* (dissolve into the air) conveys the opposite of the required meaning, and *entangle* does not make sense at all.

21. B, D, H

The word *paradoxically* is key, indicating that the sentence must describe a situation that appears to be contradictory. As a result, Blank (i) and Blank (ii) must convey contrasting ideas. In addition, the phrase *diminishing their intrusion into waking life* provides an important clue. That phrase expands on the information that immediately precedes it, so Blank (ii) must mean something like reducing. The only option that fits is *mitigate* (reduce/lessen something unpleasant), making (D) the correct answer to Blank (ii). Both *aggravate* and *spread* imply the opposite of the correct idea.

Now look at Blank (i). Logically, trying to eliminate fearful memories would lead to a decrease in those memories, but here we're looking for a *paradox*, so Blank (i) must be filled with a word meaning the opposite of decrease. *Evoke* fits that definition, making (B) the answer to Blank (i). *Disturbing* does not fit because that word does not mean the opposite of eliminate. *Soothing* does not make sense either because soothing fearful memories would seem to be an effective way of reducing them – and the sentence indicates that the correct word must convey an illogical or contradictory relationship.

For Blank (iii), the key phrase *does not actually erase the fearful memories* indicates that the correct word must describe how evoking fearful memories reduces those memories without erasing them entirely. *Powerful associations* describes a way in which that might be accomplished. If the new associations are more powerful, they would override the old ones. *Adaptive responses* does not fit because the problem is not that the old memories cannot adapt, and *comprehensive analyses* does not fit because analyses are unrelated to memories in this context. That makes (H) the answer to Blank (iii).

22. A, D, J

The fact that P.T. Barnum was a *showman* suggests that he had a positive attitude toward the theater, but make sure to read the entire sentence before you answer Blank (i). Blank (ii) is paired with the key phrase *and dissolute*, indicating that the blank must be filled with a word that is similar in meaning to *dissolute* (debased, of poor moral quality). Only *seedy* matches the required definition, making (D) the answer to Blank (ii).

Now back up and consider Blank (i). If audiences held negative attitudes toward the theater, then logically Barnum would have sought to change, i.e. *transform*, those attitudes. *Reveal* does not make sense because public attitudes are by definition widely known and thus do not need to be revealed to anyone. *Upholding* the public's negative view of the theater is precisely the opposite of what Barnum would have done. That makes (A) the answer to Blank (i).

The name *Moral Lecture Room* indicates that Barnum wanted to purge the theater of its unwholesome associations. Blank (iii) must therefore be filled with a word meaning the opposite of *seedy and dissolute*. Neither *affordable* nor *successful* matches that definition, but a *respectable* auditorium would logically appeal to the middle-class moralists. (J) is thus the answer to Blank (iii).

23. B, E, J

The information after the colon provides key information about the first two blanks. It indicates that temperatures at the lowest point of the Canyon can be extremely low, while temperatures at the highest point of the Canyon can be extremely high. That is another way of saying that they *fluctuate* (change) according to their *elevation* (height). *Develops* does not make sense since weather must exist everywhere in the Canyon, and *declines* does not fit either; both the top and the bottom of the Canyon experience extreme, uncomfortable weather. (Even if you try to interpret *weather* as temperature, *declines* still does not fit: as the elevation rises, temperatures go down, not up, as indicated by the reference to *winter snowfall*.) (B) is thus the answer to Blank (i), and (E) is the answer to Blank (ii).

Blank (iii) must refer to the weather described in the previous sentence. Temperatures cold enough to permit snowfall and 100-degree temperatures are both examples of *extreme conditions*, making (J) correct. *Stunning sights* are often associated with the Grand Canyon, but in this case the phrase is entirely off topic. Snowfall and 100 degree temperatures may also be unpredictable, but the sentence provides no information to imply that this is the case here. Likewise, *unpredictable results* does not fit – don't get distracted by the word *surprised*. There is nothing to indicate that either the snowfall or the high temperatures occur without warning, nor is extreme weather the *result* of anything discussed in the passage.

24. A, E, G

The contradictor *in spite of* sets up a contrast between *shortcomings* and Blank (i), so this blank must be filled with a positive word indicating that the book compensates for those shortcomings. *Defined* is neutral and does not convey that connotation, and *foreshadowed* (previewed) would be used to rebut the idea that the book was unexpected – not at all the case here. That leaves *redeemed*, which accurately conveys that idea that the biography's shortcomings are counterbalanced by its positive aspects. (A) is thus the answer to Blank (i).

Blank (ii), then, must be filled with a word indicating the author's positive attitude toward his subject. None of the answers is directly negative, but *exuberance* (enthusiasm) *for* is the quality that would most logically counteract the biography's shortcomings. If the author is exuberant about his subject, then it is logical that he would believe Ellington is a world-class composer. (E) is thus the answer to Blank (ii).

Warning is negative and clearly does not make sense, and *hunch* does not quite fit the context of the sentence – authors do not normally write biographies about people they only have a *hunch* are important. *Conviction* (strong belief; literally, the state of being convinced) most directly fits with the idea of exuberance, making (G) the answer to Blank (iii).

25. B, D, H

The sentence sets up an opposition between the sealed cave and the archaeologists' actions, so Blank (i) should logically mean something like discovered. Don't be fooled by *disclosed*. This word does mean revealed, but only in regard to secrets or information. A cave cannot be disclosed. *Penetrated* is a more appropriate word to indicate that the archaeologists broke through the rock hiding the cave. *Maintained* does not fit at all. (B) is thus the answer to Blank (i).

For Blank (ii), if the cave remained sealed for millennia and was not exposed to *natural damaging processes*, then the conditions inside it were both favorable and constant. *Stable* conveys that idea most effectively. The cave may have been (very cold), but there is nothing in the sentence to directly indicate that it was. A cave with *stifling* (hot, stuffy) conditions probably would not have preserved the drawings well. (D) is thus the answer to Blank (ii).

For Blank (iii), the sentence indicates that the drawings remained unaffected by *natural damaging processes* – that is, they remained in very good condition. It would be reasonable to assume that such early drawings were *primitive*, and the sentence clearly indicates that they were *ancient*, but neither word fits the clue provided by the sentence. Only *pristine* (flawless) is consistent with the idea of not being affected by damaging processes, making (H) the answer to Blank (iii).

26. A, E, G

The key word *unpalatable* (unpleasant) indicates that the government's recently instituted policy has negatively affected many voters in some way. Blank (i) must therefore be filled with a negative word. It would not make sense for voters to be upset about *emancipation* (freedom) or *indulgence* (permissiveness), but *austerity* (strictly limiting spending) would logically provoke an unpleasant reaction. (A) is thus the answer to Blank (i).

Blank (ii) must therefore be filled with a negative word meaning something like dislike. *Exploit* (take advantage of) is negative but does not make sense, and *defend* is positive. In contrast, *resent* is a word that indicates a feeling of displeasure or indignation, making (E) the answer to Blank (ii).

For Blank (iii), what type of services would voters be most likely to resent? Those that they considered indispensable, or *took for granted*. If they considered the services *superfluous* (excessive, unnecessary), they would have no reason to be upset about those services being cut. The same would be true if they regarded the services *dubiously* (doubtfully). If they took the services *for granted*, however, they would understandably be upset about their elimination. (G) is thus the most logical answer to Blank (iii).

27. B, F, H

The fact that lie detector tests have failed to *gain* something suggests that they are faulty or unreliable in some way. Blank (i) must therefore be filled with a positive word meaning something like popularity. The closest fit among the answer choices is *currency* (acceptance), making (B) the answer to Blank (i). Don't be fooled by *momentum*. Although this is a positive word that is often used with *gained*, it means speed or force, which fits far less precisely in context than *currency* does.

If lie detector tests are unreliable, then it must be because they can be fooled or misled by *people experienced at controlling their emotions*. *Distracted* is not a synonym for fooled, and a machine cannot be distracted. *Imitated* makes no sense at all. *Duped* does mean fooled, making (F) the answer to Blank (ii).

For Blank (iii), if no specific physical reactions are consistently associated with lying, then logically there is no way to tell truth-tellers from liars – that is, to *distinguish between* them. That makes (H) the answer.

28. C, D, H

For Blank (i), the sentence sets up an implicit contrast between the idea of *consum[ing] more resources* (bad) and the word in the blank (good). Conserving resources is the opposite of consuming them, and the only option consistent with that idea is *sustainable*. *Delinquent* is negative and can thus be eliminated. *Feasible* (doable) does not fit – there is no connection between consuming resources and feasibility. (C) is thus the answer to Blank (i).

The information after the colon explains the first part of the sentence, so Blank (ii) and Blank (iii) must be both positive and consistent with the idea of consuming less energy. For Blank (ii), *conserving* most directly fits that requirement. *Squandering* (wasting) is the opposite of what is needed, and *obtaining* provides no information about whether energy is saved or not. For

Blank (iii), people would logically become more *conscious* about their energy use if they are prompted to save energy by watching their neighbors. *Credible* is positive but does not make sense, and *unsound* (shaky, insecure) does not fit at all. That makes (D) the answer to Blank (ii) and (H) the answer to Blank (iii).

29. B, D, G

A logical explanation for the country's water problems would be that water is distributed *so unevenly between sectors*. Blank (i) must therefore be filled with a word meaning distributed. Only *allocated* fits that definition, making (B) the answer to Blank (i).

For Blank (ii), *accounts for* is most consistent with the idea introduced in the previous sentence: if a single sector (agriculture) is responsible for consuming 90% of water, then resources are being very unevenly allocated indeed. (D) is thus the answer to Blank (ii).

Blank (iii) describes something that cities are unable to accomplish as a result of uneven resource allocation. The reference to *electronics manufacturing and information technology* stands in contrast to the earlier reference to agriculture, and suggests that these cities are making *efforts to modernize*. (G) is thus the answer to Blank (iii).

30. B, D, G

The key phrase *power of popular opinion* indicates that people are influenced to think or behave much as their peers do. For Blank (i), only *in kind* (in the same way) conveys that idea. Responding *up front* or *on the side* are unrelated to mimicking others' behavior. (B) is thus the answer to Blank (i).

For Blank (ii), the sentence *Nevertheless, opinion has its limits* is key because it indicates that people are not always persuaded by others' opinions. Logically, the following sentence must indicate that popularity can, paradoxically, lead to poor reviews. Blank (ii) must therefore be filled with a negative word. *Improve* is positive, and *vary* is neutral, but *decline* clearly conveys the inverse relationship being described. (D) is thus the answer to Blank (ii).

For Blank (iii), consider the context: when a product receives many positive reviews, its popularity rises, and it reaches consumers with expectations and needs different from those of the original purchasers. In other words, these consumers are not the people for whom the product was *originally intended*. *Required* does not make sense because people who write reviews are not obligated to buy products, and *permitted* does not fit either – the issue is not that the consumers who write negative reviews were not originally allowed to buy the product, but rather that they did not form part of its intended market. (G) is thus the answer to Blank (iii).

Sentence Equivalences: Easy

1. In post-World War II Germany, the Allies instituted a government that would _____ power throughout the country in order to limit the influence of any single region.

   [A] legislate
   [B] disperse
   [C] exhibit
   [D] consolidate
   [E] curb
   [F] spread

2. The source of Mark Twain's (Samuel Langhorne Clemens') pen name has long been a source of perplexity to literary scholars, but new evidence suggests that this _____ may soon be resolved.

   [A] enigma
   [B] dispute
   [C] fallacy
   [D] mystery
   [E] conflict
   [F] phenomenon

3. Grizzly bears are usually solitary animals, but they _____ in groups alongside rivers when salmon come to spawn.

   [A] attack
   [B] wander
   [C] gather
   [D] prowl
   [E] lumber
   [F] congregate

4. George Washington Carver is believed to have been born in January of 1864; however, the exact date of his birth remains _____.

   [A] annual
   [B] speculative
   [C] inexplicable
   [D] official
   [E] celebratory
   [F] uncertain

5. Following the discovery that the city council president had used public funds to pay for numerous personal expenses, his constituents_____ him from office.

   [A] defended
   [B] ousted
   [C] acquitted
   [D] booted
   [E] seized
   [F] isolated

6. It is probably fair to say that, in the estimation of most critics, Stevens has _____ all of his American contemporaries; of all twentieth-century poets in English, indeed, only Yeats is consistently ranked higher.

   [A] inspired
   [B] denounced
   [C] eclipsed
   [D] excluded
   [E] challenged
   [F] surpassed

7. While the venom of a few spider species has detrimental effects on humans, the compounds contained in the poison also possess _____ properties that can be used in medications and in non-toxic pesticides.

   [A] salutary
   [B] variable
   [C] beneficial
   [D] stimulating
   [E] enduring
   [F] long-lasting

8. The theory of pragmatism resulted from the belief that ideas should not be viewed as abstract truths but rather judged by their _____ consequences.

[A] practical
[B] unintentional
[C] inevitable
[D] immediate
[E] real-life
[F] well-deserved

9. Janacek's mature compositions represent a highly original _____ of styles because they integrate musical traditions that developed independently of one another for centuries.

[A] profusion
[B] cacophony
[C] synthesis
[D] refinement
[E] blend
[F] demonstration

10. Around 10,000 years ago, early hunter-gatherers began to make _____ stone tools, but as more sophisticated technologies developed, their creations became increasingly complex.

[A] elaborate
[B] fragile
[C] impressive
[D] crude
[E] rigid
[F] primitive

11. Mitsuko Uchida is one of the most _____ pianists of her generation, having appeared with many of the world's foremost orchestras and won numerous international awards.

[A] acclaimed
[B] versatile
[C] flamboyant
[D] celebrated
[E] experimental
[F] agile

12. Much to the chagrin of developers, the city's growth has been _____ by a law restricting the construction of new skyscrapers within the city limits.

[A] streamlined
[B] hindered
[C] resisted
[D] impeded
[E] polluted
[F] exhausted

13. In spite of their obvious physical advantages and intimidating presence, bears almost never view humans as prey and rarely behave in _____ manner toward them.

[A] a bellicose
[B] an intrusive
[C] a sly
[D] an aggressive
[E] an inquisitive
[F] a cautious

14. Copernicus developed his theory of heliocentrism entirely without experimentation, but it was eventually _____ by the scientific community because his descriptions of planetary motion were more convincing than those of his predecessors.

[A] contained
[B] explored
[C] demonstrated
[D] embraced
[E] deduced
[F] endorsed

15. Spoken by fewer than 250,000 people, Tuva is nevertheless _____ in comparison to other rare languages, some of which have only a handful of remaining speakers.

[A] flourishing
[B] dwindling
[C] robust
[D] languishing
[E] convoluted
[F] arcane

16. Many children are _____ unfamiliar foods and will only agree to taste a
    new dish after they have been offered it a dozen or more times.

    [A] fond of
    [B] curious about
    [C] skeptical of
    [D] interested in
    [E] dismayed by
    [F] wary of

17. Despite the controversy surrounding it, genetic crop modification could help
    provide sustenance for fast-growing populations by creating foods _____
    to pests.

    [A] invaluable
    [B] immune
    [C] toxic
    [D] vulnerable
    [E] resistant
    [F] inaccessible

18. George Orwell was widely acclaimed for his novella *Animal Farm*, but it was the
    publication of *1984* that truly _____ his place in literary history.

    [A] solidified
    [B] signaled
    [C] clarified
    [D] cemented
    [E] subdued
    [F] dominated

19. Around 400 A.D., the Andean civilization of Tiwaniku began to shift from a locally
    dominant force to an imperialist state that conquered its neighbors and
    _____ its culture widely.

    [A] anointed
    [B] disseminated
    [C] influenced
    [D] inflicted
    [E] transmitted
    [F] proclaimed

20. The author's novels, once highly original, have unfortunately become
    _____; they now largely consist of characters, themes, and plotlines
    recycled from his earlier works.

    [A] pessimistic
    [B] succinct
    [C] uninspired
    [D] derivative
    [E] succinct
    [F] impenetrable

21. Michael Crichton's novels _____the techno-thriller genre, exploring a
    variety of failures and catastrophes that can result from human interaction with –
    and misuse of – biotechnology.

    [A] epitomize
    [B] deconstruct
    [C] embody
    [D] designate
    [E] restrict
    [F] defy

22. The Spanish Empire was not a unified monarchy with one legal system but
    rather a federation of _____ realms, each jealously guarding its own
    rights.

    [A] quarrelsome
    [B] discrete
    [C] absolutist
    [D] populous
    [E] conservative
    [F] autonomous

23. Historically, societies have developed methods of adapting their lifestyles to fit
    their environments, with acquired behaviors eventually transforming into
    _____ customs.

    [A] essential
    [B] unique
    [C] ingenious
    [D] fixed
    [E] familial
    [F] ingrained

24. In recent years, the containment of infections, coupled with efforts to purify drinking water, has resulted in a 99% decline in the number of Guinea worm cases, encouraging researchers to believe that the disease may soon be _____ entirely.

[A] eradicated
[B] alleviated
[C] overturned
[D] undermined
[E] stamped out
[F] cut off

25. Contrary to popular belief, the British government did not respond impulsively to the news of the Boston Tea Party; rather, it _____ the consequences of its reaction at considerable length.

[A] debated
[B] mulled
[C] deliberated about
[D] denounced
[E] expounded on
[F] laid out

Explanations: Easy Sentence Equivalences

1. B, F

The correct words must indicate how power was arranged in post-War Germany in order to *limit the influence of any single region*. Logically, power must have been distributed, or *spread* throughout the country, to prevent such an occurrence. [F] is a direct, straightforward match for the meaning required by the sentence. *Legislate* is related to power but has nothing to do with spreading it around, and *exhibit* does not make sense in context. *Curb* means restrain, which is the opposite of spreading. In addition, this word would simply imply that power was restrained everywhere in the country, not that it was deliberately spread around in order to prevent it from becoming concentrated. *Consolidate* implies a concentration of power – exactly the opposite of what is required. *Disperse* means scatter, which is similar to *spread* and creates the same meaning when plugged into the sentence. [B] is thus the second answer.

2. A, D

The word *perplexity* and the phrase *soon be resolved* indicate that the blank must refer to a source of puzzlement. Logically, a *mystery* would be a source of perplexity, as would an *enigma*. [A] and [D] are thus correct. Don't be fooled by *dispute* and *conflict*: although these words have the same meaning, the sentence only refers to something that literary scholars do not understand. There is no reference to a debate or argument over the source of Twain's pen name. The remaining answers do not make sense in context.

3. C, F

The contradictor *but* indicates that the two halves of the sentence will express opposing ideas. The first half of the sentence states that bears are *usually solitary animals*, so the blank must be filled with words that indicate bears are not always solitary. Both *gather* and its synonym *congregate* convey that meaning. All of the other options are words commonly associated with bears, but none fits the required definition. [C] and [F] are thus correct.

4. B, F

The key phrase *believed to have been born* implies that Carver's exact birth date is not actually known. The blank must therefore be filled with words meaning unknown. *Speculative* (based on conjecture) and *uncertain*, although not exact synonyms, both convey the idea that Carver's date of birth is open to question. [B] and [D] are thus correct. *Annual*, *official*, and *celebratory* are all words commonly associated with birthdays, but none of them fits the context of the sentence. Don't get distracted by *inexplicable*: this word describes something that cannot be explained, not something uncertain.

5. B, D

It is reasonable to assume that a city council president who used public funds for private expenses would be fired, so the blank must filled with words indicating that the president was removed from office. The correct pair is *ousted* and *booted* (forced out), both of which convey that idea. [B] and [D] are thus correct. *Defended* conveys the exact opposite meaning, and *acquitted* would very illogically imply that the city council president was found not guilty of a crime. *Seized* could plausibly fit, but it does not have a close synonym among the other choices. *Isolated* does not quite convey the necessary connotation of forcing out, nor does it have a close synonym among the other choices.

6. C, F

The sentence is constructed so that the second half of the sentence – the information after the semicolon – explains the first. The statement that only Yeats is consistently *ranked higher* than Stevens indicates that Stevens is held in higher regard than almost every other American poet. The blank must therefore be filled by positive words meaning something like outdone. *Inspired* is positive, but the sentence focuses on Stevens' popularity relative to that of other poets, not his effect on other poets. *Denounced, excluded,* and *challenged* are negative and can be eliminated on that basis. The correct pair, *eclipsed* and *surpassed*, both convey the idea that Stevens' popularity is greater than that of almost any other American poet. [C] and [F] are thus correct.

7. A, C

The contradictor *while* indicates that the two halves of the sentence are expressing opposing ideas: the first half of the sentence conveys the idea that spider venom can be *detrimental* (harmful), so the second half of the sentence must be positive and support the statement that the venom *can be used in medications and in non-toxic pesticides. Stimulating* is positive but does not directly fit the clue provided by the sentence, and *variable* is neither positive nor the opposite of *detrimental*. Although *enduing* and *long-lasting* are synonyms, they do not fit the sentence either. The correct pair, *salutary* (healthful) and *beneficial*, although not exact synonyms, both convey the idea that spider venom can have positive effects. [A] and [C] are thus correct.

8. A, E

The contradictor *but rather* indicates that the blank must be filled with words meaning the opposite of *abstract truths*. If you know the definition of *pragmatism*, that word provides another clue. *Pragmatic* means *practical*, making [A] the first answer. In the context of the sentence, *real life* also functions as an effective antonym for *abstract truths*, making [E] the second option. Although the two words are not exact synonyms, they both create the same meaning: pragmatism is about what happens in real life, not in theory.

9. C, E

The key phrase *because they integrate musical traditions* indicates that Janacek was responsible for bringing various musical traditions together. The word in the blank must therefore describe this quality of Janacek's mature compositions. Both *synthesis* and *blend* appropriately describe music that combines different styles, making [C] and [E] correct. *Cacophony* (loud and unpleasant sounds) and *refinement* clearly do not make sense in context, but be careful with the remaining answers. A *profusion* is a large quantity of something, but it is not by definition a mix. *Demonstration* could fit semi-logically into the blank, but there is no close synonym for this word among the other choices.

10. D, F

The sentence contrasts the tools made by *early hunter-gatherers* with the more complex tools made by later ones. The blank must therefore be filled with words meaning the opposite of complex – something like simple or basic. Both *crude* (unrefined) and *primitive* are consistent with that idea and have the same connotation of unsophistication. [D] and [F] are thus correct. *Elaborate* and *impressive* are inconsistent with the idea of basic tools; *fragile* makes sense but does not have a close synonym among the other answers; and *rigid* is entirely unsupported by the sentence.

11. A, D

The blank must be filled with words that describe what sort of pianist Uchida is. The fact that she has *appeared with many of the world's most celebrated orchestras and won numerous international awards* indicates that she is an extremely renowned one. The correct words must therefore be synonyms for famous. Both *acclaimed* and *celebrated* are appropriate descriptions of someone with Uchida's stature, making [A] and [D] correct. Although *versatile* and *agile* are synonyms and could very well be used to describe a musician, the sentence clearly requires words indicating fame. The remaining answers do not make sense in context.

12. B, D

The sentence indicates that the city's growth has been affected by a law *restricting* the construction of skyscrapers, so logically the blank must be filled with words meaning stopped or held back. Developers are by definition in favor of growth, so logically they would be *chagrined* (saddened) if growth were halted. Both *hindered* and *impeded* fit that idea, making [B] and [D] correct. *Streamlined* means made simpler, so [A] can be eliminated immediately. *Polluted* likewise does not make sense, eliminating [E]. *Resisted* describes a possible reaction that people could have to the passage of the law, but a city's growth cannot actually resist anything. Careful with *exhausted* (used up): it does not have quite the right connotation, and it has no close synonym among the other answers. The sentence is not saying that the city's growth has been used up, but rather that it has been held back or prevented from occurring.

13. A, D

The contradictor *despite* sets up a contrast between grizzly bears' *obvious physical advantages and intimidating presence* (negative) and their behavior, which logically must be more positive. However, the fact that these bears *rarely behave in* _____ *manner* means that the blank must be filled with negative words meaning something like frightening or threatening. *Inquisitive* (curious) is positive and *cautious* is neutral/positive, so those choices can be eliminated. *Intrusive* and *sly* are negative, but neither makes sense in context of the sentence. That leaves *bellicose* (threatening) and *aggressive*, which are general synonyms that fit the definition required by the sentence. [A] and [D] are thus correct.

14. D, F

The key phrase *more convincing than those of his predecessors* indicates that Copernicus' theory eventually met with a positive reception. The words in the blank must therefore mean something like accepted. In this context, *embraced* means accepted, making [D] the first correct answer. Although *endorsed* is not an exact synonym for *embraced*, it creates the same meaning when plugged into the sentence: Copernicus' theory was given the stamp of approval by the scientific community because it was better than anyone else's theory. That makes [F] the second answer. The scientific community clearly accepted Copernicus' theory, so *contained* is an illogical choice. Although *explored* could work (scientists would reasonably want to explore a theory developed without experimentation), this word does not have a close synonym among the other choices. The remaining answers are consistent with a discussion of scientific theories but do not fit the definition required by the sentence.

15. A, C

The contradictor *nevertheless* sets up a contrast between the phrase *Spoken by fewer than 250,000 people* and the word in the blank. The sentence also sets up an opposition between Tuva and *other rare languages, some of which have only a handful of remaining speakers*. Logically, then, the blank must be filled with positive words indicating that Tuva is more popular than it might seem. Both *flourishing* and *robust* accurately describe a tongue that, in the context of rare languages, is doing pretty well. [A] and [C] are thus correct. *Dwindling* and *languishing* have similar meanings, but both imply that Tuva is losing popularity – the opposite of what the sentence indicates. Neither *convoluted* (complex) nor *arcane* (esoteric) makes sense in context.

16. C, F

The statement that children *will only agree to taste a new dish after they have been offered it a dozen or more times* indicates a negative attitude toward new foods. The correct answers must therefore be negative and convey the idea of dislike or suspicion. When plugged in, both *skeptical of* and its synonym *wary of* create that idea, making [C] and [F] correct. *Dismayed by* is negative but does not have the necessary connotation of suspicion. The remaining answers are positive and can be eliminated on that basis.

17. B, E

The key phrase *could help provide sustenance for fast-growing populations* suggests that genetically modified foods cannot be easily destroyed by pests. The correct words must therefore convey the idea that these foods can withstand pests. Be careful with *invaluable*; although it looks negative, it's actually a positive word meaning extremely important. Foods that were invaluable to pests would attract pests, not drive them away. *Immune* makes sense, as does its synonym *resistant* – foods immune or resistant to pests could not be easily destroyed and would thus help fast-growing populations. [B] and [E] are thus correct. Be careful with both *toxic* and *inaccessible*. Both fit logically in the blank, but neither has a close synonym among the other choices. Foods that were *vulnerable* to pests would be more likely to be destroyed, so this answer does not make sense.

18. A, D

The contradictor *but* sets up a contrast between the two parts of the sentence. In this case, however, it is not the most straightforward type of contrast. Rather, the second half of the sentence is a more extreme version of the first. Essentially, it conveys the idea that *Animal Farm* helped Orwell's reputation, but *1984* confirmed his place in literary history. The correct words must therefore mean something like confirmed or ensured. *Solidified* and *cemented* both fit that definition and are the only pair of close synonyms, making [A] and [D] correct. *Signaled* and *clarified* both make sense in context, but neither has a close synonym among the other choices. *Subdued* is negative and can be eliminated on that basis, and *dominated* does not fit the required definition.

19. B, E

The fact that Tiwaniku changed from a local force to a much broader one indicates that its culture was spread much more widely. The correct words must therefore mean something like spread. That is the definition of *disseminated*, so [B] is correct. (Note that the prefix DISS- does not indicate a negative in this case.) The closest synonym is *transmitted*, which also conveys the idea that the Tiwaniku civilization passed its culture on to others. [E] is thus correct as well. *Inflicted* and *proclaimed* could plausibly fill the blank, but neither has a close synonym among the other answer choices. *Anointed* (blessed, made holy) does not make sense at all. *Influenced* could refer to the effect of the Tiwaniku civilization on its neighbors' culture, but it is does not make sense to say that the Tiwaniku civilization influenced itself.

20. C, D

The key word *unfortunately* indicates that the correct answers must be negative, and *recycled* is a clear hint that they must mean unoriginal. *Pessimistic* clearly does not fit that definition. Neither does *succinct* (brief) or *impenetrable*, although either of those words could be used to describe a novel in another context. The correct pair is *uninspired* and *derivative*, both of which convey the meaning that the author's current novels lack originality. [C] and [D] are thus correct.

21. A, C

The key phrase *exploring a variety of failures and catastrophes that can result from human interaction with – and misuse of – biotechnology* strongly implies that Crichton's novels are part of the techno-thriller genre, and the correct words must make that relationship clear. *Epitomize* and *embody* both convey it perfectly, indicating that Crichton's novels are the essence of the genre. [A] and [C] are thus correct. *Deconstruct* implies that the novels analyze the techno-thriller genre, not that they are part of the genre. *Defy* more explicitly implies that Crichton's books go against the techno-thriller genre. Neither of the remaining answers makes any sense in context.

22. B, F

The key phrases *not a unified monarchy* and *each jealously guarding its own rights* indicate that the Spanish realms were independent. *Quarrelsome* is consistent with the idea of realms jealously guarding their rights, but this word lacks a close synonym among the other choices. *Discrete* (separate; not to be confused with *discreet*) functions as an antonym for *unified* and conveys the idea that each realm was separate. [B] is thus the first answer. *Autonomous* likewise conveys the idea of a non-unified empire, making [F] the second answer. None of the remaining options fits the definition indicated by the sentence.

23. D, F

The sentence indicates that societies adapt themselves to their environments, so the correct words must suggest that *acquired behaviors* become a feature of societies' customs. In addition, the word *eventually* indicates that this process occurs over a long period. The correct pair, *fixed* and *ingrained*, is consistent with the idea of behaviors that develop out of necessity but then become set customs over an extended length of time. *Essential* and *unique* could plausibly fill the blank, but neither of these words has a close synonym among the other choices. *Familial* does not quite make sense because the sentence is talking about entire societies, not families. *Ingenious* does not fit because the sentence gives no indication that these customs are particularly clever, just that they developed as adaptations to the environment. [D] and [F] are thus correct.

24. A, E

The sentence indicates that cases of Guinea worm have dropped quite dramatically, so logically researchers would be *encouraged* by the possibility that the disease could be eliminated. The correct pair, *eradicated* and its synonym *stamped out*, clearly conveys that meaning. Be careful with *alleviated*, which is often used in the context of diseases but which does not quite fit here: the symptoms of a disease can be alleviated, but not cases of a disease. In addition, this option has no close synonym among the other choices. *Undermined* could plausibly fit, but there is likewise no close synonym for that word. A decision can be *overturned*, but not a disease, and *cut off* does not mean eliminated. [A] and [E] are thus correct.

25. B, C

The sentence states that *the British government did not respond impulsively to the news of the Boston Tea Party*, and the transition *rather* indicates that the blank must specify what the British government did do. The correct words must therefore mean the opposite of responding impulsively. *Denounced* does not fit at all, but *debated*, *laid out*, and *expounded on* are all entirely reasonable choices. The problem is that no two of those words are close enough synonyms or create the same meaning when plugged into the sentence. Don't be distracted by *debated* and *expounded on*: the former implies a clash of viewpoints, while the latter simply means talking at length about. *Mulled* and *deliberated about* are the only pair of close synonyms that also set up an effective contrast with the idea of impulsivity. [B] and [C] are thus correct.

Text Completions: Medium

1. The moralized world of the late Middle Ages did wane, but not as a result of the Reformation. Rather, medieval society was _____ by the growth of technical literacy across all areas of culture.

| (A) permeated |
| (B) eroded |
| (C) forestalled |
| (D) compounded |
| (E) adapted |

2. Unlike other authors, who portray the security officers at Robert Oppenheimer's laboratory as either mindless bureaucrats or paranoid witch-hunters, Ray Monk offers a much more _____ depiction of the workers who ensured the secrecy of the Manhattan Project.

| (A) nuanced |
| (B) skillful |
| (C) erratic |
| (D) skeptical |
| (E) provocative |

3. In recent years, few major hurricanes have struck the most exposed sections of the Atlantic coast in the United States; however, _____ coastlines in other regions have not been spared the effects of serious storms.

| (A) barren |
| (B) populous |
| (C) isolated |
| (D) unspoiled |
| (E) susceptible |

4. Throughout Dante's work, there is a constant back-and-forth between his personal predicament as an impoverished exile and his reflections on the nature of human society, with an inevitable tension between the conclusions he has genuinely reached and those he merely considers _____ to state.

| (A) natural |
| (B) imperative |
| (C) thorny |
| (D) convenient |
| (E) unnecessary |

5. William Jennings Bryan's speech at the 1896 Democratic National Convention _____ Bryan's supporters, adding new vigor to a campaign that had previously been quite staid.

| (A) elucidated |
| (B) galvanized |
| (C) placated |
| (D) enervated |
| (E) pandered to |

6. Mental telepathy has been a staple of science fiction for decades, featuring prominently in the plots of books, movies, and comics, yet mainstream scientific consensus dismisses the phenomenon as nothing but _____.

| (A) egotism |
| (B) profligacy |
| (C) chicanery |
| (D) frustration |
| (E) equivocation |

7. Napoleon's 1812 invasion of Russia was _____ moment because the French army, once considered invincible, never fully recovered from the damage it withstood during the course of the campaign.

| (A) a divisive |
| (B) an ineffable |
| (C) a fortuitous |
| (D) a coveted |
| (E) a watershed |

8. In the decades following the introduction of the printing press, hand-illustrated parchment came to be viewed as _____, a relic of a pre-technological age.

(A) a paragon
(B) an anachronism
(C) a deficit
(D) a debacle
(E) an endeavor

9. Many primate species are terrestrial rather than _____, but unlike humans, all great apes possess physiological adaptations that allow them to climb trees.

(A) arboreal
(B) omnivorous
(C) predatory
(D) aquatic
(E) nomadic

10. Linguists sometimes feel discomfort when inventing scripts for traditionally oral languages because the very idea of an alphabet alters the language and converts the inventor from observer to _____.

(A) activist
(B) analyst
(C) mimic
(D) bystander
(E) defender

11. That the Higgs boson truly existed was an idea traditionally (i) _____ by the majority of the scientific community; only in recent years has the notion that the particle is real gained widespread (ii) _____ among physicists.

Blank (i)	Blank (ii)
(A) panned	(D) parlance
(B) espoused	(E) compensation
(C) squandered	(F) traction

12. Public health officials often describe risks in (i) _____ jargon, using metrics such as odds ratios, relative risks, and standardized mortality ratios. Unfortunately, these metrics, which are standard fare for epidemiologists and other scientists, often do not (ii) _____ into public discourse.

Blank (i)	Blank (ii)
(A) obfuscating	(D) split clearly
(B) hybrid	(E) buy fully
(C) idealistic	(F) translate easily

13. Even though language assists the thinking process by providing categories and concepts, it is now widely accepted that language is not a (i) _____ thought. Studies have repeatedly demonstrated that children who have not yet begun to speak can follow complex situations, indicating that cognition is (ii) _____ from language.

Blank (i)	Blank (ii)
(A) detriment to	(D) distinct
(B) precondition for	(E) derived
(C) component of	(F) evident

14. Since the eighteenth century, science has been based on the notion that scientific truth is straightforward and (i) _____, devoid of the (ii) _____ found in literature and in other humanistic fields.

Blank (i)	Blank (ii)
(A) lofty	(D) intensity of emotion
(B) adaptive	(E) ambiguities of interpretation
(C) unequivocal	(F) keenness of observation

15. In her book *The Idealist*, which follows humanitarian Jeffrey Sachs in his quest to reduce poverty in Africa, Nina Munk conveys her subject's (i) _____ as well as his consequent unwillingness to (ii) _____ any flaws in the implementation of his projects.

Blank (i)	Blank (ii)
(A) intransigence	(D) sweep aside
(B) affluence	(E) concede to
(C) erudition	(F) call on

16. In response to the candidate's attempt to present herself as (i) _____, her opponents have denounced her public displays of generosity as nothing but political (ii) _____.

Blank (i)	Blank (ii)
(A) an ideologue	(D) machination
(B) a sycophant	(E) parrying
(C) an altruist	(F) equivocation

17. New, more accurate techniques for measuring the ever-increasing size of the cosmos suggest that the universe is expanding at a rate five to nine percent faster than the rate indicated by previous data. This (i) _____ may be due to a simple misunderstanding that, when resolved, will allow scientists to (ii) _____ the two sets of figures.

Blank (i)	Blank (ii)
(A) innovation	(D) marry
(B) discrepancy	(E) quantify
(C) convergence	(F) regulate

18. The masks used by actors in ancient Greece were (i) _____ objects: constructed from (ii) _____ materials, they were traditionally burned as sacrifices on the altar of Dionysus after being used in performance.

Blank (i)	Blank (ii)
(A) grotesque	(D) rare
(B) malleable	(E) perishable
(C) ephemeral	(F) exquisite

19. The Roman historian Plutarch rarely touched on weighty events, recounting (i) _____ anecdotes because he believed that they would reveal more about his subjects than lists of (ii) _____ accomplishments would.

Blank (i)	Blank (ii)
(A) frivolous	(D) sporadic
(B) banal	(E) marginal
(C) private	(F) venerable

20. Despite much speculation, it is unclear which English-language book has sold the greatest number of copies. There are no (i) _____ sales figures for books published more than a few decades ago, and works that are out of copyright frequently exist in (ii) _____ editions and translations. Nevertheless, some sources have continued to make the (iii) _____ assertion that Dickens' *A Tale of Two Cities* holds the honor, followed by Tolkien's *Lord of the Rings*.

Blank (i)	Blank (ii)	Blank (iii)
(A) projected	(D) slick	(G) audacious
(B) independent	(E) myriad	(H) unsubstantiated
(C) comprehensive	(F) annotated	(J) calculated

21. The senator is notorious for his (i) _____ speeches, but colleagues now dismiss his (ii) _____ rhetoric as nothing but bluster. Indeed, they have learned to react to his diatribes with utter (iii) _____.

Blank (i)	Blank (ii)	Blank (iii)
(A) laconic	(D) uplifting	(G) nonchalance
(B) bombastic	(E) overblown	(H) bemusement
(C) resentful	(F) resounding	(J) apprehension

22. It is often claimed that Kant was a late developer – that he only became an important philosopher in his mid-50s, after rejecting his earlier views. Although it is true that Kant wrote his greatest works relatively late in life, there is often an unmerited tendency to (i) _____ the value of his earlier works. In recent years, however, Kant scholars have begun to (ii) _____ these "pre-critical" writings and have even identified some (iii) _____between these works and Kant's mature work.

Blank (i)	Blank (ii)	Blank (iii)
(A) esteem	(D) pay more attention to	(G) ruptures
(B) underestimate	(E) deny the validity of	(H) continuities
(C) describe	(F) uphold the authenticity of	(J) collaborations

23. Although the study of modern literature was (i) _____ in the late nineteenth century, it still was met with widespread skepticism about its validity as branch of scholarship. Even Matthew Arnold, who famously (ii) _____ literary education, expressed concern that it might not prove substantial enough to be (iii) _____ as an independent discipline.

Blank (i)	Blank (ii)	Blank (iii)
(A) legitimized	(D) fended off	(G) solvent
(B) reviled	(E) agitated for	(H) cognizant
(C) contrived	(F) prevailed upon	(J) viable

24. Air creates a naturally (i) _____ formation, with cooler layers sinking to the bottom and warmer ones rising above them. Ceiling fans are normally used to cool rooms by pushing warm air down to create a draft; however, when set counter-clockwise, they can also heat rooms by (ii) _____ warm air from the ceiling toward the floor. In some cases, this technique can significantly reduce heating costs, while in others it may result in only (iii) _____ savings.

Blank (i)	Blank (ii)	Blank (iii)
(A) permeable	(D) amplifying	(G) relative
(B) volatile	(E) circulating	(H) marginal
(C) stratified	(F) boosting	(J) essential

25. Some companies succeed in achieving such complete (i) _____ of a market that their brand name becomes virtually (ii) _____ a product itself. Few people, for example, request facial tissues when they have a cold; rather, they (iii) _____ ask for Kleenex®.

Blank (i)	Blank (ii)	Blank (iii)
(A) valuation	(D) synonymous with	(G) reflexively
(B) monopolization	(E) comparable to	(H) intentionally
(C) appraisal	(F) suggestive of	(J) offhandedly

26. Groups "transmit" preferences to other groups, but the opposite is also true: preferences help create groups. When the latter occurs, small, seemingly (i) _____ differences have the potential to become genuine (ii) _____. The more people who have access to what is considered proper taste, the finer these (iii) _____ become.

Blank (i)	Blank (ii)	Blank (iii)
(A) laconic	(D) points of contention	(G) rebellions
(B) indelible	(E) forms of appeasement	(H) exceptions
(C) trivial	(F) statements of opinion	(J) gradations

27. One popular theory holds that if the poliovirus arrives in infancy, it produces mild if any symptoms. If it arrives later in childhood or in adulthood, however, prognosis is generally far more (i) _____. Thus, the polio outbreaks that left thousands paralyzed in the United States during the mid-twentieth century most likely signaled improving sanitary conditions rather than a new (ii) _____. Children were (iii) _____ smaller amounts of dangerous bacteria and encountering the poliovirus later and later.

Blank (i)	Blank (ii)	Blank (iii)
(A) grave	(D) diagnosis	(G) shedding
(B) encouraging	(E) expertise	(H) imbibing
(C) unpredictable	(F) pandemic	(J) uncovering

28. The poetry world has long (i) _____ the problem of accessibility. Since audiences are smaller than they are in other genres, the assumption is that many readers are tuning out because they find the work (ii) _____. The conventional logic is that many contemporary poems are too conceptual for the public, just as abstract art is too (iii) _____.

Blank (i)	Blank (ii)	Blank (iii)
(A) reveled in	(D) enticing	(G) permissive
(B) fretted over	(E) inscrutable	(H) esoteric
(C) alluded to	(F) germane	(J) myopic

29. Isabella Stewart Gardner's (i) _____ eccentricity as well as her tendency to (ii) _____ social conventions made her the subject of much gossip. Her exploits, which included walking a pair of lions in Boston's Public Gardens and sporting a headband emblazoned with "Oh, you Red Sox" to the symphony, provoked much (iii) _____ among the more upright members of society.

Blank (i)	Blank (ii)	Blank (iii)
(A) confrontation with	(D) condone	(G) consternation
(B) rancor toward	(E) grasp	(H) penitence
(C) penchant for	(F) flout	(J) ambivalence

30. Characterized by an aloof and (i) _____ style, the author's new novel lacks the sort of emotional (ii) _____ that her readers have come to expect. It is therefore unsurprising that sales of the book have been at best (iii) _____.

Blank (i)	Blank (ii)	Blank (iii)
(A) detached	(D) restraint	(G) stellar
(B) caustic	(E) poignancy	(H) incremental
(C) florid	(F) manipulation	(J) tepid

Explanations: Medium Text Completions

1. B

The contradictor *rather* indicates that the second sentence is offering a different explanation for why *the moralized world of the late Middle Ages wane[d]* than the one presented in the first sentence. What explanation is presented in the first sentence? The growth of technical literacy rather than the Reformation caused the medieval world to wane (gradually disappear). The blank must therefore be filled with a synonym for *waned*. Be careful with (A): the late Middle Ages may have been *permeated* by the growth of technical literacy, but the second sentence must explain why the *moralized world* disappeared, and *permeated* does not mean. Don't be fooled by *forestalled* (prevented) either: the society in question disappeared – it was not prevented from occurring in the first place. *Compounded* (augmented) means the opposite of the required word, and *adapted* does not make sense at all. The only word that fits is *eroded*, which echoes the idea of disappearance conveyed in the first sentence. (B) is thus correct.

2. A

The key word *unlike* indicates that the sentence will focus on the difference between Ray Monk and other authors who write about Robert Oppenheimer. The sentence tells us that the other authors portray the security officers at Oppenheimer's lab in stark, black-or-white terms (*mindless bureaucrats or paranoid witch hunters*), so the blank must be filled with a positive word that implies Monk took a contrasting approach. The answer that matches that criterion most precisely is *nuanced*, which implies a perspective that examines a broad spectrum of behaviors. The remaining answers do not fit the definition required by the sentence. (A) is thus correct.

3. E

The sentence sets up a contrast between the relative freedom from major hurricanes experienced by the most exposed sections of the Atlantic coastline in the United States, and the damage caused by serious storms along comparable coastlines elsewhere. Logically, then, the blank must be filled with a word similar to *exposed*. Be careful with *barren*: this word simply means empty, and a coastline that is empty can easily be struck by storms. Likewise, a coastline can be both isolated and exposed to storms – one factor does not affect the other. *Populous* and *unspoiled* do not fit at all. Whether a coastline is developed/inhabited does not affect its likelihood of being struck by storms. A coastline that is exposed, however, is also the type of coastline that is most *susceptible* (vulnerable) to storms. So even though *susceptible* is not an exact synonym for *exposed*, the two words convey the same idea: the coastlines in the United States most likely to be hit by hurricanes have been spared in recent years, but coastlines elsewhere have not been so lucky. (E) is thus correct.

4. D

The phrase *with an inevitable tension between* indicates that the two ideas that follow must be opposing or contradictory in some way. The first idea involves *conclusions he has genuinely reached*, implying that the second idea must involve conclusions that are not genuine. The only option that conveys this idea is (E): if Dante stated conclusions only because they were *convenient*, he was not stating something he sincerely believed – rather, he was acting based on practical concerns.

5. B

The fact that Bryan's speech had the effect of *adding new vigor* (energy) *to a campaign that had previous been quite staid* (unexciting) indicates that the blank must be filled with a positive word consistent with the idea of reinvigorating. *Elucidated* (clarified) is positive but does not make sense, and supporters who were *enervated* (drained of energy) or *placated* (calmed) would make a campaign less vigorous. Don't get distracted by (E) – although supporters who were *pandered to* might respond enthusiastically, this word is a less direct match than *galvanized*, which exactly fits the definition of *adding new vigor*. (B) is thus correct.

6. C

The fact that mental telepathy is associated with science fiction, as well as the fact that it is dismissed by *mainstream scientific consensus*, indicates that the blank must be filled with a negative word roughly meaning nonsense. Although all of the options are negative, the only word that matches the necessary definition is *chicanery* (fakery). Scientists would logically consider mental telepathy to be a fraudulent phenomenon. (C) is thus correct.

7. E

The sentence indicates that Napoleon's army was permanently changed by the 1812 invasion of Russia, so clearly that campaign had a significant (negative) impact on the army. The blank must therefore be filled with a word indicating that profound effect. *Divisive* implies that the members of the army turned against one another, not that the army as a whole sustained permanent damage. *Ineffable* (inexpressible), *fortuitous* (occurring by chance), and *coveted* (in high demand) all do not fit. A *watershed* moment is a key moment, and the phrase *never fully recovered* clearly supports the idea that the 1812 invasion was a crucial turning point. Although this word is not explicitly negative, it is the best fit for the sentence, making (E) correct.

8. B

Logically, hand-illustrated parchment would have been regarded as old-fashioned after the introduction of the printing press, an idea that is reinforced by the phrase *a relic of a pre-technological age*. The blank must therefore be filled with a negative word meaning something like irrelevant. *Paragon* (perfect example), *deficit*, and *endeavor* (undertaking) all clearly do not fit. Be careful with *deficit*: it is both negative and generally consistent with the idea of irrelevance, but *anachronism* (something that does not belong in a given time period) fits the sentence perfectly. (B) is thus correct.

9. A

The sentence sets up a contrast between *terrestrial* and the blank, providing a further clue with the reference to tree-climbing. Logically, the blank must be filled with a word that refers to living in trees. The only possibility is (A); even if you are unfamiliar with the word *arboreal*, the root ARBOR- (tree) provides an important clue.

10. A

The key word, *alters*, indicates that linguists who invent alphabets for existing languages are changing those languages, so the blank must be filled with a word consistent with the idea of change. In addition, the phrase *converts the inventor from observer to _____* indicates that the correct word must mean the opposite of *observer*. Although you may be more familiar with the term *activist* in a political context, the word is used here in its literal definition – that is, a person who takes action. *Activist* thus fits the required definition, making (A) correct. *Analyst* could make sense as the opposite of *observer*, but a person who invents a language is actually creating, not just analyzing. *Mimic* does not make sense because imitating is not the same thing as creating. A *bystander* is similar to an observer, so (D) can be eliminated. In some contexts, *defender* could be construed as the opposite of *observer*, but here the sentence focuses on creating, not defending.

11. A, F

The sentence sets up a contrast between how the Higgs boson was viewed traditionally and how it has been viewed more recently. The word *gained* offers a subtle clue that the word in Blank (ii) should be positive, so you can assume that the word in Blank (i) should be negative. For Blank (i), *espoused* is positive and can be eliminated, but the other answers are both negative. *Squandered* (wasted, thrown away) does not make sense; the blank must be filled with a word meaning something more like rejected. *Panned* (disparaged) is a much better fit, making (A) the answer to Blank (i).

If the idea that the Higgs Boson existed was rejected in the past, then Blank (ii) must convey that it has been more recently accepted. *Traction* is accurately used as a synonym for acceptance here – "gained traction" is a common expression used to indicate that an idea is increasing in popularity. *Parlance* (speech) does not make sense at all, and *compensation* does not fit either – an idea cannot be compensated. That makes (F) the answer to Blank (ii).

12. A, F

Blank (i) must be filled with a word that describes the type of jargon public health officials use, so consider the reference to *odd ratios, relative risks, and standardized mortality ratios*. Those are technical terms that would be largely meaningless to most people. *Hybrid* (made up of parts from different sources) and *idealistic* (impractical, starry-eyed) are both inconsistent with that idea, but *obfuscating* (making unclear) fits with the technical terminology used. (A) is thus the answer to Blank (i).

Blank (ii) indicates a difference between how the jargon is perceived by epidemiologists and other scientists vs. how it is perceived by the public. For the former, it is *standard fare*, i.e. everyday language. Logically, though, this type of technical speech would not carry over well into public discourse – that is, it would not *translate easily*. Although it is possible for a language to *split clearly* into different components, that meaning does not make sense here. It is also impossible for a language to *buy fully into* anything. (F) is thus the answer to Blank (ii).

13. B, D

The first sentence sets up a contrast between two ideas: the first half indicates that language *assists the thinking process,* and the second half indicates a relationship between language and thought that does *not* exist. The implication is that language and thought have a close relationship but are not precisely the same thing. Be careful with (A). It is true that if language is an aid to the thinking process, then it is not a detriment to that process; however, this idea does not really make sense in context. The word in Blank (i) is referring to a belief that recently became accepted (*now widely accepted*), and if the relationship between language has been firmly established *since the eighteenth century,* it would not make sense to say that people previously believed language impeded thought. (C) does not fit: if language helps people think, then the idea that language is not a *component of* thought is entirely illogical.
(B) is supported by the remainder of the passage: if children who cannot yet speak *can follow complex situations,* then language must not be a *precondition for thought* – that is, people can think before they can talk. That idea also implies that language and thought are *distinct,* processes, making (D) the answer to Blank (ii).

14. C, E

Blank (i) must be filled with a word that describes science and means something similar to straightforward. *Lofty* (high-minded) and *adaptive* are both words that could be used to describe science, but neither is consistent with the idea of straightforwardness. *Unequivocal* (absolute) does, however, fit that idea, making (C) the answer to Blank (i).

Blank (ii) must be filled with a word indicating something that science is *devoid of* – that is, something it lacks – but that literature possesses. *Keenness of observation* is a quality associated with science, but it is not the opposite of *unequivocal.* Be careful with (D): it might seem reasonable that literature would involve more emotion than science would, but the opposition is between the absolute, black-and-white nature of science and the word in the blank. In order for (D) to be correct, the sentence would have to highlight the unemotional quality of science, but that is not the case here. (E) is much more directly consistent with the focus of the sentence: a field that deals in absolutes, by definition, does not deal in *ambiguities of interpretation.* The latter is also a key feature of literature and humanistic fields. That makes (E) the answer to Blank (ii).

15. A, E

The word *consequent* indicates that Blank (ii) must be filled with a word indicating a result of the word in Blank (i); however, the sentence provides no information about the definition of either word. As a result, you must work entirely from the relationship. The only pair of words that logically conveys a cause/effect relationship is *intransigence* (extreme stubbornness) and *concede to* (admit to). A person who is extremely stubborn is someone who is unlikely to admit to flaws in a project. (A) is thus the answer to Blank (i), and (E) is the answer to Blank (ii).

16. C, D

Blank (i) must be filled with a word that describes how the candidate sought to portray herself. Since politicians typically try to present themselves in a positive light, it is reasonable to assume that the answer to Blank (i) must be positive. *Sycophant* (suck-up) is negative, and *ideologue* is neutral, with a slightly negative connotation. Only *altruist* (someone who performs good works out of a genuine desire to do so) describes the type of person a candidate would clearly go out of her way to present herself as.

For Blank (ii), the blank must be filled with a word indicating what the candidate was *denounced* for, suggesting that the correct answer will be negative and mean something like showing off or self-promoting. Although there is no direct match for those definitions, *machination* (crafty maneuvering) comes closest, making (D) correct. *Parrying* (evading, warding off) does not make sense; the sentence does not indicate that the candidate presented herself well in an attempt to evade anything. *Equivocation* (vacillating, being inconsistent) also does not quite fit. Although this is something politicians are often accused of, there is nothing here to directly indicate that the candidate behaved in a contradictory or inconsistent manner. We only know that she presented herself in a particular way publicly, and assuming anything more than that involves reading beyond what the sentence implies.

17. B, D

Blank (i) must be filled with a word that refers to the situation described in the previous sentence. What is that situation? New data about the expansion of the universe indicates that this phenomenon is occurring at faster rate than that indicated by earlier data. In other words, there is a *discrepancy* between the two sets of data. (B) is thus the answer to Blank (i). Be careful with *innovation*, though. Although the first sentence does refer to *new, more accurate techniques*, the phrase *simple misunderstanding* in the second sentence indicates a focus on the fact that there are two contradictory sets of data. In order for the problem to be resolved, scientists must be able to make sense out of the two data sets – that is, to bring them together or reconcile them in some way. The answer most consistent with that idea is (D). Used in this context, *marry* is synonym for bring together. Neither *quantifying* nor *regulating* the two sets of figures would allow scientists to resolve the problem. That makes (D) the answer to Blank (ii).

18. C, E

The fact that Greek theater masks were *traditionally burned as sacrifices* after use indicates that they were not intended to be preserved, a meaning that the word in Blank (i) must convey. Only *ephemeral* (short-lived) matches that definition, making (C) the answer to Blank (i).

Blank (ii) must refer to a quality of the masks that would make them short-lived. There is no direct connection between being *rare* or *exquisite* and lasting for a short time, but *perishable* materials would by definition not last very long. That makes (E) the answer to Blank (ii).

19. A, F

The sentence sets up an implicit contrast between *weighty events* and the type of anecdotes Plutarch did recount. Blank (i) must therefore mean the opposite of *weighty* (serious), i.e. light. *Banal* (boring, unoriginal) does not fit at all. Although *private* is consistent with the idea of revealing information about subjects, it is not the opposite of *weighty*, nor is it the opposite of any of the options for Blank (ii). *Frivolous* (not serious) is a much better fit, making (A) the answer to Blank (i).

For Blank (ii), *venerable* (honorable, serious) echoes the word *weighty* and serves as an effective antonym for *frivolous*. *Sporadic* (occasional) does not fit at all, and *marginal* (unimportant, non-essential) is more of a synonym to *frivolous* than its opposite. (F) is thus the answer to Blank (ii).

20. C, E, H

The first sentence provides key information for filling in the blanks. The fact that it is <u>unclear which English-language book has sold the greatest number of copies</u> suggest that no reliable sales figures are available. A lack of *comprehensive* sales figures would certainly lead to a state of uncertainty about which book holds that honor. *Independent* does not fit at all for, but don't be distracted by *projected* – the sentence is describing a situation resulting from existing sales figures, not figures based on speculation. *Comprehensive* is much more directly consistent with the focus of the sentence. (C) is thus the answer to Blank (i).

For Blank (ii), the correct answer must also convey the lack of clarity over the top selling English-language book. Logically, the presence of *myriad* (many) editions would add to the difficulty of tracking sales at a large scale over time, making (E) the answer to Blank (ii). Neither *slick* nor *annotated* editions would have any effect on the tracking of book sales.

Blank (iii) reiterates the idea presented in the first sentence: people have speculated that either *A Tale of Two Cities* or *Lord of the Rings* is the best selling English-language book, but there is no evidence for that claim – that is, it is *unsubstantiated*. The claim might also be either *audacious* (daring) or *calculated*, but the sentence provides no information to directly support either of those possibilities. (H) is thus the answer to Blank (iii).

21. B, E, G

The key phrase *nothing but bluster* and the key word *diatribes* make it clear the senator is inclined to angry outbursts. *Bombastic* for Blank (i) and *overblown* for Blank (ii) convey that meaning most directly – bombastic speeches are by definition overblown. *Laconic* (using few words) clearly does not fit, but don't get distracted by *resentful*. Although that word fits with the idea of diatribes, resentful speeches would not necessarily be overblown, and neither *resounding* nor *uplifting* makes sense. (B) is thus the answer to Blank (i), and (E) is the answer to Blank (ii).

Blank (iii) describes the colleagues' reaction to the senator's speeches. If the colleagues consider the speeches *nothing but bluster* (that is, a bunch of hot air), then they must not take the speeches very seriously. Neither *bemusement* (puzzlement) nor *apprehension* (anxiety) accurately describes that type of reaction. *Nonchalance* (casualness) fits the idea of not demonstrating a strong reaction to the speeches, so (G) is the answer to Blank (iii).

22. B, D, H

The sentence sets up a contrast between attitudes toward Kant's greatest works, which are generally acknowledged to have been written late in his life, and attitudes toward his earlier works which, the sentence implies, were less great. The phrase *although it is true that Kant wrote his greatest works relatively late in life* suggests that the statement that follows will present a contrasting idea – that is, it will suggest that Kant's earlier works were better than they are usually recognized to be. The *unmerited tendency* must therefore refer to the tradition of viewing Kant's earlier works negatively, and Blank (i) must be filled with a word conveying that idea. *Esteem* is positive and can thus be eliminated, and *describe* is positive/neutral and does not fit at all – the issue is that Kant's earlier works are not held in high regard, not that they have not been described. *Underestimate* accurately conveys the idea that the value of Kant's earlier works is often unfairly overlooked. (B) is thus the answer to Blank (i).

Blank (ii) indicates a reversal of the situation in Blank (i): Kant scholars used to view Kant's earlier works as unworthy of study, but now they are reconsidering that perspective and taking a closer look at them. The blank should therefore be filled with a phrase indicating this newly positive attitude. *Deny the validity of* is negative, and *uphold the authenticity of* is positive but off-topic – the issue is not whether Kant's earlier works were truly written by Kant, but rather whether they are worthy of study. *Pay more attention to* is most directly consistent with the idea that scholars are seeing new value in Kant's earlier works, making (D) the answer to Blank (ii).

Why would scholars pay new attention to Kant's earlier works? Logically, because they have recognized that these works are similar to – that is, they contain *continuities* with – Kant's later, greater works. *Ruptures* conveys the exact opposite of what is required. Be careful with *collaborations*, though: people can collaborate with one another to write works, but works themselves cannot collaborate. (H) is thus the answer to Blank (iii).

23. A, E, J

The first sentence sets up a contrast between something that was done to the study of modern literature in the nineteenth century and the skepticism with which that action was received. Because skepticism indicates a negative attitude, Blank (i) must be filled with a positive word. *Reviled* (detested) is negative and can be eliminated. *Legitimized*, however, is positive and creates a logical meaning when plugged into the sentence: in the nineteenth century, literature came to be viewed as a legitimate area of study for the first time, but people still remained wary of it. Be careful with *contrived* (thought up): although it is in fact true that the study of modern literature was invented in the nineteenth century, this answer does not fit with the context of the sentence. The phrase *skepticism about its validity* indicates that the sentence is focusing on whether literature was a valid field of study – that is, one that deserved to be *legitimized*, so (A) is the best match for Blank (i).

For Blank (ii), the word *even* is key. It indicates that the second sentence will reaffirm the idea presented in the first sentence, and will emphasize the extent to which the study of literature was viewed suspiciously. To make that point clearly, Blank (ii) must be filled with a word indicating that Arnold's attitude toward the study of modern literature was generally positive. *Fended off* is negative and can be eliminated, and *prevailed upon* (convince) does not make sense – a person can only prevail upon another person, not an academic discipline. Don't be fooled by (E). Although *agitate* normally has a negative meaning, *agitate for* is actually a positive expression meaning *fight for*. (E) is thus the answer to Blank (ii).

Blank (iii) refers to Arnold's concern that the study of modern literature would be unable to stand on its own as a discipline. Logically, the blank must be filled with a positive word meaning something like strong. *Solvent* is a word indicating that a person or company has sufficient funds to pay all of their debts; it makes no sense here. Likewise, *cognizant* (aware) does not fit – only a person can be cognizant, not a field of study. That leaves *viable* (workable), which fits. (J) is thus the answer to Blank (iii).

24. C, E, H

For Blank (i), the phrase *with cooler layers sinking to the bottom and warmer ones rising above them* provides a clear illustration of what the correct word must mean. The only option corresponding to this definition is *stratified*, which means layered. Although air is *permeable* (porous, able to be passed through), that word does not correspond to the idea of layers. The same is true for *volatile* (unstable). (C) is thus the answer to Blank (i).

Blank (ii) must be filled with a word that describes how ceiling fans create heat by moving warm air toward the floor. *Amplifying* is something that is done to sound to make it louder; it does not apply to moving air. *Boosting* is illogical: something that is boosted moves up, whereas ceiling fans move air down (*toward the floor*). That leaves *circulating*, which accurately describes the movement of air caused by a fan. (E) is thus the answer to Blank (ii).

For Blank (iii), the sentence sets up a contrast between the outstanding results of using ceiling fans to heat rooms (*significantly reduce heating costs*) that are obtained in some cases, and the less outstanding results that are obtained at other times. Logically, this blank must be filled with a word meaning small or modest. The word that most directly conveys this idea is *marginal* (slight or insignificant), making (J) the answer to Blank (iii).

25. B, D, G

The sentence offers few direct clues about the required definitions, so you must work primarily from the relationships between the words and sentences. For Blanks (i) and (ii), the basic construction *such complete _____ that _____* indicates that Blank (ii) must be filled with a word indicating a result of the word in Blank (i). The only pair that conveys this relationship is *monopolization…synonymous with*, making (B) the answer to Blank (i) and (D) the answer to Blank (ii). If a company has an extreme monopoly on a product, then logically the product becomes identified with the company to the point at which they are indistinguishable. Kleenex™ is provided as an example of that phenomenon, and the word *reflexively* (automatically) accurately conveys the lack of distinction between company and product. In most consumers' minds, facial tissue *is* Kleenex™, and most people unthinkingly use the brand name to ask for the product – indeed, they may be unaware that Kleenex™ is a brand name and not the product itself. *Intentionally* conveys just the opposite idea, namely that people deliberately conflate Kleenex™ and facial tissues. This answer is incorrect because the whole point is that most people automatically conflate the product and brand. *Offhandedly* (casually) is incorrect because that word does not convey the implication of doing something automatically. (G) is thus the answer to Blank (iii).

26. C, D, J

Blank (i) must be filled with a word that is similar to *small* and that is used to characterize what some differences appear to be. Neither *laconic* (using few words) or *indelible* (unable to be removed) is consistent with the idea of small differences, but *trivial* (very minor, insignificant) fits well. (C) is thus the answer to Blank (i).

For Blank (ii), consider the context: the sentence must describe what happens when preferences create groups – that is, when people associate with others based on mutual preferences. Logically, such groups are more likely to reject conflicting points of view or preferences. Differences that are initially small can blow up and become major sources of conflict, i.e. *points of contention*. That makes (D) the answer to Blank (ii). (E) implies exactly the opposite of the required meaning. If a group is based on similar likes among its members, differences are likely to cause conflict rather than *appeasement* (making concessions to preserve the peace). (F) does not make any sense: differences can provoke opinions, but they do not *become* opinions.

Blank (iii) must be filled with a word that refers to differences. If a lot of people buy into an accepted group preference or manner of behaving (*proper taste*), then membership must become based on ever *finer* (more precise) criteria in order for the group to maintain its exclusivity. A word meaning something like differences is therefore required. Neither *rebellions* nor *exceptions* matches that definition, but *gradations* fits: the more specifically acceptable taste is defined, the more gradations emerge. (J) is thus the answer to Blank (iii).

27. A, F, H

In the second sentence, the contradictor *however* sets up a contrast with the first sentence. The first sentence indicates that polio produces *mild if any* symptoms in infants, so the second sentence must indicate that polio is more serious in older children – that is, its prognosis is *far more grave*. That makes (A) the answer to Blank (i).

For Blank (ii), the fact that thousands of children were left paralyzed by polio during the mid-twentieth century suggests that older children were contracting the disease. Why were older children contracting the disease? Because of *improved sanitary conditions*, a phrase that is contrasted with the blank. The implication is that older children began falling ill because of this environmental factor rather than because of an entirely new outbreak, i.e. a *pandemic*, of the disease. That makes (F) the answer to Blank (ii).

For Blank (iii), the passage states that children were *encountering the poliovirus later and later*, so the blank must be filled with a word that describes how children became infected. *Shedding* implies exactly the opposite of the required meaning: children must have been absorbing or ingesting the bacteria, not giving it off. *Uncovering* bacteria would also not necessarily make someone ill. *Imbibing* (ingesting) harmful bacteria, however, would most likely lead to serious illness. (H) is thus the answer to Blank (iii).

28. B, E, H

Blank (i) describes the poetry world's reaction to the *problem of accessibility*, so it is reasonable to assume that the blank should be filled with a negative word meaning something like worried about. *Reveled in* (enjoyed) is strongly positive, and although poetry does often *allude* (refer) *to* things, this phrase does not make sense here. *Fretted over* means worried, so (B) is the answer to Blank (i).

For Blank (ii), the phrase *tuning out* indicates that readers are likewise having a negative reaction to poetry – some features of that genre cause them to stop paying attention. *Enticing* work would draw readers in, not push them away, as would *germane* (relevant) work. Work that readers found *inscrutable* (impenetrable, inaccessible) would, however, result in a lack of interest. (E) is thus the answer to Blank (ii).

For Blank (iii), the key phrase *just as* indicates that the sentence is drawing a parallel between a feature of poetry that makes the genre inaccessible (*too conceptual*) and a feature of abstract art that has a similar effect. The blank must therefore be filled with a word that would logically describe an inaccessible genre like abstract art and convey an idea similar to *conceptual*. *Permissive* and *myopic* (short-sighted) are both words that could be potentially be used to describe abstract art, but *esoteric* (extremely specialized, understood by only a select few) is most consistent with the idea that this form of art is inaccessible to the public. (H) is thus the answer to Blank (iii).

29. C, F, G

For Blanks (i) and (ii), the description *the subject of much gossip* provides an important clue. Logically, Gardner was a source of gossip because she behaved in an eccentric manner and defied social conventions. *Penchant for* (tendency toward) is the best fit for Blank (i) because it indicates that Gardner was inclined to act in an eccentric manner. *Rancor toward* implies exactly the opposite – someone who hated eccentricity would be a far less likely source of gossip. Likewise, a person who had a *confrontation with* eccentricity would logically be opposed to it, which was not at all the case for Gardner. (C) is thus the answer to Blank (i).

For Blank (ii), *flout* (openly go against) perfectly conveys the idea that Gardner behaved in an unusual manner and disregarded social consequences. *Condone* (approve of) and *grasp* both imply the opposite. That makes (F) the answer to Blank (ii).

Blank (iii) describes the reaction of *the more upright members of society* to Gardner's outrageous exploits (walking a pair of lions in the Public Garden, attending the symphony while decked out in a headband emblazoned with the name of a baseball team). Logically, those members of society would have been horrified, a reaction conveyed by *consternation*. They would not have been *penitent* (apologetic) or *ambivalent* (uncertain). (G) is thus the answer to Blank (iii).

30. A, E, J

Blank (i) is paired with *aloof* (unemotional, standoffish), indicating that it must be filled with a word that has a similar meaning. This implication is reinforced by the statement that the novel is emotionally lacking in some way. *Caustic* (harsh) is far too negative, however, and a *florid* (flowery) style would be the opposite of an *aloof* one. *Detached* is far more consistent with the description provided in the sentence, making (A) the answer to Blank (i).

Blank (ii) describes an emotional quality that the novel lacks. Logically, it should be filled with a word meaning something like impact or effect, and should emphasize the detached quality of the novel. A novel that lacked *restraint* would by definition be an emotional one, so this answer does not fit. *Manipulation* is too negative and has the wrong connotation: an author who was manipulative would be unlikely to acquire regular readers – something the sentence implies this particular author has done. The sentence also suggests that readers are disappointed by this novel because they have come to value a positive emotional connection with the author's work. A work that lacked a negative quality such as manipulation would please rather than displease readers. That leaves *poignancy* (being deeply touching). Logically, a work that lacked the ability to move people emotionally could be characterized as aloof and would be off-putting to readers. (E) is thus the answer to Blank (ii).

For Blank (iii), the key phrase *at best* suggests that the novel's sales have been weak, an interpretation supported by the fact that it lacks key features that readers expect. *Stellar* (outstanding) implies exactly the opposite of what is required, and *incremental* (little by little) does not fit at all. *Tepid* (middling, lukewarm) accurately conveys the idea of weak sales, making (J) the answer to Blank (iii).

Sentence Equivalences: Medium

1. Charles Mingus's music _____ the listener in the blues rituals of African American life, while at the same time depicting those rituals from a playful distance.

   [A] engages
   [B] immerses
   [C] pulls
   [D] conceals
   [E] steeps
   [F] situates

2. Following revelations that they had authorized the purchase of stolen antiquities, senior museum administrators were immediately _____ by the board of directors.

   [A] rebuked
   [B] exasperated
   [C] booted
   [D] censured
   [E] mollified
   [F] evaluated

3. While physics and art may outwardly appear to have little in common, they do have some _____ similarities because both are grounded in mathematical principles.

   [A] recurring
   [B] latent
   [C] potent
   [D] vestigial
   [E] underlying
   [F] potential

4. The origin of heavy metals such as gold and platinum is a source of debate among astronomers, but one theory suggests that these substances were _____ by collisions between stars.

    [A] pulverized
    [B] expelled
    [C] created
    [D] altered
    [E] forged
    [F] modified

5. Angela Carter's works are widely taught in schools and universities, but many critics find it difficult to _____ them within a particular tradition: Carter has literary offspring but few antecedents.

    [A] surround
    [B] situate
    [C] reify
    [D] administer
    [E] represent
    [F] contextualize

6. If it is to succeed, any new paradigm for resolving disputes between workers and management must include a less _____ review board, one with members who are independent and neutral experts.

    [A] litigious
    [B] formal
    [C] biased
    [D] partisan
    [E] entrenched
    [F] disinterested

7. Pauline Kael is often viewed as _____ because she not only re-invented film criticism as an art form but also pioneered an entirely new style of writing.

    [A] a dilettante
    [B] a purveyor
    [C] an aesthete
    [D] a phantasm
    [E] a maverick
    [F] an iconoclast

8. As bits and pieces left over from the formation of the solar system, near-Earth objects provide important insights into the environment of the _____ planets.

   [A] nascent
   [B] indigenous
   [C] extant
   [D] far off
   [E] newly formed
   [F] long awaited

9. When the first European settlers arrived in Australia, the country's abundant trees and lush plant life _____ them into overestimating the amount of food that could easily be produced.

   [A] startled
   [B] intimidated
   [C] seduced
   [D] unnerved
   [E] emboldened
   [F] deluded

10. Intended to be discarded after a single use, the Dixie Cup was created by public health workers order to _____ the transmission of disease at public water sources.

    [A] chart
    [B] mitigate
    [C] bait
    [D] stanch
    [E] trace
    [F] rescind

11. Edmund Burke transcended his reputation for stubbornness, even _____, eventually wining fame for the brilliance and eloquence of his political writings.

    [A] mendacity
    [B] resilience
    [C] obtuseness
    [D] intransigence
    [E] munificence
    [F] obstinacy

12. The multiple perspectives presented in Siri Hustvedt's novel never _____ into a single view, creating an atmosphere of ambiguity and flux.

    [A] coalesce
    [B] distort
    [C] crystallize
    [D] expand
    [E] morph
    [F] venture

13. The brain undergoes more _____ maturation than any other bodily system, with the prefrontal cortex undergoing substantial changes from the time a person is born until he or she is well over 20 years old.

    [A] protracted
    [B] complex
    [C] innate
    [D] spontaneous
    [E] drawn-out
    [F] wide-ranging

14. In 1982, the personal computer was named Machine of the Year by *Time* magazine, a choice that turned out to be _____ given that a publicly available internet did not yet exist.

    [A] brazen
    [B] sweeping
    [C] controversial
    [D] prescient
    [E] prevalent
    [F] prophetic

15. A source of dispute for decades, the scientist's theory has finally been _____ by compelling new evidence that appears to confirm it once and for all.

    [A] extrapolated
    [B] vindicated
    [C] revised
    [D] substantiated
    [E] hypothesized
    [F] deduced

16. The intensity of Beethoven's *Eroica* symphony makes hearing the piece a
_____ experience that leaves listeners both utterly exhausted and devoid
of emotion.

   [A] riveting
   [B] cathartic
   [C] sensational
   [D] draining
   [E] tedious
   [F] profound

17. As agricultural societies grew in size and complexity during the Neolithic period,
rivalries within groups had to be _____ so that the larger collective could
flourish.

   [A] sanctioned
   [B] exorcised
   [C] diverted
   [D] sustained
   [E] quelled
   [F] exonerated

18. A ballooning body of research shows that moral judgments are not always the
product of careful deliberation: we make snap decisions and then later construct
justifications for those _____ reactions.

   [A] habitual
   [B] excessive
   [C] preliminary
   [D] universal
   [E] intuitive
   [F] visceral

19. Since the 1970s, the country's government has been more willing to refer
disputes to independent tribunals and commissions for resolution, but these
efforts have been _____ by the growth of state-based political parties that
appeal to specific ethnic and linguistic groups.

   [A] thwarted
   [B] decimated
   [C] frustrated
   [D] touted
   [E] endorsed
   [F] regulated

20. With the exception of full-fledged language, many of the behaviors once thought to be the exclusive _____ of humans have now been observed in animals: the ability to consider the past and the future, to demonstrate self-awareness, and to anticipate the motives of others.

[A] province
[B] expression
[C] pastime
[D] domain
[E] innovation
[F] disposition

21. Research suggests that exposure to infectious agents can affect moral judgment: people who are reminded of the threat of disease are more inclined to _____ conventional values and express greater disdain for those who flout societal norms.

[A] deplore
[B] counteract
[C] espouse
[D] confer
[E] extol
[F] adhere to

22. Beginning in the mid-1920s, people in the United States embraced unpolished forms of expression, perceiving in them an authenticity that more _____ discourse lacked.

[A] mundane
[B] refined
[C] novel
[D] inspired
[E] pompous
[F] nuanced

23. As writing developed, first in the ancient Near East and soon after in Greece, old habits of thought began to _____, while other, previously latent mental faculties began to appear.

[A] struggle
[B] predominate
[C] dissipate
[D] protrude
[E] atrophy
[F] catch up

24. The notion that people who live alone are happier than those who do not is viewed with derision because no known civilization has _____ solitary living as a social ideal.

   [A] proposed
   [B] touted
   [C] bestowed
   [D] stipulated
   [E] lauded
   [F] salvaged

25. Some members of the class Crustacea possess sensors so _____ that they can perceive fine distinctions between waves made by prey and those made by predators.

   [A] acute
   [B] discreet
   [C] malleable
   [D] pliable
   [E] ubiquitous
   [F] discriminating

Explanations: Medium Sentence Equivalences

1. B, E

The key phrase *while at the same time* suggests that the two halves of the sentence express opposing ideas. The second half indicates that Mingus's music *depict[s] those ritual from a playful distance*, so logically, the first half must convey a lack of distance between listeners and Mingus's music. *Immerses* (surrounds completely) is clearly consistent with that idea, making (B) the first correct answer. When used as a verb, *steep* is a synonym for *immerses*, so (E) is the second answer. Be careful with [A]: *engages* would also imply an elimination of the distance between the listener and Mingus's music, but this word does not have a close synonym among the answer choices. Of the remaining answers, neither fits logically with the idea of eliminating the distance between listeners and Mingus's music.

2. A, D

The fact that museum administrators *authorized the purchase of stolen antiquities* suggests that they were punished. Although you might be tempted by *booted* (that is, fired) this word does not have a close synonym among the other choices. *Exasperated* (frustrated, outraged) is a word that would be more aptly applied to the board of directors, not the administrators. *Mollified* (pacified) does not fit at all, and *evaluated* is too neutral. *Rebuked* (harshly scolded) and *censured* (punished) both indicate that the administrators faced negative consequences for their actions, making [A] and [D] correct.

3. B, E

The key phrase *grounded in* provides a subtle clue, indicating that both physics and art share fundamental similarities. The word most directly consistent with that idea is *underlying*, which is the first answer. The other answer, *latent* (present but not visible), is not a precise synonym for *underlying*, but it does create the same meaning when plugged in – both words imply that physics and art have similarities that lurk beneath the surface but that are not apparent at a superficial level. [B] and [E] are thus correct. *Recurring* could also fit, but this word does not have a close synonym among the other options. *Vestigial* (leftover) and *potential* do not fit either because the sentence is referring to qualities of physics and art that actually exist, not to ones that existed in the past or could exist in the future.

4. C, E

The key word is *origin* – the first half of the sentence indicates that this aspect of heavy metals is unclear, and the second half of the sentence provides a possible explanation. The blank must therefore be filled by words described how the metals came into existence. *Created* is a clear fit for this definition, making [C] the first answer. *Pulverized* and *expelled* are words that would logically describe the result of collisions between stars, but they have nothing to do with origins, and neither has a close synonym among the other choices. *Altered* and *modified* are synonyms but are inconsistent with the idea of origins. Only *forged* (produced – note the second meaning) creates the same meaning as *created* when plugged into the sentence, making [E] the second answer.

5. B, F

The information after the colon provides an important clue, namely that Carter influenced writers who came after her but was herself influenced by few writers. Logically, then, the blank should be filled with words indicating that Carter's work is difficult to place or understand within a particular tradition. *Surround* does not convey that meaning, and *reify* (transform into an object) and *administer* do not make any sense. *Represent* could plausibly fit, but this word does not have a close synonym among the other choices. *Situate* and *contextualize* are synonyms that create a logical meaning when plugged into the sentence: because Carter's works were largely self-generated, they cannot be easily placed within an existing tradition. [B] and [F] are thus correct.

6. C, D

The fact that *independent and neutral experts* are required for successful labor/management relations implies that the problem with the current review board is that it is insufficiently neutral. The sentence, however, asks for a word that describes a quality that the review board must possess *less* of. More neutral = less *biased*, making [C] the first answer. The closest synonym for that word is *partisan*. By definition, making the board less partisan would make it more neutral. [D] is thus the second answer. *Litigious* and *formal* do not fit at all, but be careful with *entrenched* and *disinterested*. It is true that a less entrenched review board would be a more independent one, but this answer does not have a close synonym among the other choices. For *disinterested*, be careful not to get confused by the double negative. A less disinterested board would be a *more* biased one, so this answer actually conveys exactly the opposite of the required meaning.

7. E, F

The key phrase *reinvented film criticism as an art form and pioneered an entirely new style of writing* explains why Kael is considered the word in the blank. Logically, the correct answers must have something to do with innovating or pioneering. A *dilettante* (dabbler), *a purveyor* (provider), and *a phantasm* (apparition, illusion) all clearly do not fit. Be careful with [C]: although someone who reinvented an art form could reasonably be considered an *aesthete* (a person who appreciates beauty), the focus here is on the fact that Kael did things that were new. Both *maverick* (a person who pursue nonconformist or disruptive policies) and *iconoclast* (a person who attacks traditional ways of doing things) are much more consistent with that idea, making [E] and [F] correct.

8. A, E

If near-Earth objects are *left over from the formation of the solar system*, then they must provide important insights into the nature of the early planets. The blank must therefore be filled with words meaning early. *Nascent* (just born) and *newly formed* both fit that definition, making [A] and [E] the answers. *Indigenous* (native), *far off*, and *long awaited* all do not make sense. *Extant* (existing) could plausibly fit, but this word does not have a close synonym among the other choices.

9. C, F

The key phrase *abundant trees and lush plant life* strongly suggests that the first European settlers in Australia received a very (falsely) positive impression of their ability to easily grow food in that country. Even though *intimidated* and *unnerved* are general synonyms, there is nothing in the sentence to indicate that the settlers were frightened. On the contrary, they felt reassured by the apparent bounty of natural resources. *Startled* does not make sense because the sentence does not at all indicate that the settlers were surprised. *Emboldened* could plausibly fit, but this word does not have a close synonym among the other choices. Though not exact synonyms, *seduced* and *deluded* both convey the idea that the settlers were falsely lulled into thinking that food would be easy to grow. [C] and [F] are thus correct.

10. B, D

Given the context of disease transmission at public water sources, the invention of a cup *intended to be discarded after a single use* would logically hinder transmission and result in fewer cases of the disease. The correct words must therefore have something to do with stopping or reducing. *Chart* and *trace* are synonyms, but they would imply that the Dixie Cup was invented to keep track of disease transmission, not to stop it. *Bait* (attract) is exactly the opposite of what is required, and *rescind* (take back) does not make sense – it is not possible to take back the transmission of a disease. That leaves *mitigate* (reduce) and *stanch* (stop the flow of), which create the same meaning when plugged into the sentence: the Dixie Cup was invented to help stop disease transmission. [B] and [D] are thus correct.

11. D, F

The word *even* is an important clue, indicating that the blank must be filled with words that are stronger versions of *stubborn*. Both *intransigence* and *obstinacy* indicate extreme stubbornness, making [D] and [F] the answers. *Mendacity* (lying), *resilience* (the ability to bounce back from hardship), *obtuseness* (mental dullness), and *munificence* (generosity) all do not make sense.

12. A, C

The sentence indicates the multiple perspectives in Hustvedt's novel do *not* do something, an absence that creates *an atmosphere of ambiguity and flux*. Logically, the blank should be filled with words indicating that the novel's multiple perspectives do not cohere into a single view. *Coalesce* (come together) and *crystallize* (give definite form to) both convey a feature of multiple perspectives that, if lacking, would cause the narrative to remain ambiguous. [A] and [C] are thus correct. *Distort, expand,* and *morph* (change) all fail to imply that the various perspectives come together in a clear way. *Venture* (dare to go) does not have quite the right connotation; it also lacks a close synonym among the other choices.

13. A, E

The fact that the prefrontal cortex is not fully developed until a person is *well over 20 years old* suggests that the brain takes a very long time to develop. Both *protracted* and *drawn-out* convey this idea, making [A] and [E] correct. Be careful with *complex*: it is true that such a long development period would be consistent with complex maturation, but this word does not have a close synonym among the other choices. It may also be true that the brain undergoes *spontaneous* maturation, but this word does not fit the clues in the sentence. The same is true of *wide-ranging* and *innate*.

14. D, F

The clues in this sentence are the date *1982* and the statement that *a publicly available internet did not yet exist.* In that context, the decision to designate the personal computer Machine of the Year showed remarkable foresight, anticipating the influence that the computer would eventually wield. *Prescient* and *prophetic* have similar meanings and correctly convey that idea. The decision may have also been *brazen* (bold) or *controversial*, but there is nothing in the sentence to directly indicate that that was the case. *Sweeping* and *prevalent* have similar meanings but are not supported by the context of the sentence. [D] and [F] are thus correct.

15. B, D

The key phrase *compelling new evidence that appears to confirm it once and for all* indicates that the scientist's theory has finally been proven, and that the blank must be filled with words indicating that fact. *Vindicated* (justified, upheld) and *substantiated* (proven) both convey that meaning, making [B] and [D] correct. *Revised* would not make sense because the new evidence confirms that the theory is correct as is, and the remaining answers do not make sense in context.

16. B, D

The key phrase *utterly exhausted and devoid of emotion* indicates the effect that the *Eroica* symphony has on listeners. The blank must therefore be filled with an adjective describing the type of experience that would produce that effect. *Draining* would logically describe an experience that leaves listeners *devoid of* (emptied of) emotion, as would *cathartic* (emotionally draining). *Riveting, sensational,* and *profound* are all words that could reasonably be applied to a symphony, but none fits the clues provided in the sentence. *Tedious* could describe the reaction of a concert-goer who found the *Eroica* symphony unpleasant, but again, this word does not match the key phrase as precisely as *draining* and *cathartic* do. It also lacks a close synonym among the other choices. [B] and [D] are thus correct.

17. B, E

The cause-and-effect phrase *so that* indicates that the *flourishing of the larger collective* was the result of something being done to *rivalries within groups.* Logically, rivalries were eliminated because infighting was a threat to the stability of the larger group. The blank must therefore be filled with negative words meaning eliminated. Be very careful with *sanctioned*: although *sanctions* are penalties for breaking the law, the verb *sanction* means approve or permit. *Sustained* is also positive and can be eliminated. *Diverted* and *exonerated* (freed from blame) both do not make any sense in context. That leaves *exorcised* and *quelled.* Although not exact synonyms, both words produce the logical implication that rivalries needed to be eliminated in order for larger societies to be healthy. [B] and [E] are thus correct.

18. E, F

The words in the blank must support the idea that people do not always think through matters carefully when making moral judgments. The construction _____ *reactions* also refers back to *snap decisions*, so the blank must logically be filled with synonyms for *snap* (instantaneous). *Habitual, excessive,* and *universal* all do not fit that definition. Be careful with *preliminary*. Although this word accurately describes a reaction that is not thought out carefully, it lacks a close synonym among the other choices. *Visceral* (literally, from the gut; the root VISC- means gut) and *intuitive*, however, have similar definitions and create the same meaning when plugged into the sentence: moral judgments tend to be instinctive.

19. A, C

The contradictor *but* indicates that the two halves of the sentence express opposing ideas. The first half presents a generally positive idea (the government is willing to refer to bodies outside itself to help people resolve disputes), so the second half must present a negative idea and describe a way in which that scheme is ineffective or falls short. The phrase *that appeal to specific ethnic and linguistic groups* also suggests that the tribunals and commissions are biased and thus unable to carry out justice effectively. The blank must therefore be filled with words meaning stopped or prevented. *Touted* (promoted), *endorsed*, and *regulated* clearly do not fit, but be careful with *decimated* (destroyed completely): although this word could plausibly be used to fill the blank, it lacks a close synonym among the other choices. Only *thwarted* (prevented) and *frustrated* (note the second meaning) have very similar definitions and produce a logical meaning when plugged into the sentence.

20. A, D

The sentence describes behaviors that were once thought to be displayed only by humans but that other animals are now understood to display as well. The blank must be filled with words supporting that idea. Both *province* and *domain* effectively convey the idea of an area no longer considered specific to one species. Note that in this case, the correct words are used somewhat figuratively – that is, they do not refer to literal pieces of land, but rather to realms of ability. (Note that it is relatively common for both of these words to be used in this way.) [A] and [D] are thus correct.

If you are unable to fill in a word, you can work from the answer choices. Although *expression* and *innovation* make sense in context, both words lack a close synonym among the other choices. *Pastime* (hobby) and *disposition* (prevailing mood) both do not fit. Even if you are unsure about *province* and *domain*, they are the only pair with similar meanings.

21. C, E

People who *express greater disdain for those who flout societal norms* are most logically people who are also the most in favor of traditional values. The blank must therefore be filled with positive words indicating appreciation. *Deplore* (bemoan) and *counteract* are both negative, and *confer* (bestow), although positive, does not make sense in context. Be careful with *adhere to* (follow closely): this answer fits extremely well – people who disdain those who flout societal norms would logically adhere to traditional values themselves – but it lacks a close synonym among the other choices. In contrast, *espouse* (proclaim) and *extol* (praise) create the same meaning when plugged into the sentence: people who tout the importance of traditional values are more likely to look down on those who go against those values. [C] and [E] are thus correct.

22. B, F

The sentence sets up an opposition between *unpolished forms of expression* and *more _____ discourse*. In addition, we are told that the latter was lacking in authenticity. Logically, then, the blank must be filled with words meaning more polished. *Refined* is a synonym for *polished*, making [B] the first answer. *Mundane* (quotidian, run-of-the-mill), *novel*, *inspired*, and *pompous* (arrogant) all do not fit the necessary definition, nor do they have similar definitions to *refined*. Even though *nuanced* (subtle, including fine gradations) is not an exact synonym for *refined*, it functions effectively as the opposite of *unpolished* and produces the same meaning when plugged into the sentence: people were turned off by forms of expression that seemed too overtly highbrow or sophisticated because they seemed inauthentic. [B] and [F] are thus correct.

23. C, E

The contradictor *while* indicates a contrast between *old habits of thought* and *other, previously latent faculties*. The sentence tells us that the latter *began to appear*, suggesting that the former declined. The blank must therefore be filled with words meaning decline. *Predominate* conveys the opposite, and *protrude* (stick out) and *catch up* do not make sense. *Struggle* could potentially fit, but this word lacks a close synonym among the other choices. Only *dissipate* (gradually vanish; the root DISS- suggests a negative word) and *atrophy* (wither away) have sufficiently similar definitions and produce the same meaning when plugged into the sentence. [C] and [E] are thus correct.

24. B, E

Logically, the idea that *people who live alone are happier than those who do not* would be viewed suspiciously if no known civilization had been in favor of solitary living. The blank must therefore be filled with positive words indicating a favorable attitude toward solitary living. *Proposed* could plausibly work, even if it is not the strongest fit; however, this word lacks a close synonym among the other choices. *Bestowed* (granted), *stipulated* (required), and *salvaged* (saved) all do not make sense. Only *touted* and *lauded* (praised) are both synonyms and create a logical meaning when plugged into the sentence, making the answers [B] and [E].

25. A, F

The construction *so _____ that they can perceive fine distinctions* indicates that the blank must be filled with words describing a quality of the sensors that makes members of the class Crustacea (crabs) capable of recognizing small differences between waves made by prey and waves made by predators. *Discreet* (reserved, diplomatic) does not quite fit as a way to describe sensors, so this answer can be eliminated. Although *pliable* and *malleable* are synonyms, neither makes sense in context. *Ubiquitous* does not fully make sense – even if the creatures in question had sensors everywhere, that quality would not necessarily allow them to perceive tiny differences between wave types. Only *acute* (highly sensitive) and *discriminating* (able to perceive fine distinctions) have similar definitions and create the same meaning when plugged into the sentence, so [A] and [F] are correct.

Text Completions: Hard

1. The philosopher and cultural critic Walter Benjamin, who frequently lamented his _____, was actually quite prolific as a writer, producing a number of major essays as well as several important translations.

(A) indolence
(B) temerity
(C) idiosyncrasies
(D) intensity
(E) convictions

2. The contemporary author Jonathan Raban has called water the most _____ of all symbols: a volatile element, it reshapes itself for every writer and every generation.

(A) protean
(B) transparent
(C) pendulous
(D) hackneyed
(E) bucolic

3. The historian's observations in any given moment are invariably edifying, whereas the lessons he draws from those observations are for the most part remarkably _____.

(A) trite
(B) lucid
(C) timorous
(D) novel
(E) succinct

4. The historical understanding of books as physical locations, within which one might store practical information, legal documentation, jokes, and ownership lists, challenges the contemporary ideal of equating _____ margins with value.

(A) annotated
(B) prominent
(C) broad
(D) unsullied
(E) narrow

5. Snow's richest metaphorical potential probably lies in its capacity to accurately convey states of mental _____, from torpor to catatonia, through its utter blankness.

(A) fortitude
(B) depravity
(C) acuity
(D) precariousness
(E) desolation

6. It is clear that a combination of circumstances can go far to explain what has gone wrong in science. Systems of controls and rewards that evolved under earlier conditions have in many ways become counterproductive, creating _____ incentives that lead researchers to publish even dubious findings.

(A) sporadic
(B) perverse
(C) recondite
(D) extrinsic
(E) assiduous

7. Non-compete agreements, proponents say, can protect valuable trade secrets and motivate employers to invest in worker training because such arrangements _____ the possibility that employees will resign and go to work for rival companies.

(A) subsidize
(B) renege on
(C) mitigate
(D) exacerbate
(E) violate

8. Long touted as _____ for a wide range of ills, the gel obtained from the leaves of the aloe vera plant has been a staple of herbal medicines since the first century A.D.

(A) a substitute
(B) an etiology
(C) a corollary
(D) a panacea
(E) a dogma

9. Some global historians _____ the tendency to create oceanic as well as continental divisions, arguing that our globe is dominated by one great seamless body of water that covers seven-tenths of the planet's surface and affects weather, climate, and life on land as well as at sea.

(A) account for
(B) sum up
(C) abide by
(D) pander to
(E) chafe at

10. When Alexander von Humboldt arrived in North America, he and his fellow explorers carried the finest scientific equipment as well as something even more valuable: Spanish passports. A _____ rarely granted to foreigners, the documents assured them safe passage through Spain's New World viceroyalties.

(A) boon
(B) denizen
(C) harbinger
(D) foible
(E) predicament

11. Observing that their experiment was failing to yield any significant data, the researchers elected to (i) _____ it until they were able to devise a more (ii) _____ methodology.

Blank (i)	Blank (ii)
(A) table	(D) empirical
(B) rebut	(E) efficacious
(C) castigate	(F) systematic

12. There is a sense in which the history of literary criticism is one of (i) _____. Each new movement or school of thought advances an implicit – and very often explicit – (ii) _____ for its existence; each makes its own claim to methodological, empirical or philosophical rigor.

Blank (i)	Blank (ii)
(A) ongoing struggle	(D) rationale
(B) frequent disappointment	(E) regard
(C) self-justification	(F) atonement

13. Earthquakes, which can be triggered by the movement of magma within a volcano, are frequently considered (i) _____ of disaster, their shockwaves indicating that a major eruption is (ii) _____.

Blank (i)	Blank (ii)
(A) catalysts	(D) catastrophic
(B) paragons	(E) ostensible
(C) harbingers	(F) imminent

14. Willa Cather's novels are often viewed reverently as the embodiment of life in the American Midwest during the late nineteenth century; however, this (i) _____ perspective conflicts with the reality that Cather was a highly (ii) _____ writer.

Blank (i)	Blank (ii)
(A) astute	(D) compelling
(B) parochial	(E) cosmopolitan
(C) wry	(F) didactic

15. Helen Thomas, who worked as a United Press International correspondent for nearly six decades, demonstrated a (i) _____ asking blunt questions that made her a (ii) _____ figure among Washington politicians.

Blank (i)	Blank (ii)
(A) antipathy toward	(D) polemical
(B) predilection for	(E) revered
(C) caution in	(F) heretical

16. The idea that history is infinitely (i) _____ is by no means the exclusive property of totalitarian governments. Until recently, it was common to assert that history is a "narrative," and that the facts themselves must not dictate what version of history we ought to (ii) _____.

Blank (i)	Blank (ii)
(A) dialectical	(D) appraise
(B) malleable	(E) realize
(C) reductive	(F) adopt

17. Although Benjamin Barber and Pierre Manent's studies of contemporary urbanism contain similar theses, the former seems (i) _____, even callow, while the latter is a work of (ii) _____.

Blank (i)	Blank (ii)
(A) naïve	(D) sophistry
(B) buoyant	(E) erudition
(C) terse	(F) ostentatiousness

18. According to one school of thought, no particular linguistic dialect can be considered (i) _____ because language is not immutable and, moreover, it is constantly (ii) _____.

Blank (i)	Blank (ii)
(A) definitive	(D) above reproach
(B) convoluted	(E) under siege
(C) abstruse	(F) in flux

19. Before the nineteenth century, attitudes toward the oceans were primarily (i) _____; bodies of water were explored only as a means to reach distant lands. Little attention was paid to the waters, which were deemed (ii) _____ literary or artistic representation.

Blank (i)	Blank (ii)
(A) prescriptive	(D) unfit for
(B) utilitarian	(E) devoid of
(C) ambivalent	(F) conducive to

20. Every time the company raises another enormous sum of money, venture capitalists and other investors may find themselves less (i) _____ backing one of its many rivals. Essentially, the organization seeks to dominate through (ii) _____, starving its competitors of resources so that they are forced to remove themselves from the market.

Blank (i)	Blank (ii)
(A) averse to	(D) attrition
(B) zealous about	(E) chicanery
(C) censured for	(F) subterfuge

21. It is curious that something as ostensibly harmless as poetry could (i) _____ such derision, and yet denunciations of the genre are nothing new. Beginning with Plato's argument that an ideal society would banish its poets, many criticisms have been (ii) _____ over the centuries, some more (iii) _____ than others.

Blank (i)	Blank (ii)	Blank (iii)
(A) inspire	(D) undermined	(G) propitiatory
(B) berate	(E) forfeited	(H) vitriolic
(C) declaim	(F) lobbed	(J) sycophantic

22. According to the primatologist Frans de Waal, it is not the tendency to (i) _____ but rather the unwillingness to (ii) _____ the human-like traits of animals that too often defines people's attitudes toward other species. This phenomenon is a relatively recent development: in medieval and early modern Europe, the animal mind was considered sophisticated enough that (iii) _____ dogs, pigs, and other domesticated animals could be put on trial for crimes.

Blank (i)	Blank (ii)	Blank (iii)
(A) anthropomorphize	(D) determine	(G) errant
(B) substantiate	(E) acknowledge	(H) feral
(C) exonerate	(F) dispel	(J) stealthy

23. Even though some contemporaries of the Algonquin Round Table (i) _____ the group during its existence, its reputation remained mostly (ii) _____ after its dissolution in 1929. Indeed, a number of its members became (iii) _____ in the entertainment industry, making lasting contributions to the stage and screen.

Blank (i)	Blank (ii)	Blank (iii)
(A) savaged	(D) inchoate	(G) provocateurs
(B) lauded	(E) unscathed	(H) luminaries
(C) accompanied	(F) murky	(J) monoliths

24. *Telenovelas*, the popular soap operas that draw millions of viewers throughout Central and South America, are often denigrated for their outrageous plotlines and (i) _____; nevertheless, some media scholars argue that this form of entertainment can offer (ii) _____, even (iii) _____ social commentary.

Blank (i)	Blank (ii)	Blank (iii)
(A) attention to detail	(D) sharp	(G) explicit
(B) wooden acting	(E) skeptical	(H) trenchant
(C) brisk style	(F) provocative	(J) sanctimonious

25. Human beings have an innate liking for both familiarity and novelty, but these preferences express themselves in (i) _____ ways. While the initial surge of appreciation for what is new and exciting quickly tapers, our enjoyment of familiar things does not (ii) _____ – a contrast that may reflect an inborn biological prejudice against (iii) _____.

Blank (i)	Blank (ii)	Blank (iii)
(A) conflicting	(D) wane	(G) objectivity
(B) imperceptible	(E) deepen	(H) disorder
(C) surprising	(F) advance	(J) extremes

26. Modern medicine, singularly focused on the microscopic, is poorly (i) _____ to grasp relationships between internal and external factors; however, most new infections defy disciplinary boundaries. Diseases in animal populations, studied by veterinarians, (ii) _____ into human populations, studied by physicians. But because these workers rarely interact, the crossovers (iii) _____.

Blank (i)	Blank (ii)	Blank (iii)
(A) situated	(D) plummet	(G) cease to exist
(B) executed	(E) spill	(H) occur only rarely
(C) conceived	(F) transfigure	(J) escape detection

27. In the late nineteenth century, when British culture was still held up as an ideal for Americans to (i) _____, the very humor of Twain's *A Connecticut Yankee in King Arthur's Court* was built on the (ii) _____ of an American influencing British ways. In Twain's time, this (iii) _____ was merely amusing. But during the Jazz Age the joke became reality, and on a far grander scale than Twain or any of his contemporaries could have imagined.

Blank (i)	Blank (ii)	Blank (iii)
(A) emulate	(D) dichotomy	(G) genre
(B) contest	(E) distinction	(H) archetype
(C) satirize	(F) incongruity	(J) reversal

28. The accumulation of water on arctic ice is a self-perpetuating process that
(i) _____ as it (ii) _____. Water facilitates melting by decreasing the
reflectivity, or albedo, of white ice. The dark pools of water on the ice's surface
absorb greater amounts of energy from the sun, promoting more melting and
causing the albedo to (iii) _____.

Blank (i)	Blank (ii)	Blank (iii)
(A) abates	(D) progresses	(G) suddenly flare up
(B) accelerates	(E) contracts	(H) decline even further
(C) stagnates	(F) adapts	(J) expand more rapidly

29. Throughout history, scapegoating has been a common response to the outbreak
of disease. Because epidemics caused by novel pathogens so often strike
societies with weak and corrupt social institutions, they are especially
(i) _____ disrupting people's sense of control over their environments. At
the same time, these illnesses' (ii) _____ are not inescapable, like the
effects of wars or floods. Certain people are struck, while others are not,
suggesting some form of (iii) _____, however opaque.

Blank (i)	Blank (ii)	Blank (iii)
(A) focused on	(D) ravages	(G) mendacity
(B) constrained by	(E) vulnerabilities	(H) penitence
(C) adept at	(F) proclivities	(J) complicity

30. Nowadays, it seems that anything and everything can qualify as a masterpiece:
a hit single, a theme park, even a video game. While the (i) _____ merits
of some of these works can be defended, it is tempting to suggest that the word
itself has become debased to the point of (ii) _____ by indiscriminate
usage. But the fact that most people still feel the need for such a word in
everyday discourse suggests that the idea of the masterpiece is not yet entirely
(iii) _____.

Blank (i)	Blank (ii)	Blank (iii)
(A) intrinsic	(D) extinction	(G) devoid of meaning
(B) aesthetic	(E) vacuity	(H) beyond consideration
(C) cumulative	(F) incredulousness	(J) within our grasp

Explanations: Hard Text Completions

1. A

The answer to this question hinges on the key word *prolific* (productive). That quality is contrasted with a personal quality that Benjamin *lamented*, so the blank must be filled with a negative word meaning unproductive or lazy. *Indolence* does in fact mean lazy, making the answer (A). *Temerity* (daring), *idiosyncrasies* (eccentricities), and *convictions* (strong beliefs) all do not fit, and *intensity* is exactly the opposite of the required word.

2. A

The key phrase *it reshapes itself for every writer and every generation* implies that the blank must be filled with a word indicating the ability to change – something like flexible. *Protean* means changeable, which fits perfectly and makes (A) the answer. *Transparent* is a quality associated with water, but here it does not fit the clues provided by the sentence. *Pendulous* (heavy) and *bucolic* (related to country life) do not make sense at all. *Hackneyed* (trite) may accurately describe how some people view the use of water as a symbol, but again, that interpretation is not supported by the information in the sentence.

3. A

The sentence sets up a contrast between the historian's edifying observations and the lessons he draws from them. *Edifying* is a positive word meaning enlightening, so the blank must be a negative word meaning the opposite. *Lucid* (clear), *novel* (new), and *succinct* (concise) are all relatively positive and can thus be eliminated. *Trite* (cliché, unoriginal) and *timorous* (fearful) are both negative, but the latter does not fit because fearful is not the opposite of enlightening. That leaves *trite*, which fits because ideas that are tired and clichéd would do little to enlighten. (A) is therefore correct.

4. D

The key word *challenges* sets up a contrast between the two ideas presented in the sentence. The first idea indicates that the books were traditionally treated as *physical locations*, to be filled with a range of commentary. If that conception has been challenged, then the *contemporary ideal* – and the blank – must involve NOT regarding books as repositories for this type of information. You can try plugging in a word like *blank* or *empty*. *Annotated* is precisely the opposite of the required word: the sentence indicates that margins were traditionally covered in annotations. If this use has been challenged, then it is no longer the case. *Prominent* and *broad* do not fit: these types of margins would encourage readers to mark up their books. Besides, when two answer choices in a text completion have similar definitions, both will usually be wrong. *Narrow* could seem to fit – narrow margins would be more difficult to make notes in – but the focus of the sentence is not really on the size of the margins. For this answer to be correct, the first part of the sentence would have to focus on how large margins used to be. *Unsullied* (unmarked) is much more directly consistent with the information in the sentence and produces the most logical meaning: in the past, people considered it normal to mark up their books, but now clean books are held up as the ideal. (D) is thus correct.

5. E

The phrase *from torpor to catatonia* describes the range of mental states to which the word in the blank can refer. *Torpor* (extreme sluggishness) and *catatonia* (utter frozenness) are both adjectives that would describe someone who is extremely depressed, so the blank must be filled with a negative word similar to depression. *Fortitude* (strength; FORT-, strong) is exactly the opposite of what is required, and *acuity* (sharpness) is positive and does not fit. *Depravity* (wickedness, perversion) is strongly negative, but a depraved person would not necessarily experience torpor or catatonia. Be careful with *precariousness*: this word means fragility, and although a person who was mentally precarious might topple over into a depressive state, this word is not quite strong enough to fit the sentence. In contrast, *desolation* (extreme solitude, devastation) is a logical description of a mental state that would cause a person to freeze completely. (E) is thus correct.

6. B

The first sentence indicates that something is very wrong with the scientific world, suggesting that the focus of the passage will be negative. The assertion that *systems of controls and rewards...have in many ways become counterproductive* provides a further clue, indicating that scientists' motivations for conducting research are compromised in some way. Finally, the statement that *researchers may publish even dubious* (questionable*) findings* implies that the pressure to publish research is so great that the act of publishing itself has become more important than whether the research being published is valid. The blank must therefore be filled with a negative word that means something like twisted or unfair. *Sporadic* (occasional), *recondite* (esoteric), and *assiduous* (hard-working, diligent) all do not convey that idea. Be careful with *extrinsic* (external): while it can be assumed that the incentives offered to scientists are not self-created, this type of incentive would not necessarily lead to the publication of poor data. A system of *perverse* incentives, however, would encourage researchers to publish findings of questionable validity, making (B) the correct answer.

7. C

This is a fairly complicated sentence, so try to focus on the basics of what it's saying: non-compete agreement reduce the possibility that employees will resign and go to work for competing organizations. Logically, then, the blank must be filled with a word meaning lessen or reduce. That is essentially the definition of *mitigate* (reduce something bad), so (C) is correct. A non-compete agreement itself cannot *renege on* (back out of) anything – only a person can do that. *Exacerbate* (make worse) means exactly the opposite of the required word. *Subsidize* and *violate* simply do not make sense in context.

8. D

The key phrase *a staple of herbal medicines* indicates that the gel from the aloe vera plant has long been used as a cure for many diseases. A *panacea* is a cure-all, making (D) the only possible answer.

9. E

This question has the potential to be tricky because you have to read quite far into the sentence in order to obtain clues to the blank. Let's break this down logically: first, the sentence tells us that some global historians react in a particular way (the word in the blank) to *the tendency to create oceanic as well as global divisions*. Next, the sentence explains why they react in this way – that is what they believe. What do they believe? That *our globe is one great seamless body of water*. Logically, then, these historians would resist or dislike the tendency to create divisions between oceans. The blank must therefore be filled with a negative word indicating this dislike. *Account for* (explain) and *sum up* are neutral words that do not convey the idea of dislike. *Abide by* (adhere to) and *pander to* (suck up to) would indicate a positive attitude and can thus be eliminated. That leaves *chafe at* (be irritated by), which describes a logical reaction that the historians might have to an idea that they oppose.

10. A

The sentence indicates that Spanish passports were even more valuable than *the finest scientific equipment*, and that they ensured that the members of von Humboldt's expedition would receive safe passage in the New World. The blank must therefore be filled with a strongly positive word meaning something really great or helpful. The only word consistent with that definition is *boon* (gift, good fortune), making (A) correct. *Denizen* (inhabitant), *harbinger* (warning), *foible* (weakness), and *predicament* (difficult situation) all do not fit.

11. A, E

If the experiment was not providing any useful results, then the researchers would logically have decided to set it aside until they could find a better way of working. For Blank (i), it would not make nearly as much sense for the researchers to *rebut* (refute) or *castigate* (harshly criticize) their own experiment as it would for them to *table* (stop) it while attempting to find a better approach. For Blank (ii), *efficacious* (effective) most logically describes the type of methodology the researchers would want to devise.

12. C, D

The first sentence provides no information about Blank (i); rather, it is necessary to work backwards from Blank (ii). The primary clue for Blank (ii) also comes after that blank. The parallel construction *Each...advances; each makes* indicates that the information after the semicolon is expanding on the information before the semicolon. The information after the semicolon indicates that *each [new movement or school] makes its own claim to methodological or empirical rigor*, so Blank (ii) must be filled with a word that similarly conveys the idea of making a claim to validity. Logically, a movement that wanted to promote itself would seek to explain the *rationale* (reason) for its existence. It would certainly not *atone (repent) for* its existence – expressing guilt is not normally an aspect of self-promotion. Likewise, it probably would not express *regard for* its own existence; doing so would convince few people outside the movement of the movement's value. (D) is thus the answer to Blank (ii).

For Blank (i), consider that the first sentence serves to set up the second – that is, it makes a general statement that the second sentence then expands upon. Logically, then, the first sentence must convey an idea similar to that contained in the second sentence. There is nothing in the passage to suggest *frequent disappointment*, eliminating (B), but be very careful with (A): it is true that a field whose movements must continually put forth reasons for their own existence is engaged in a sort of *ongoing struggle*, but the focus here is really on the fact that each school or movement is itself responsible for explaining why it should exist – that is, its need to engage in constant acts of *self-justification*. In particular, the phrase *each makes its own claim* directly supports this idea. (C) is thus the strongest answer to Blank (i).

13. C, F

The structure of the sentence provides an important clue: the information after the comma is used to modify or expand on the preceding statement, so the words in the blanks must serve to convey similar ideas. In addition, the fact that earthquakes *can be triggered by the movement of magma within a volcano* indicates that earthquakes can signal disaster. If earthquakes occur because magma is moving, then they must signal that a volcano is about to erupt. For Blank (i), the word most consistent with that idea is *harbingers* (warnings). *Paragons* (perfect examples) does not fit at all, but be very careful with *catalysts*: a catalyst is something that sets off an event/chain of events, but the sentence indicates the opposite: earthquakes are the *result* of volcanic eruptions rather than the cause. (C) is thus the answer to Blank (i).

That meaning is further supported by *imminent*, the answer to Blank (ii). If earthquakes occur when volcanoes are about to erupt, then by definition, the eruption must be *imminent*. Earthquakes are indeed *catastrophic*, but this word is not supported by the sentence, and *ostensible* (appearing to be true) does not make sense. (F) is thus the answer to Blank (ii).

14. B, E

Blank (i) must be filled with a word describing the perspective indicated in the first half of the sentence – namely that Cather's novels are thought to embody life in a particular location, the American Midwest. The statement that these novels are often viewed in a way that *conflicts with* reality suggests that the answer to Blank (i) is negative, or at least not positive. *Astute* (highly observant) is very positive, and *wry* (dryly humorous) does not fit. *Parochial* (local, narrow-minded) is consistent with the idea of being rooted in one place.

Blank (ii) must be filled with a word indicating the opposite – that Cather had a broader perspective. The opposite of *parochial* is *cosmopolitan* (worldly), making (E) the answer to Blank (ii). Cather may have been *compelling* or *didactic* (instructive), but neither of those answers is supported by the sentence.

15. B, D

The key phrase *that made her* indicates that the word in Blank (ii) must be the result of the word in Blank (i). Logically, a journalist would have been inclined to *[ask] blunt questions*, so you can assume Blank (i) should be filled with a positive word. *Antipathy toward* (dislike) or *caution in* are negative and can be eliminated. It would be much more reasonable for a journalist to demonstrate a *predilection* (liking) *for* asking blunt questions. A journalist who asked such questions would probably not be *revered* (worshiped) by politicians, but neither would she be considered *heretical* (someone who defies official dogma). Doing so could easily have made her a *polemical* (controversial) figure, however. (B) is thus the answer to Blank (i), and (D) is the answer to Blank (ii).

16. B, F

The reference to totalitarian governments is key. What does this type of government do to history? It twists it, or rewrites it, in order to suit its own ends. Logically, then, Blank (i) must be filled with a word consistent with that idea. Neither *dialectical* (analytical) nor *reductive* makes sense at all; these words are simply plausible-sounding placeholders. Only *malleable* (flexible, bendable) conveys the idea that a government can distort history to fit its needs, making (B) the answer to Blank (i).

The second sentence expands on the first by explaining the assertion that the malleability of history is not the exclusive property of totalitarian governments – that is, totalitarian governments are not the only entities to consider historical truth flexible. The discussion of viewing history as a "narrative" is used to illustrate that idea. Essentially, this sentence is saying that until recently, interpreting history was considered more a question of advancing a particular theoretical framework or understanding of events, and that the actual facts of what happened were given less importance. Given that the discussion focuses on how historical truth is created, Blank (ii) must be filled with a word meaning something like accept. *Realize* and *appraise* (evaluate) do not make sense, but *adopt* describes something that people might do to a particular viewpoint or interpretation of historical events. (F) is thus the answer to Blank (ii).

17. A, E

The sentence sets up a clear contrast between Barber and Manent's studies, indicating that the words in the two blanks must express opposing ideas. The only clue provided in regard to actual definitions, however, is *callow* (juvenile, unsophisticated). The construction *the former seems _____, even callow* indicates that the blank must be filled with a less extreme version of *callow*. Neither *buoyant* (cheerful, light) nor *terse* (succinct) makes sense, but *naïve* fits perfectly, making (A) the answer to Blank (i).

Blank (ii) must be filled with a word that conveys the opposite – that Manent's work is profound or sophisticated. Be very careful with *sophistry*. Although this word looks like *sophisticated*, it actually refers to superficiality or important sounding nonsense. *Ostentatiousness* (flashiness) does not make sense in context. *Erudition* (profound knowledge), accurately describes a characteristic that is the opposite of naïve, so (E) is the answer to Blank (ii).

18. A, F

The continuer *moreover* indicates that the two halves of the sentence must convey similar ideas, with the second half providing a stronger statement than the first. The major potential point of confusion here involves the double negative *not immutable. Immutable* = unchangeable, so *not immutable* = able to be changed. If language can be changed, then no particular dialect can be *definitive* – that is, absolute. *Convoluted* (complicated) and *abstruse* (esoteric) do not make sense. (A) is thus the answer to Blank (i).

Because the information after *moreover* reaffirms the idea presented before that transition, Blank (ii) must be filled with a phrase that conveys the changing nature of language. The only answer consistent with that idea is *in flux* (in motion), making (F) the answer to Blank (ii).

19. B, D

The first sentence provides no information about Blank (i), so look to the second sentence for a clue. The key phrase *only as a means to reach distant lands* indicates that bodies of water were valued only for their capacity to bring about a specific result. That is not a *prescriptive* (authoritative) attitude because nothing is being dictated or ordered, nor is it an *ambivalent* (uncertain) one. It is, however, a *utilitarian* one, valuing the usefulness of bodies of water above all else. (B) is thus the answer to Blank (i).

If bodies of water were only considered in terms of their practical value, then they were <u>not</u> thought of in terms of their aesthetic value – that is, in terms of *literary or artistic representation*. Blank (ii) must therefore be filled with a word indicating a negative attitude. *Conducive to* (helpful to) is positive and clearly does not fit, but be very careful with *devoid of* (lacking). Although this expression is negative, it is illogical to imply that the waters themselves were considered to be missing artistic representation – artistic representation is not a characteristic that an object can lack. Rather, the issue is that the waters were not considered an appropriate subject, i.e. were *deemed unfit for*, artistic representation. (D) is thus the answer to Blank (ii).

20. B, D

If the company were regularly raising enormous sums of money, as the phrase *every time* would imply, then investors would become less inclined to back the company's rivals. That is a negative idea, but the presence of the negation *less* means that Blank (i) must be filled with a positive word. *Averse* and *censured* (punished) are negative, leaving *zealous* (extremely enthusiastic) as the only possibility. (B) is thus the answer to Blank (i).

Blank (ii) must be filled with a word describing how the organization (that is, the company referred to in the previous sentence) operates. The phrase *forced to remove themselves from the market* provides an important clue. If competitors are removing themselves, they are dropping out. Dropping out = *attrition*. Although the company's tactics could be considered ruthless, there is nothing in the passage to directly indicate that the company operates through fraud or trickery, which would be implied by both *chicanery* and *subterfuge*. (D) is thus the answer to Blank (ii).

21. A, F, H

The first sentence sets up an opposition between something as *ostensibly* (seemingly) *harmless as poetry* and a negative reaction (*derision*), clearly implying that one paradoxically provokes the other. Blank (i) must therefore be filled with a word meaning causes or leads to. Even though the idea is negative, the word itself must be neutral or even positive. *Berate* (harshly criticize) is negative and can be eliminated. Although *declaim* (recite) is something that is often done to poetry, it does not make sense here. Only *inspire*, which serves as a synonym for *cause*, fits. (A) is thus the answer to Blank (i).

Blank (ii) refers to the criticisms that have been offered up over the centuries. Again, negative idea, neutral/positive word. *Undermined* (destroyed by underhanded means) does not fit, nor does *forfeited* (passed up). Only *lobbed* works. Literally, this word means thrown or tossed, but in the context of an idea, it can be used figuratively to mean proposed.

Blank (iii) describes the criticisms and so must be negative. *Propitiatory* (conciliatory; PRO- suggests a positive word) and *sycophantic* (flattering, sucking up) both indicate positive attitudes. *Vitriolic* (harsh, nasty) is strongly negative and is a logical way to describe criticisms. (H) is thus the answer to Blank (iii).

22. A, E, G

Although the key word *but* indicates that the words in Blank (i) and Blank (ii) must be opposites, there is no way to determine the meaning of either based on the first sentence. Rather, you must start with Blank (iii) and work backwards from the end of the passage.

Blank (iii) refers to animals *put on trial*, so it must mean something like bad or criminal. Only *errant* (ERR-, like error) makes sense, so (G) is the answer to Blank (iii). *Feral* (wild) is a word often associated with animals, but it does not carry a specific connotation of wrongdoing. Likewise, *stealthy* (secretive) is often associated with wrongdoing, but someone who is stealthy is not necessarily doing anything illegal.

Now consider the relationship between the first two blanks and the rest of the passage. The second sentence is important because it indicates that *this phenomenon is a relatively recent development* – the key is to recognize that *this phenomenon* refers back to the situation described in the first sentence.

The problem, however, is that the first sentence itself provides no information. As a result, it is necessary to infer the idea that the sentence must convey by looking later in the passage. The third sentence describes the situation in *medieval and early modern Europe* – the opposite of a recent development. So the phenomenon described in the first sentence must be the opposite of the phenomenon described in the third sentence.

The third sentence indicates that animals were once considered to have sophisticated mental capabilities, so logically, the first sentence must present the idea that animals do <u>not</u> have sophisticated mental capabilities. Basically, the passage is saying that a long time ago, people thought that animals thought like humans, whereas now people are more likely to think that animals don't think like humans.

Now consider the first sentence. Blank (ii) is more straightforward than Blank (i), so start with it. Blank (ii) describes something that people are <u>un</u>willing to do in regard to animals' human-like traits. Because the sentence must convey the idea that people disregard human-like traits in animals, you can infer that people would be unwilling to *acknowledge* those traits. *Dispel* implies the opposite, and *determine* does not make sense. (E) is thus the answer to Blank (ii).

For Blank (i) reiterate what the sentence is saying: human attitudes toward non-humans are defined by the fact that people do not acknowledge animals' human traits, NOT that people _____ animals. Blank (i) must therefore convey the opposite idea of Blank (ii) – that is, it must refer to the acknowledgement of human traits in animals. That is the definition of *anthropomorphize*, so (A) is correct for Blank (i).

Note that the easiest way determine that answer is to focus on the fact that Blank (i) must mean the opposite of Blank (ii). If you think too hard about all the negatives, you are likely to end up confused about what the sentence is actually saying.

23. A, E, H

The contradictor *even though* indicates that Blank (i) and Blank (ii) must be filled with words that have opposite meanings. Unfortunately, the first sentence offers no clues as to what those meanings might be. In order to answer the question, it is thus necessary to work backwards from Blank (iii). The key phrase *making lasting contributions* indicates that the Algonquin Round Table's members were successful, so Blank (iii) must be filled with a positive word. *Luminaries* (people who have achieved prominence in a field) fits perfectly, whereas *provocateurs* (people who deliberately stir up controversy) and *monoliths* (large groups that act uniform blocs) do not make sense in context. That makes (H) the answer to Blank (iii).

For Blanks (i) and (ii), the transition *indeed* is key because it indicates that the second sentence is reinforcing the idea presented in the first sentence. The first sentence must therefore also convey the idea that members of the Algonquin Round Table achieved great success, and Blank (ii) must be filled with a word indicating a positive reputation. This is where prefixes can get you into trouble: *inchoate* (unformed) is indeed negative, but *unscathed* (unharmed) is actually positive. *Murky* is negative as well, making *unscathed* correct. (E) is thus the correct answer to Blank (ii).

Now look at Blank (i). You know that it means the opposite of Blank (ii), so logically you need a negative word that means something like insulted. The sentence is essentially saying that the Algonquin Round Table had a bad reputation during its existence but that its members did pretty well afterward. *Lauded* (praised) is positive and can be eliminated. *Accompanied* is neutral/positive and does not fit either. That leaves *savaged* (attacked viciously), which fits and makes (A) the answer to Blank (i).

24. B, D, H

Logically, *telenovelas* would be *denigrated* (put down) for something bad, so Blank (i) must filled with a negative phrase. *Attention to detail* is clearly positive, and *brisk style* is neutral – it could inspire criticism, but it would not necessarily do so. In contrast *wooden* (stiff, unnatural) *acting* is clearly negative, making (B) the most logical fit for Blank (i).

The contradictor *nevertheless* indicates a contrast between the preceding information and the information that follows. Since the preceding information focuses on negative aspects of *telenovelas*, the following information must be positive. Furthermore, the word *even* indicates that Blank (iii) must be filled with a word that is a more extreme version of the word in Blank (ii).

For Blank (ii), *skeptical* has a distinctly negative implication, but after that, you need to be very careful. *Provocative* could indeed be plausibly filled into Blank (ii), but there is no option for Blank (iii) that is a more extreme synonym for that word. *Sharp* might not immediately strike you as a positive word, but in the context of criticism, it implies a high degree of observation and can be a synonym for words such as *astute* and *penetrating*. Furthermore, *trenchant* (acerbic, extremely incisive) is a more extreme version of *sharp*. Both of those words create a logical meaning when plugged into the sentence: even though *telenovelas* might seem silly and superficial, they actually offer smart, pointed observations about how society operates.

25. A, D, J

For Blank (i), the sentence contrasts *an innate liking for both familiarity and novelty* with the blank, implying that it must be filled with a word indicating a difference in the ways these likings are expressed. In addition, the contradictor *while* in the following sentence reinforces the idea that people's reactions to new things differ from their reactions to familiar ones. *Conflicting* perfectly captures that meaning, making (A) the correct answer to Blank (i).

For Blank (ii), the sentence sets up an opposition between the brief enjoyment of new things and the _____ enjoyment of familiar ones. Logically, then, this sentence must convey the idea that enjoyment of familiar things is long-lasting. Watch out for the negative, though: you are asked to fill Blank (ii) with a word describing what enjoyment of familiar things does NOT do. Logically, if enjoyment is long-lasting, then that enjoyment does not decrease. Blank (ii) must thus be filled with a word meaning decrease. The only option to convey that meaning is *wane*; *deepen* and *advance* imply the opposite. (D) is thus the answer to Blank (ii).

For Blank (iii), the key word *prejudice* indicates that this blank must be filled with a word referring to people's rapidly decreasing interest in novel items. The best fit here is *extremes* – something that is new and exciting is much more extreme than something familiar and comfortable. *Objectivity* does not make sense at all, but be careful with *disorder*. Although it might seem logical to associated novelty with disorder, the passage provides no information directly connecting those two concepts. (J) is thus the answer to Blank (iii).

26. A, E, J

The blank must be filled with a word indicating a negative quality of modern medicine. Logically, if that field focused exclusively on one internal feature (*the microscopic*) of organisms, it would not be well placed, i.e. *situated*, to deal with situations involving both internal and external qualities. Note that the references to spatial relationships (*internal*, *external*, and *boundaries*) serve as an important clue here; only *situated* is consistent with that type of language. (A) is thus the answer to Blank (i).

For Blank (ii), the statement that *most new infections defy disciplinary boundaries* is an important clue, implying that animal diseases cross over into humans. There is nothing in the sentence to connote dropping or declining, so *plummet* does not make sense, but be careful with *transfigure* (transform): when plugged in, that word would indicate the animals diseases themselves become humans populations, not human diseases – a thoroughly illogical meaning. *Spill* fits as a synonym for cross over, making (E) the answer to Blank (ii).

Blank (iii) indicates a result of *these workers'* (that is, veterinarians' and physicians') failure to interact. Logically, if physicians and veterinarians do not discuss diseases with one another, than they will remain unaware of the fact that animal diseases are turning into human ones. As a result, the crossovers will go unnoticed, i.e. *escape detection*. They do not *cease to exist* simply because experts remain ignorant of them, nor do they *occur only rarely* for that reason – the lack of interaction between veterinarians and physicians has no effect on the frequency or the existence of animal-to-human disease transmission. It only results in experts remaining unaware of the situation. (J) is thus the answer to Blank (iii).

27. A, F, J

The fact that *British culture was held up as an ideal* implies that Americans were expected to admire or look up to it, so it is reasonable to assume that Blank (i) should be filled with a positive word. *Emulate* (copy) makes sense because people would logically be encouraged to model themselves after an ideal, but both *contest* (a verb meaning dispute) and *satirize* (parody, send up) are negative. (A) is thus the answer for Blank (i).

For Blank (ii), if Americans were expected to copy the British, then it can be assumed the humor in Twain's novel resulted from the fact that Twain played with or inverted that model – that is, it involved the British copying Americans. Blank (ii) must therefore be filled with a word indicating the odd nature of that situation. A *dichotomy* is a situation in which two things are set in apparent opposition to one another, with no obvious way of being reconciled. That is not quite what is being described here. *Distinction* does not fit at all – the correct word must logically describe a situation that is unexpected or strange, and *distinction* implies an honor. *Incongruity* (inconsistency) is a word that would accurately describe a situation in which the normal cultural hierarchy was reversed, making (F) the answer to Blank (ii).

Blank (iii) must be filled with a word that refers to the "incongruity" in Blank (ii) – namely, the fact that the British characters in Twain's novel were copying the American ones. The correct word must therefore mean something generally similar to incongruity. *Genre* refers to an entire category of literature and is far too broad; the correct word must describe one particular feature of the novel in question. An *archetype* refers to a standard pattern or model, but the word required here must indicate an exception to the norm. Only *reversal* is consistent with the idea that Twain's novel inverts normal social relations. (J) is thus the answer to Blank (iii).

28. B, D, H

The construction _____ *as it* _____ is the only clue provided for Blanks (i) and (ii), indicating that the process changes in some way while it is occurring. For more specific information about what happens to the process, it is necessary to look to the following sentences and work backwards from Blank (iii). Think carefully about what the second and third sentences are saying: the implication is that arctic ice has a high albedo, remaining frozen because it deflects light. As the ice melts, however, the ice becomes less reflective, and its albedo declines. Ice that is less reflective absorbs more energy from the sun and melts even more. More melt = even lower albedo, i.e. the albedo *declines even further*. (H) is thus the answer to Blank (iii).

Now go back and think about the first two blanks in terms of what has been determined about the melting process. Logically the more ice melts, the lower the albedo drops, causing the ice to melt even more and the albedo to drop even more – that, in turn, causes the ice to melt even more, and so on. The more ice melts, the faster the melting process goes. In other words, the process *accelerates as it progresses*. It certainly does not *abate* (subside) or *stagnate* (lose momentum), nor does it *contract* or *adapt*. It just keeps turning ice into water at an increasingly rapid pace. (B) is thus the answer to Blank (i), and (D) is the answer to Blank (ii).

29. C, D, J

Although the first sentence does not contain any blanks, it is key because it sets up the scenario that follows. What does that sentence tell us? People often react to outbreaks of disease by blaming others for their misfortune, regardless of whether those individuals are actually responsible for infecting anyone.

For Blank (i), illnesses that struck already vulnerable societies would logically be very good at making people feel as if they lacked control over their environments. Even though the idea is negative, the blank must be filled with a positive word meaning good or skillful. Although *focused on* indicates a positive attitude, diseases lack the agency to focus on anything. *Constrained by* (limited) implies exactly the opposite of the required word. *Adept* is a synonym for skillful and provides a logical description of how pathogens are able to effectively exploit a weakness of vulnerable populations. (C) is thus the answer to Blank (i).

For Blank (ii), be careful with the double negative: *not inescapable* means that a disease <u>can</u> be escaped. The phrase *Certain people are struck, while others are not* in the following sentence reinforces that idea. Blank (ii) refers to some quality of an illness, logically a negative one. *Proclivities* (preferences; PRO-, in favor of) is clearly positive and can be eliminated. *Vulnerabilities* is negative, but the passage is discussing a category of people vulnerable to disease, not the vulnerabilities of diseases themselves. *Ravages* (destructions) fits perfectly as a negative quality of disease that some people but not others are able to escape.

For Blank (iii), if you find the phrase *however opaque* confusing, try not to get distracted by it. Instead, focus on the meaning of the passage as a whole. Remember that the first sentence indicates that epidemics provoke *scapegoating*. The answer to Blank (iii) must be consistent with that idea. Given that context, the fact that certain people fall ill while others do not is not suggestive of *mendacity* (lying) or *penitence* (repentance). It does, however, suggest some form of *complicity* – that is, some people become ill because they are involved in (complicit in), something bad and are being punished as a result. (Alternately, this statement could be interpreted to suggest that some people are spared from disease for unnatural reasons, but this does not affect the answers in any way.) *However opaque* implies that the exact reasons for the punishment may be extremely unclear (opaque), but that they exist nonetheless. After all, that is the definition of scapegoating: shifting the blame for unpleasant events onto other people and thus justifying their punishment.

30. B, E, G

The key word in the passage is *masterpiece*, i.e. a monumental <u>artistic</u> achievement. In the first sentence, the writer complains that anything can be granted this title, providing three examples of works that are not normally associated with the term. The construction *While the _____ merits of some of these works can be defended* at the beginning of the second sentence signals a concession – an admission that a hit single, a theme park, and a video game can possess a value associated with masterpieces. Blank (i) must therefore be filled with a word referring that value. Be very careful with *intrinsic* (innate). Although this option might seem appealing, a work can possess intrinsic value without being a masterpiece; there is no automatic connection between the two things. Likewise, whether some of the merits of the works mentioned are *cumulative* is entirely irrelevant to whether they are masterpieces. Only *aesthetic* value (value relating to beauty) is consistent with the discussion of masterpieces. (B) is thus the answer to Blank (i).

For Blank (ii), the key word *debased* (degraded) indicates that the blank must be filled with a negative word indicating that the word *masterpiece* has lost its meaning. *Extinction* does not make sense because clearly, the term is still being used. *Incredulousness* does not fit either – a word that is overused would not become incredulous (disbelieving) as a result. A word cannot believe or disbelieve in anything. In contrast, a frequently overused term could easily be described as vacuous (empty; *vacuity* = emptiness). When any old work can be described as a masterpiece, then the term ceases to have an impact. (E) is thus the answer to Blank (ii).

For Blank (iii), if people are still using the word *masterpiece*, then logically the concept of such extraordinary work must still exist. That suggests the term has not yet lost its meaning entirely – that is, it is not *entirely devoid of meaning*. The other answers do not fit at all, making (G) the answer to Blank (iii).

Sentence Equivalences: Hard

1. Although Jackson Pollock's early work is in some ways very _____, it nevertheless hints at some of the more avant-garde aspects of Pollock's emerging artistic personality.

    [A] amorphous
    [B] trite
    [C] captivating
    [D] unique
    [E] prosaic
    [F] enthralling

2. Toward the end of his career, the psychologist became fascinated with psychics as well as a variety of other mystical phenomena, an interest that his more incredulous colleagues dismissed as pure _____.

    [A] charlatanism
    [B] impudence
    [C] chicanery
    [D] esotericism
    [E] pedantry
    [F] revisionism

3. Even after hours of questioning, the detectives remained unable to comprehend the suspect's motives, which, to their chagrin, remained bafflingly _____.

    [A] opaque
    [B] incoherent
    [C] impulsive
    [D] deviant
    [E] ignorant
    [F] inscrutable

4. Unhampered by cumbersome equipment, post-Impressionist painters used some of the first handheld cameras to observe rapid light effects previously too _____ to capture.

   [A] stunning
   [B] fleeting
   [C] evanescent
   [D] unstable
   [E] subdued
   [F] daunting

5. Although the term "banana" refers to a soft, sweet fruit, while "plantain" refers to a firmer, starchier one, they are genetically indistinguishable, the distinction between them being essentially _____.

   [A] suspect
   [B] arbitrary
   [C] restrictive
   [D] clandestine
   [E] semantic
   [F] benign

6. Dorothy Parker's biting wit earned her great fame, but she was eventually fired from *Vanity Fair* because the magazine's editors believed that some readers were put off by her excessively _____ style.

   [A] bombastic
   [B] contemplative
   [C] caustic
   [D] erudite
   [E] crude
   [F] acerbic

7. Throughout the Inca's quest to extend their empire into territory controlled by the Mapuche people in modern-day Chile, the Mapuche thwarted all attempts at subjugation and refused to _____.

   [A] capitulate
   [B] persevere
   [C] abscond
   [D] endure
   [E] acquiesce
   [F] reconcile

8. Even the most seasoned members of the orchestra were rattled by the _____ of the conductor's commentary; he made no attempt to mitigate his condescension toward their playing.

[A] banality
[B] callousness
[C] astuteness
[D] vitriol
[E] disinterest
[F] intensity

9. As Georgia O'Keefe aged, her ability to paint was _____ by vision problems, although she continued to work in pencil and charcoal until she was more than ninety years old.

[A] demeaned
[B] marred
[C] assuaged
[D] exacerbated
[E] aggravated
[F] tarnished

10. Progress in developing more effective global health programs has been consistently undermined by the _____ of systematic large-scale approaches to improving program design.

[A] tumult
[B] inefficiency
[C] paucity
[D] surfeit
[E] complexity
[F] dearth

11. In the sixteenth century, the first museums fed _____ public interest in the categorization and display of natural history and material culture as visitors flocked to see these "cabinets of curiosities," as they were then called.

[A] a disquieting
[B] an onerous
[C] an auspicious
[D] a burgeoning
[E] a fleeting
[F] an incipient

12. When evidence of a collision between black holes was first reported, it was rumored that the discovery was not _____ – other gravitational-wave cataclysms had also been detected.

[A] a recurrence
[B] a fluke
[C] an impediment
[D] a permutation
[E] an anomaly
[F] a revelation

13. The notion that authors should write about what they know is often scorned for leading to the kind of literary _____ toward which many novels and memoirs exhibit a pronounced tendency.

[A] pedantry
[B] solipsism
[C] obscurity
[D] collusion
[E] narcissism
[F] omniscience

14. When asked to predict the outcome of the election, the journalist _____, first predicting that the current front-runner would win and then suggesting that a lesser-known candidate would be more likely to prevail.

[A] equivocated
[B] demurred
[C] vacillated
[D] opined
[E] dissented
[F] complied

15. Translators of movie subtitles are frequently overlooked or, if they are recognized, receive no more than _____ attribution after the rest of the closing credits have finished rolling.

[A] a cursory
[B] a discreet
[C] an apparent
[D] a meandering
[E] an unobtrusive
[F] an effusive

16. Many neuroscientific theories about music's effects on the brain – for example, Steven Pinker's assertion that music is "auditory cheesecake," a biologically useless pleasure – ignore how personal tastes affect our processing of musical information; a genre that agitates one person may have _____ effect on another.

    [A] a mollifying
    [B] a gratifying
    [C] a placating
    [D] an invigorating
    [E] an ephemeral
    [F] a humbling

17. Ethical principles are most commonly ascribed to the operations of reason, but the imagination also plays an important role because without it, we would remain _____ by our experiences, acting out only against wrongs that we ourselves have endured.

    [A] blemished
    [B] lulled
    [C] vitiated
    [D] bound
    [E] circumscribed
    [F] inundated

18. When a team of archaeologists first began exploring the hypogeum, the labyrinthine structure under the floor of the Coliseum, they were baffled by its disarray, which reflected some 1,500 years of neglect and _____ construction projects, one layered on top of the other.

    [A] sparse
    [B] abstruse
    [C] haphazard
    [D] slapdash
    [E] scant
    [F] rudimentary

19. In oral cultures, which lack fixed, textual anchors for words, there is often a sense that words, when spoken, can call a new state of affairs into existence: they do not so much describe as _____.

[A] conjure
[B] decry
[C] persuade
[D] clarify
[E] invoke
[F] titillate

20. Illegal dogfighting remains a serious problem in some regions, but new technologies have allowed investigators to become _____ about identifying participants, making the phenomenon less widespread than it used to be.

[A] cannier
[B] surlier
[C] warier
[D] stealthier
[E] fiercer
[F] savvier

21. Although the book is exceptionally well-written, the author is strikingly reticent when it comes to stating his convictions, a strategy that consistently _____ any understanding of what he truly believes.

[A] precludes
[B] expedites
[C] appeases
[D] forestalls
[E] bolsters
[F] accounts for

22. One reason sound is such a potent force is that it can pass through walls, _____ a space, and technical advances have only served to increase its invasive powers.

[A] modulating
[B] dominating
[C] permeating
[D] insulating
[E] suffusing
[F] beguiling

23. Among Pluto's most peculiar features is Sputnik Planum: its smooth, softly pitted face is continually _____ by warm nitrogen ice; the jagged craters that typically accumulate on ancient planetary surfaces are entirely absent.

[A] rejuvenated
[B] bombarded
[C] burnished
[D] submerged
[E] illuminated
[F] scoured

24. Protagonists of superhero franchise movies are typically depicted as rebels against weak or corrupt civic authority and, at the same time, as avatars of a less accountable form of power whose exercise is _____ by the need to combat absolute evil.

[A] vindicated
[B] mitigated
[C] perpetuated
[D] justified
[E] resolved
[F] stipulated

25. If the singer's last comeback was an unequivocal triumph of quality in an evolving but still-receptive market, success is liable to prove more _____ this time around, even though the ingredients remain the same.

[A] assiduous
[B] enduring
[C] quantifiable
[D] tenuous
[E] remunerative
[F] elusive

Explanations: Hard Sentence Equivalences

1. B, E

The sentence sets up a contrast between a _____ aspect of Pollock's early work and the fact that that work foreshadows the more innovative work to come. The blank must therefore be filled with words meaning something like traditional. Both *trite* and *prosaic* mean unoriginal/cliché, making [B] and [E] correct. Although *captivating* and *enthralling* have similar meanings, they are incorrect because they do not describe work that is the opposite of innovative. Neither *amorphous* (shapeless; A-, not + MORPH-, shape) nor *unique* fits.

2. A, C

The reference to *psychics and mystical phenomena*, coupled with the fact that the psychologist's *more incredulous* (skeptical) *colleagues dismissed* this interest, strongly implies that the blank should be filled with words meaning something like nonsense. *Charlatanism* and *chicanery* are synonyms meaning fraud or trickery, words that skeptical people would logically use to describe things like psychics and mysticism. Be careful with [D]: although *esotericism* accurately describes the mystical phenomena referred to, the words in the blank must describe the "incredulous" colleagues' reaction rather than the phenomena themselves. None of the other answers makes any sense in context. [A] and [C] are thus correct.

3. A, F

The fact that the detectives were unable to determine the suspect's motives indicates that those motives were unclear, so the blank must be filled with words meaning something similar to unclear. Both *opaque* and *inscrutable* fit those definitions, indicating that the suspect's motives remained entirely incomprehensible. [A] and [F] are therefore correct. *Incoherent* would be consistent with the idea of motives that were difficult to understand, but that word does not have a close synonym among the other choices. *Impulsive* and *deviant* are both words often associated with criminals, but neither adequately characterizes the suspect's motives here. In addition, neither has a close synonym among the other choices. *Ignorant* describes the detectives' state of mind – they remained ignorant of the suspect's motives – but the motives themselves could not be characterized that way.

4. B, C

The key phrase *rapid light effects previously too _____* indicates that the blank must be filled with words meaning something similar to fast. Both *fleeting* and *evanescent* (short-lived) fit that definition and create a logical meaning: new, handheld cameras allowed post-Impressionist painters to capture light effects that in the past would have vanished too quickly to be recorded. [B] and [C] are thus correct. *Unstable* would also be consistent with the idea of something that disappeared too quickly to be captured, but there is no close synonym for that word among the choices. It also does not have quite the right connotation: something can be both unstable and long-lasting. *Subdued* light would be hard to capture, but it would not necessarily disappear quickly. Neither of the other choices accurately describes something that disappears too quickly to capture.

5. B, E

The sentence indicates that the banana and the plantain are genetically identical, even though they have some differences in taste and texture. The fact that they are indistinguishable on a structural level suggests that the differences between them cannot be objectively determined. In other words, those differences are *arbitrary*, making [B] the first answer. Although *semantic* might not be considered a typical synonym for *arbitrary*, it creates the same meaning as that word when it is plugged into the sentence. Literally, *semantic* refers to the fact that the only real difference between the banana and the plantain is that the two foods are referred to by different words – again, the implication is that there is no biological distinction between them. [E] is thus the second answer. *Suspect* (questionable, fishy) does not fit because there is nothing to suggest that distinguishing between bananas and plantains involves some sort of illicit activity, as that word would imply. The remaining answers do not make any sense in context.

6. C, F

The key phrase *biting wit* provides an explanation for why some readers found Parker off-putting. Logically, then, the blank must be filled with a word indicating that Parker's wit was excessively sharp or biting. Both *caustic* and *acerbic* (harsh, witheringly sarcastic) convey that idea, making [C] and [F] correct. Readers might also be put off by a *bombastic* (over-the-top) or a *crude* style, but neither of those words is consistent with the idea of an excessively harsh wit. While *contemplative* and *erudite* (possessing profound knowledge) have somewhat similar meanings, neither is at all consistent with the implied meaning of the sentence.

7. A, E

If the Mapuche *thwarted* (prevented) all of the Inca's attempts to *subjugate* (conquer) them, then the blank must be filled with words indicating that this people refused to give in. *Capitulate* and *acquiesce* both mean give in, so [A] and [E] are correct. *Abscond* (leave quickly and in secret) makes a reasonable amount of sense in context, but it lacks a close synonym among the other choices. *Persevere* would imply exactly the opposite – if the Mapuche refused to persevere, that would imply that they <u>did</u> give in. *Endure* creates the same problem, and *reconcile* implies that the Mapuche refused to make up with the Incas, not that they resisted being conquered.

8. B, D

The fact that *seasoned* (experienced) players were *rattled* (shaken) by the conductor's comments, and that the conductor did not even try to *mitigate* (soften) his condescension, suggests that his words were very harsh indeed. Comments characterized by their *banality* (lack of inspiration) or *astuteness* (perceptiveness) would certainly not elicit such a reaction from the players. Be careful with *disinterest*: this word means objectivity, not a lack of interest. *Intensity* does not necessarily denote something positive or negative. Only *callousness* (cruelty) and *vitriol* (nastiness) have similar meanings and fit with the players' reaction as well as the idea of extreme condescension. [B] and [D] are thus correct.

9. B, F

Logically, O'Keefe's ability to paint must have declined as a result of her vision problems, so the blank must be filled with negative words meaning reduced. *Aggravated* and *exacerbated* (made worse) are synonyms that could perhaps describe what happened to the vision problems themselves, but they do not convey the idea of reduction. *Assuaged* (soothed) is positive and does not make sense at all. Although not exact synonyms, *marred* (damaged, sullied) and *tarnished* (impaired) both convey the same logical result of an aging artist's vision problems on her ability to paint. [B] and [F] are thus correct.

10. C, F

The statement that progress has been *consistently undermined* indicates that efforts to develop more effective global health systems have faced serious impediments to success. As a result, the blank must be filled with negative words. *Tumult* (turmoil), *inefficiency*, and *complexity* all logically describe systems that lack effectiveness, but none of these words has a sufficiently close synonym among the other choices. *Surfeit* could almost make sense – an excess of large-scale programs might lead to conflict and difficulty in implementing solutions – but it is a bit of a stretch, and this word too lacks a synonym. *Paucity* and *dearth* (lack of) are synonyms that create a straightforwardly logical meaning: the lack of systematic approaches to improving global health problems has hindered the effectiveness of those programs. [C] and [F] are thus correct.

11. D, F

The only real clue provided by the sentence is the word *first*, indicating that the *categorization and display of natural history and material* was a novel phenomenon in the sixteenth century. The blank must therefore be filled with words consistent with the idea of newness. The only options consistent with that criterion are *burgeoning* (sprouting) and *incipient* (just beginning). There is nothing in the sentence to suggest that the interest in classifying objects was *disquieting* (disturbing), *onerous* (burdensome), *auspicious* (boding well) or *fleeting* (brief). [D] and [F] are thus correct.

12. B, E

The sentence is constructed so that the statement after the dash is used to clarify the information before the dash. The fact that <u>other</u> *gravitational-wave cataclysms had also been detected* implies that the incident described earlier in the sentence (*a collision between black holes*) might have occurred before. Remember, though, that the sentence is asking for what the incident was NOT – that is, a new or isolated phenomenon. *Recurrence* could only describe something that <u>had</u> happened before, so this word does not fit. Likewise, there is no indication that the discovery would be an *impediment* (obstacle) to any further research. *Permutation* does not fit at all. *Revelation* could plausibly fit – if similar phenomena had been observed, this one would not be nearly so earth-shattering – but this word lacks a close synonym among the other choices. *Fluke* (chance occurrence) and *anomaly* (something out of the ordinary) both convey the idea that the discovery of the collision was not a quirk of the calculations but rather part of a pattern of similar discoveries. [B] and [E] are thus correct.

13. B, E

Logically, the idea that authors should *write about what they know* could, if pushed to an extreme, result in authors having a tendency to focus excessively on themselves. The only answers to imply that kind of navel-gazing are *solipsism* (egoism) and *narcissism*. *Omniscience* and *collusion* both imply the involvement or recognition of other people/points of view, and the remaining answers are entirely unsupported by the context. [B] and [E] are thus correct.

14. A, C

The key takeaway from the sentence is that the journalist changed his mind, initially predicting one outcome and then later predicting a different one. In other words, the prediction was inconsistent. Although it is true that the journalist *complied* with the request to predict the election's outcome and *opined* in the sense that he or she provided an opinion, neither word fits the clues in the sentence or has a close synonym among the other choices. The journalist did not *demur* (refrain from commenting) because clearly an opinion was given, nor is there any indication that the journalist *dissented*. In contrast, *equivocated* (talked out of both sides of one's mouth) and *vacillated* (wavered) both accurately describe the type of contradictory discourse referred to in the sentence, making [A] and [C] correct.

15. B, E

The sentence states that subtitle translators are often *overlooked*, so the blank must be filled with adjectives indicating that these individuals do not receive prominent attribution. *Cursory* (brief) fits perfectly but lacks a close synonym among the other choices, and *effusive* means exactly the opposite of the required words. *Meandering* (wandering) and *apparent* do not make sense at all. An attribution that was *discreet* or *unobtrusive* would by definition be easily overlooked, however, so [B] and [E] are correct.

16. A, C

Even though this sentence is quite long and complex, it is really only necessary to focus on the very end. The reference to *one person* and *another* sets up an implicit contrast, so the blank must be filled with words conveying the opposite of agitation. An *invigorating* effect would make a person more energized – although this word has a more positive connotation than *agitating* does, it is too similar to accurately work as an antonym. *Gratifying* (rewarding) could plausibly fit, but this word has no close synonym among the other choices. *Ephemeral* (short-lived) and *humbling* make no sense at all. *Mollifying* and *placating* both mean calming, which is the logical opposite of agitating. [A] and [C] are thus correct.

17. D, E

The beginning of the sentence is dense and confusing, but you only need the basics to answer the question. To sum up, it is saying that the imagination plays an important role in ethics because without it, people could only think about wrongdoing in terms of what they have directly experienced. Given that context, the blank must be filled with words indicating that people would be defined or limited in some way by their experiences. People who remained *blemished* (stained) could logically be expected to *act out against wrongs [they] have endured*, but this word lacks a close synonym among the other choices and is inconsistent with the idea of being limited. *Lulled* (soothed), *vitiated* (drained of energy), and *inundated* all do not make sense. Only *bound* and *circumscribed* (limited) are consistent with the meaning the blank must logically convey, making [D] and [E] correct.

18. C, D

The key words *disarray* and *neglect* imply that the construction projects that took place under the Coliseum were disorganized or even chaotic. The blank must be filled with words conveying that idea. *Sparse* and *scant* (meager) are synonyms, but they do not convey the idea of disorganization and are inconsistent with the idea of 1500 years worth of construction projects layered on top of one another. *Rudimentary* (basic) could plausibly fit, but this word lacks a close synonym among the answer choices. *Abstruse* (abstract, esoteric) does not really make sense. That leave *haphazard* and *slapdash*, both of which mean sloppy or carelessly done, and fit perfectly with the idea of disarray. [C] and [D] are thus correct.

19. A, E

Try not to get too hung up on the beginning of the sentence, which is somewhat abstract and potentially confusing. The key phrases are *call a new state of affairs into existence*, which is roughly equivalent to the meaning of the words in the blank; and *they do not so much describe*, which must mean the opposite of the words in the blank. Words that *decried* (denounced), *persuaded*, or *titillated* (tantalized) would not call anything into existence. In contrast, *conjure* and *invoke* would do precisely that. [A] and [E] are thus correct.

20. A, F

The key phrases *new technologies* and *making the phenomenon less widespread* suggest that investigators have improved their ability to catch participants in dogfighting. The blank must therefore be filled with words conveying the idea of something better or more effective. *Surlier* (grouchier) is clearly negative and makes no sense. Be careful with *warier*: although the investigators might become more suspicious about certain individuals they suspect are involved in illicit activity, the fact that dogfighting has declined suggests that the investigators have been more aggressive, not less, about identifying participants. *Fiercer* would be a good fit, but this word lacks a close synonym among the other choices. The same is true for *stealthier* – it is reasonable that investigators who behaved in a more discreet manner would be more effective – but again there is no close synonym. Only *cannier* and *savvier* (more resourceful) are both synonyms and convey a logical meaning: new technologies have allowed investigators to do their jobs more intelligently, making them more effective.

21. A, D

The fact that the author is *strikingly reticent* (shy, reluctant) *when it comes to stating his convictions* (beliefs) indicates that it is extremely difficult to determine what he actually thinks. As a result, the blank must be filled with words meaning something like prevents or obstructs. *Precludes* and *forestalls* both mean prevents, making [A] and [D] correct. *Expedites* (speeds up), *appeases* (calms), and *accounts for* all do not make sense; *bolsters* (supports, props up) means exactly the opposite of the required words.

22. C, E

The sentence indicates that sound is *potent* (powerful) because it can *pass through walls* and is becoming increasingly *invasive*. Logically, then, the blank must convey the idea that music can take over a space. *Modulating* (regulating, balancing) and *beguiling* (charming) do not fit at all, and *insulating* gets the relationship backwards: rooms are insulated to protect sound from getting out. Sound itself does not insulate a room. *Dominating* is a clear match for the clues, but this word lacks a close synonym among the other choices. Only *permeating* and *suffusing* (seeping into) have similar meanings and fit the clues provided by the sentence. [C] and [E] are thus correct.

23. A, C

Make sure you take the entire sentence into account here. If you only focus on the information before the semicolon, you might think that *bombarded* is a logical choice because the sentence is suggesting that the warm nitrogen ice causes deformations (*soft pits*) in Sputnik Planum's surface. However, the information after the semicolon implies exactly the opposite: jagged craters are *entirely absent* from Sputnik Planum's surface. The focus is actually on the fact that the pits here are *smooth*. Given that, the blank must be filled with words conveying the idea of smoothing. *Bombarded* has the wrong connotation, implying that Sputnik Planum is being violently hit. *Illuminated* does not make sense because the sentence says nothing about light. *Submerged* could plausibly fit, but it does not have a close synonym among the other choices. Although *rejuvenated* and *burnished* are not exact synonyms, they both convey the same idea when plugged into the sentence: Sputnik Planum's surface is continually renewed and smoothed over by the warm nitrogen ice, removing the signs of wear typically found on the surface of a celestial body. [A] and [C] are thus correct.

24. A, D

The sentence indicates that superheroes have two major characteristics: they rebel against corrupt authority, and they represent (act *as avatars of*) a *less accountable* type of power – that is, power unconnected to formal authority. The phrase with the blank describes the second type of power, and the word *need* is an important clue indicating that the focus is on why that power is important or necessary. *Mitigated* (reduced) and *resolved* do not make sense at all. *Perpetuated* would be a logical fit – the need to combat *absolute evil* would certainly lead to the perpetuation (continuation) of this type of power – but this word lacks a close synonym among the other choices. *Stipulated* (required) has the same problem. In contrast, *vindicated* (proven right) and *justified* have very similar definitions and create the same logical meaning when plugged into the sentence: because it is necessary to fight against absolute evil by any means available, superheroes' exercise (use) of power that operates outside the bounds of traditional authority is justified.

25. D, F

The word *if* at the beginning of the sentence is used to imply a potential contrast between the straightforward success (*unequivocal triumph*) of the singer's previous comeback and the greater challenges this time around. Logically, then, the blank must be filled with negative words denoting difficulty. *Assiduous* (hardworking), *enduring* (long-lasting), and *remunerative* (well-paying) are all positive and can be eliminated. *Quantifiable* (measurable) is neutral and does not make any sense in context. Although they have somewhat different meanings, *tenuous* and *elusive* both accurately convey the idea that the success of this comeback is less certain than the success of the previous one.

Part 3

....

Mixed Practice Sets

In this section:

- 15 practice sets

- 6 Text Completions and 5 Sentence Equivalences per set

- Questions presented in order of difficulty within each type

Set 1

1. In the past, maps often reflected the diverse perspectives of their creators, but the use of computers and satellites to ensure accuracy has in recent years rendered them increasingly _____.

(A) complex
(B) sleek
(C) uniform
(D) colorful
(E) eclectic

2. In spite of his role as the head of an international fashion empire, Christian Fabré leads _____ existence, subsisting on only the most basic necessities.

(A) a serene
(B) an eccentric
(C) a staid
(D) an ostentatious
(E) an ascetic

3. The scientist's work, once widely praised for its precision and attention to detail, is now being (i) _____ in some quarters as the (ii) _____ of shoddiness.

Blank (i)	Blank (ii)
(A) ransacked	(D) bane
(B) pilloried	(E) epitome
(C) extolled	(F) antithesis

4. Accused of (i) _____ by members of the opposing party, the candidate refused to   admit to any form of wrongdoing and in fact protested that she had always been entirely (ii) _____.

Blank (i)	Blank (ii)
(A) punctiliousness	(D) terse
(B) waffling	(E) thorough
(C) obfuscation	(F) frank

5. To be accepted as a (i) _____, a theory must seem superior to its competitors, but it need not, and in fact never does, (ii) _____ all the facts with which it could possibly be (iii) _____.

Blank (i)	Blank (ii)	Blank (iii)
(A) conviction	(D) abide by	(G) subsumed
(B) paradigm	(E) account for	(H) confronted
(C) consequence	(F) relate to	(J) entertained

6. Economists say years of economic mismanagement have (i) _____ the nation's food supply. Sugar fields in the country's agricultural center remain (ii) _____ for lack of fertilizers, and unused machinery decays in shuttered factories. Staples including corn and rice, once exported, must now be imported, arriving in quantities that persistently (iii) _____ what is needed.

Blank (i)	Blank (ii)	Blank (iii)
(A) confounded	(D) overrun	(G) measure up to
(B) girded	(E) unwieldy	(H) double down on
(C) devastated	(F) fallow	(J) fall short of

7. The association between meditation and mindfulness naturally leads the two terms to be frequently _____ when in fact they are distinct.

[A] conflated
[B] divulged
[C] explained
[D] defined
[E] confused
[F] qualified

8. Recent studies suggest that many cases of cancer are preventable, but this revelation has inflamed as much as it has _____ people's fears.

[A] stoked
[B] assuaged
[C] revealed
[D] alleviated
[E] compelled
[F] aggravated

9. Because antibiotics are only used for a short time, there is little market incentive for pharmaceutical companies to develop new ones; the market value of a brand-new antibiotic is just $50 million, _____ sum for a company, considering the research and development costs incurred by the creation of such treatments.

   [A] a staggering
   [B] an unfathomable
   [C] a manageable
   [D] an impressive
   [E] a meager
   [F] a paltry

10. Citrus greening, thought to be caused by the bacterium *Candidatus Liberibacter asiaticus*, is capable of _____ entire groves in only a few months and has become a scourge for orange growers throughout much of southeastern United States.

   [A] obliterating
   [B] anchoring
   [C] fortifying
   [D] decimating
   [E] penetrating
   [F] surrounding

11. Saul Bellow's early novels were perspicacious if rarely _____: they reflected his keen sense of observation but were entirely lacking in economy of expression.

   [A] lucid
   [B] prolix
   [C] succinct
   [D] inane
   [E] facetious
   [F] laconic

Explanations: Set 1

1. C

The sentence sets up a contrast between the *diverse perspectives* represented by maps in the past, and the increasingly _____ quality of maps today. Logically, the blank must be filled with a word meaning the opposite of diverse. Only *uniform* (alike, standardized) fits that requirement exactly, making (C) the answer. *Eclectic* is a synonym for *diverse*, and none of the other choices makes sense in context.

2. E

The key phrase is *subsisting on only the most basic necessities*, which indicates that Fabré leads an extraordinarily plain lifestyle, despite his position. The blank must therefore be filled with a word meaning something similar to plain or basic. *Staid* (conventional) clearly does not fit, and *ostentatious* (showy) means exactly the opposite of the required word. Although a lifestyle that does not include many possessions could be very *serene*, it would not necessarily have this quality. While *eccentric* could justifiably be used to describe the head of an international fashion empire who spurns all luxuries, the most direct match for the clue is *ascetic*, which means practicing extreme self-denial. (E) is thus correct.

3. B, E

The statement that the scientist's work was *once widely praised for its attention to detail* implies that this is no longer the case, and that the work is now characterized by its *shoddiness* (poor quality). Blank (i) should therefore be filled with a negative word meaning attacked or criticized. *Ransacked* (plundered) is negative but can only refer to a physical action and cannot refer to criticism. *Extolled* (praised) is positive and clearly does not fit. That leaves *pilloried* (ridiculed, derided), which logically describes the reaction against a scientist accused of doing shoddy work. (B) is thus the answer to Blank (i).

The meaning of Blank (ii) is less clear, but the correct word must indicate an association between the scientist's work and shoddiness. *Bane* (cause of distress) does not fit; the sentence is saying that the work *is* shoddy, not that it ruins shoddiness. And *antithesis* (opposite) implies that the scientist's work is not shoddy. However, work that was the *epitome* (essence) of shoddiness would draw criticism. (E) is thus the answer to Blank (ii).

4. C, F

The fact that the politician was *accused* of something, and that she would not *admit to any form of wrongdoing*, indicates that Blank (i) must be filled with a negative word. *Punctiliousness* (meticulousness) is not a notably negative quality in a politician, so this answer can be eliminated. *Waffling* (wavering, being indecisive) is a plausible answer, but there is no option for Blank (ii) that means decisive. *Obfuscation* (covering up) fits and is the only option that has a direct opposite for Blank (ii): someone accused of presenting the issues in an unclear or confusing way would logically protest by claiming that she had been clear and direct, i.e. *frank*. (C) is thus the answer to Blank (i), and (F) is the answer to Blank (ii).

5. B, E, H

The phrase *a theory must seem superior to its competitors* is presented as a condition for Blank (i), indicating that the blank must be filled with a positive word meaning something like fact. It would not make sense to say that a theory must outdo its competitors in order to be accepted as a *conviction* or a *consequence*. A theory that was clearly superior to rival theories could, however, be accepted as a *paradigm* (model). (B) is thus the answer to Blank (i).

The sentence does not provide any direct information about the definitions of Blanks (ii) and (iii), although the contradictor *but* does indicate that the second half of the sentence will convey an idea that contrasts with the idea in the first half. Since the first half focuses on what a theory must do correctly in order to be accepted (be better than other theories), the second half must discuss what it does NOT need to do nearly as well. Given that context, *account for* and *confronted* create the most logical meaning when plugged into the sentence: although a theory must provide the most convincing explanation for a phenomenon in order to be accepted as a standard model, it need not be perfect or absolutely comprehensive – that is, it need not take into consideration (*account for*) every fact that is related to it, or that could *confront* it. (E) is thus the answer to Blank (ii), and (H) is the answer to Blank (iii).

6. C, F, J

If the country has been mismanaged economically for years, then presumably the nation's food supply has declined. *Confounded* (confused) makes no sense, and *girded* (supported) means exactly the opposite of the required word. *Devastated* (utterly ruined) describes a result that years of economic mismanagement would logically have on the food supply, making (C) the answer to Blank (i).

For Blank (ii), if the country's food supplies have been destroyed, then the sugar fields must be empty or unproductive. A lack of fertilizers would not make the fields *overrun* or *unwieldy* (cumbersome, difficult to manage), but it would make them *fallow* (neglected).

Blank (iii) must be filled with a word reinforcing the idea that the country's food supply is lacking. Imports of staple items that *measure up to* or *double down on* (become more persistent in) what is needed would not lead to a food shortage, but ones that *persistently fall short* would indeed have that effect. (J) is thus the answer to Blank (iii).

7. A, E

The key phrase *when in fact they are distinct* sets up a contrast between that statement and the blank, implying that *meditation* and *mindfulness* are frequently believed to mean the same thing. In other words, they are *confused* for one another, i.e. *conflated*. [A] and [E] are thus correct. Although the answers are not exact synonyms, in this context both accurately convey the idea that the terms in question are used interchangeably. None of the other answers creates a logical meaning that corresponds to the clues in the sentence.

8. B, D

The construction *inflamed as much as it has* _____ implies that the blank must be filled with words meaning the opposite of inflamed – something like calmed or soothed. *Assuaged* and *alleviated* both fit that definition, making [B] and [D] correct. *Stoked* (incited) and *aggravated* have similar meanings in this context, but both convey the opposite of the required definition. The remaining answers all do not make sense.

9. E, F

To say that there is *little market incentive for drug companies to develop new [drugs]* is another way of saying that new drugs don't make drug companies much money. Even though a $50 million market value might seem large, the key word *just* implies that this figure is actually quite small. The blank must therefore be filled with words meaning something like small. *Staggering, unfathomable,* and *impressive* would all more logically be used to describe a very large sum, so these words can be eliminated. *Manageable* does not fit because a sum that is *manageable* is one that is affordable, and here the focus is on how much new antibiotics are worth to drug companies, not how much those companies can afford to pay. This word also has a more positive connotation than what is required here. In contrast, an antibiotic whose worth was *meager* or *paltry* (scanty, insignificant) would not be of very much value to a drug company at all. [E] and [F] are thus correct.

10. A, D

The fact that citrus greening is caused by a *bacterium* and has become a *scourge* (pest, affliction) suggests that is very bad for orange growers indeed. It is therefore reasonable to assume that the blank should be filled with negative words. *Anchoring* makes no sense, and the definition of *fortifying* (strengthening) is the opposite of what is required. *Penetrating* and *surrounding* could both plausibly fit, but neither of these words has a close synonym among the other choices. The correct answers, *obliterating* and *decimating*, refer to destroying something thoroughly. Logically, citrus greening would be considered a scourge if it thoroughly destroyed citrus groves, making [A] and [D] correct.

11. C, F

Watch out for the negative – the blank must be filled with words describing a quality that Bellow's novels *rarely* possessed. The key information comes after the colon, with the two pieces of information running parallel to the two descriptors before the colon: *perspicacious* (perceptive) = keen sense of observation, and the blank = *entirely lacking in economy of expression*. *Economy of expression* means not using a lot of words (*economy* = thrift), so to say that a book lacks economy of expression is a fancy way of saying that it is wordy. The sentence, however, asks for words indicating what Bellow's works are NOT – that is, the opposite of wordy. The opposite of wordy is concise, i.e. *succinct* or *laconic*. *Prolix* means wordy, and the other answers do not make sense in context.

Set 2

1. Political parties and other formal groupings are often as much tribal as they are ideological: families, corporations, even whole cities tend to show their allegiance _____.

(A) belatedly
(B) prominently
(C) collectively
(D) immediately
(E) sporadically

2. Because the reactions that cause ozone to be destroyed require sunlight, the thinning of the ozone layer begins each year in late August, when winter in the Southern Hemisphere is ending, and reaches its _____ in December, when the days are longest.

(A) boundary
(B) cusp
(C) stature
(D) zenith
(E) altitude

3. Failure to recognize the power of broad context can create considerable misunderstanding, from assuming that accidents were (i) _____ to crediting people with earning success as a result of factors that were in reality (ii) _____.

Blank (i)	Blank (ii)
(A) catastrophic	(D) unique to them
(B) random	(E) beyond their control
(C) deliberate	(F) within their grasp

4. One of the most surprising findings to emerge from human gene-sequencing data in the past decade is that human evolution has been accelerating in recent times. In fact, adaptive mutations in our species' genome have (i) _____ a hundred times more quickly since farming got underway than at any other period in human history, and the closer we move to the present, the faster the adaptive mutations (ii) _____.

Blank (i)	Blank (ii)
(A) dissembled	(D) zero in
(B) accumulated	(E) come apart
(C) mobilized	(F) pile up

5. Explaining why people might be induced to cooperate is not an easy task. Indeed, it has (i) _____ many an evolutionary theorist. The (ii) _____ of the problem is this: by nature, we are not (iii) _____.

Blank (i)	Blank (ii)	Blank (iii)
(A) stymied	(D) extent	(G) loners
(B) deranged	(E) plight	(H) dissenters
(C) entranced	(F) crux	(J) altruists

6. The pleasure involved in making aesthetic judgments cannot be completely (i) _____. Otherwise, the claim that everyone should agree about the value of a work could not even (ii) _____, and there would be no need to (iii) _____.

Blank (i)	Blank (ii)	Blank (iii)
(A) subjective	(D) arise	(G) break it down
(B) ephemeral	(E) expand	(H) quarrel over it
(C) inconsistent	(F) abate	(J) hand it over

7. In some ways, presidential memorabilia is a subsection of Americana or antiques. But given the _____ supply of presidential material, the uniqueness of the objects available for acquisition attracts people with very specific interests.

   [A] copious
   [B] significant
   [C] limited
   [D] antiquated
   [E] minute
   [F] restricted

8. No publication can fully capture the cultural or political spirit of its time; history will inevitably judge it and find it _____ in some way or another.

   [A] lacking
   [B] momentous
   [C] exclusive
   [D] wanting
   [E] perplexing
   [F] indefensible

9. It is dispiriting to see how the identities of old-fashioned chain stores can become _____ as the companies seek to remain vital in what is becoming an ever more competitive retail culture.

   [A] ossified
   [B] distorted
   [C] derivative
   [D] expendable
   [E] warped
   [F] imperiled

10. The springtime blizzard was _____ occurrence: not for more than a century had a major snowstorm taken place so late in the season.

   [A] a scandalous
   [B] an anomalous
   [C] a peripheral
   [D] a fortuitous
   [E] an exceptional
   [F] a disquieting

11. Like many of the characters that would eventually populate his novels, Dickens was raised in _____ family and even left school to work in a factory after his father was thrown into a debtor's prison.

   [A] an indigent
   [B] a chaotic
   [C] a ruthless
   [D] an impecunious
   [E] a supercilious
   [F] an imprudent

Explanations: Set 2

1. C

The statement that formal groups are *as much tribal as they are ideological* suggests that their members tend to act together and in similar ways. The only answer consistent with that idea is *collectively* – a group that behaves tribally is a group that acts as a whole. The other answers do not describe this type of group behavior. (C) is thus correct.

2. D

Don't get too thrown off by the references to the end of winter in August and long days during December in the southern hemisphere. What's important here is the fact that sunlight destroys ozone, and more sunlight = more destruction. Logically, the most ozone is destroyed when the amount of sunlight is greatest, i.e. in December, when days are longest. The correct answer must therefore refer to the fact that the ozone layer is thinnest at that time. *Boundary* refers to a limit beyond which something cannot pass, but the sentence is not referring to the thinnest point that could possibly ever be reached. Although the events described are occurring at a very high *altitude,* that word cannot logically refer to the extreme thinning of the ozone layer itself. *Stature* refers to the height of a person, and *cusp* means verge, neither of which makes any sense in context. *Zenith* refers to the highest point and is a logical way to describe the time when the thinning of the ozone layer is most extreme. (D) is thus correct.

3. C, E

The key phrase *considerable misunderstanding* indicates that the reality of the two phenomena indicated (accidents, people being credited with earning success) is actually the opposite of what it appears to be. If the cause of an accident – by definition, something that does not happen on purpose – were misunderstood, then people would believe that the accident occurred *deliberately* rather than *randomly. Catastrophic,* a word that is often associated with accidents, does not fit at all. (C) is thus the answer to Blank (i).

For Blank (ii), the key phrase is *crediting people with earning success* – that is, people are believed to have gained success through their own efforts. If the reality were the opposite, then people would have earned success not because of their own hard work but rather because of other, external factors. The only option consistent with that idea is *beyond their control.* People whose success was due to factors beyond their control would by definition not be responsible for their own success. (E) is thus the answer to Blank (ii).

4. B, F

Even though the first sentence does not contain a blank, it still provides key information that sets up the sentence that follows. The first sentence indicates that *human evolution has been <u>accelerating</u> in recent times,* and Blank (i) indicates that *mutations in our species' genome* have been affected in some way. Logically, the blank must be filled with a word consistent with the idea of getting faster. The only option to directly fit that idea is *accumulated* – if evolution is speeding up, then genetic mutations must logically be increasing as well. *Dissembled* (conceal one's true motives) clearly does not fit, and *mobilized* (set in motion) does not quite make sense. (B) is thus the answer to Blank (i).

Blank (ii) must be filled with a word whose meaning is similar to accumulate. If evolution is occurring even more quickly now than it did in the recent past, then adaptive mutations must be appearing faster as well. Mutations themselves cannot *zero in* (focus in) on anything, and *come apart* is the opposite of *accumulate*. *Pile up*, however, describes the logical effect of an accelerated evolution process on genetic mutations. (F) is thus the answer to Blank (ii).

5. A, F, J

If *explaining why people might be induced to cooperate* is such a difficult task, then evolutionary theorists would likely struggle with it. Blank (i) must therefore be filled with a word meaning something like stumped. *Deranged* (insane) is far too strong – trying to solve such a knotty problem would understandably make evolutionary theorists irritated, but it would probably not make them crazy. Certain evolutionary theorists might also find the problem *entrancing*, but this answer is a less direct fit for the idea of something not being difficult than is *stymied*, which means blocked or thwarted. (A) is thus the answer to Blank (i).

Blank (ii) must be filled with a word that describes some quality of the problem referred to in the previous sentence – that is, how to explain why people cooperate. If the type of word you're looking for isn't clear enough, skip to Blank (iii). Logically, it would be difficult to explain why people cooperate with one another if people were inclined to compete *by nature*. Watch out for the negation, though: Blank (iii) must be filled with a word that describes what people are *not*. *Loners* and *dissenters* are exactly the opposite of what is required: people who were not either of these things by nature could be easily induced to cooperate. An *altruist* is someone who performs good works selflessly, and this word fits: if people were not naturally altruistic, they find would it difficult to put aside their own needs and work with others. As a result, it would be difficult to explain why they might be induced to cooperate. (J) is thus the answer to Blank (iii).

In that context, the phrase that includes Blank (ii) must logically set up the statement that follows – that is, the central reason that evolutionary theorists struggle to explain why people cooperate. *Crux* refers to an essence or central issue in a problem, making (F) the most logical choice for Blank (ii).

6. A, D, H

Blank (i) must be filled with a word describing something that the *pleasure involved in making aesthetic judgments* lacks. The reference to aesthetic judgments is an important clue because questions of artistic beauty or value involve personal preferences by definition ("beauty is in the eye of the beholder"). The only answer to fit that idea is *subjective*. Neither *ephemeral* (short-lived) nor *inconsistent* is relevant. (A) is thus the answer to Blank (i).

With that context in mind, consider Blanks (ii) and (iii). The transition *otherwise* indicates that the second sentence is discussing an alternative to the situation in the previous sentence – that is, what would happen if aesthetic judgments were purely subjective. If that were the case – that is, if everyone's opinion of a work was so different that there was no possibility that two people could perceive it similarly – then there would be no need to even claim that people should agree about the work's value. Sustained debates could not even come up, i.e. *arise*, in the first place. And, by extension, there would be no need to argue about that value, i.e. *quarrel over it*. (D) is thus the answer to Blank (ii), and (H) is the answer to Blank (iii).

7. C, F

The key phrase *uniqueness of the objects available* and the reference to collectors with very specific interests suggest that presidential memorabilia is both in short supply and lacking in broad appeal. *Copious* and *significant* both describe plentiful things – exactly the opposite of what is required. *Antiquated* would be a logical way to describe antiques, but it provides no information about items' availability. *Minute* (very small) would logically describe a supply of items with unique appeal, but this word lacks a close synonym among the other choices. In contrast, *limited* and *restricted* have the same meaning and convey the idea that the memorabilia is only interesting to a small number of collectors. [C] and [F] are thus correct.

8. A, D

The key piece of information is that no publication can fully capture the spirit of its time. In other words, there are always aspects of an era that a book, magazine, newspaper, etc. fails to convey. The blank must be filled with negative words indicating that information will always be missing from these types of publications. That would not describe *momentous* works (hugely significant ones), nor would it apply to *exclusive* ones. Be careful with *perplexing*: it only implies that a work would be puzzling, not that it would fail to capture certain characteristics of a time period. *Indefensible* is too strongly negative and does not fit the clue. That leaves *lacking* and *wanting* (note the second meaning), synonyms that clearly convey the idea that no publication can fully reveal a given time period. [A] and [D] are thus correct.

9. B, E

The key word *dispiriting* implies that an increasingly competitive retail culture has negatively affected old-fashioned chain stores. Logically, then, the blank must be filled with negative words meaning something similar to lost or changed. *Ossified* (hardened; OS-, bone) does not fit at all. *Expendable* (disposable) and *imperiled* (endangered) both create logical meanings when plugged into the sentence, but those meanings are not similar enough to make them the answers. *Derivative* (unoriginal, copied) makes sense as well, but this word lacks a close synonym among the other choices. In contrast, *distorted* and *warped* are synonyms that convey the logical idea that the existing identities of chain stores have been twisted as a result of the stores' being forced to compete with bigger rivals. [B] and [E] are thus correct.

10. B, E

The information after the colon provides a definition for the words in the blank. The fact that a major springtime snowstorm had not occurred for more than a century suggests the blizzard in question was a highly unusual occurrence. The blizzard may have been *scandalous* or *disquieting*, but those words do not accurately describe something unusual. *Peripheral* (not central) and *fortuitous* (by chance) do not fit either. Only *anomalous* and *exceptional* both describe an event that is out of the ordinary, making [B] and [E] correct.

11. A, D

The passage indicates that Dickens *left school to work in a factory* and that his *father was thrown into a debtor's prison*, strongly implying that the author's family was impoverished. The blank must therefore be filled with words describing the family's lack of money. The only two choices that convey this meaning are *indigent* and *impecunious*, both of which mean poor. [A] and [D] are thus correct.

Set 3

1. The whale is _____ navigator, driven by instinct to migrate thousands of miles each year and always arriving in precisely the same spot.

(A) a timid
(B) an expert
(C) a flexible
(D) a blatant
(E) an indifferent

2. Although the fear of wolves is _____, present in virtually every society around the world, wolf attacks against humans are actually quite rare and typically occur only when an animal is sick or provoked.

(A) ubiquitous
(B) relative
(C) insidious
(D) distressing
(E) overwhelming

3. Although psychologists once (i) _____ fiction as a way of understanding people's actions, they have recently developed a new (ii) _____ for the insight that stories can provide into human behavior.

Blank (i)	Blank (ii)
(A) broke down	(D) contempt
(B) inquired about	(E) appreciation
(C) scoffed at	(F) classification

4. The idea that art is inherently good took hold only in the past few centuries. Philosophers of prior eras tended to view it as (i) _____ for unrest that had to be properly channeled in order to prevent social (ii) _____.

Blank (i)	Blank (ii)
(A) a catalyst	(D) contamination
(B) a penchant	(E) exclusion
(C) a distaste	(F) discord

5. The problem with confirmation bias is not only that it causes people to
(i) _____ notice and remember only the subset of evidence that
(ii) _____ their assumptions, but that it also leads them to dismiss
information that contradicts what they (ii) _____.

Blank (i)	Blank (ii)	Blank (iii)
(A) impartially	(D) bolsters	(G) expect to see
(B) allegedly	(E) mitigates	(H) want to understand
(C) selectively	(F) defies	(J) struggle to convey

6. The term "emerging viruses" is a (i) _____. In reality, these
microorganisms have existed for millennia, but overpopulation and the
progressive (ii) _____ of human habitation on their environments are only
now forcing them (iii) _____.

Blank (i)	Blank (ii)	Blank (iii)
(A) paradox	(D) insistence	(G) into the open
(B) misnomer	(E) fixation	(H) onto the brink
(C) pretext	(F) encroachment	(J) out of sight

7. Many major food manufacturers are _____ to put the words "genetic engineering" on labels for fear of conveying the impression that the foods are suspect.

[A] compelled
[B] loath
[C] reluctant
[D] eager
[E] fortunate
[F] wont

8. In the two-dimensional world of maps, sharp lines are used to demarcate where one country ends and another begins, but in reality borders are far more _____.

[A] porous
[B] impregnable
[C] salient
[D] fluid
[E] elaborate
[F] defensive

9. Kyoto's 2,000 temples and shrines, not to mention its numerous gardens, make the city's 17 World Heritage sites a _____ percentage of the city's cultural offerings.

[A] reductive
[B] substantive
[C] discrete
[D] negligible
[E] cumulative
[F] trivial

10. The ancient Greeks _____ the mythical figure of Orpheus as the greatest of all poets and musicians, frequently holding festivals in honor of his art.

[A] imbued
[B] depicted
[C] excoriated
[D] contemplated
[E] extolled
[F] venerated

11. Critics' praise for the artist's most recent exhibition was unqualified: it was entirely _____ any disparaging commentary.

[A] dependent on
[B] unmarred by
[C] adapted to
[D] devoid of
[E] unequal to
[F] mitigated by

Explanations: Set 3

1. B

A creature that is always able to arrive in *precisely the same spot* after migrating thousands of miles is clearly an exceptionally good navigator. The blank must be filled with a word describing that fact. *Timid* (shy), *blatant* (direct, in-your-face), and *indifferent* (uninterested) clearly do not fit. Although whales might in fact be *flexible* navigators, the sentence provides no information to support that idea. If anything, the fact that whales perform this extraordinary feat by instinct suggests that they act according to some sort of inflexible auto-pilot. Only *expert* logically describes the ability of an animal that can consistently travel thousands of miles to the exact same spot, making (B) the answer.

2. A

The key phrase *present in virtually every society* indicates that the fear of wolves is an exceedingly widespread phenomenon. The blank must be filled with a word conveying that fact. The rest of the sentence simply serves to emphasize the contrast between the extent of people's fears about wolves and the actual scarcity of wolf attacks. *Relative* does not make sense: the sentence is not making a comparison between the fear of wolves and any other kind of fear. *Insidious, distressing,* and *overwhelming* may accurately describe some people's fear of wolves, but none of these words emphasizes the widespread nature of the fear. Only *ubiquitous* (omnipresent) would logically describe a fear that was present in every human society.

3. C, E

The sentence provides more information about the meaning of Blank (ii) than about Blank (i), so start with Blank (ii).

The key word *insight* strongly suggests that psychologists have developed a newly positive attitude toward reading fiction as a way of understanding human behavior. *Contempt* is strongly negative, and *classification* does not make sense, but *appreciation* logically refers to an attitude psychologists would have toward a tool that helped them better do their jobs. (E) is thus the answer to Blank (ii).

For Blank (i), the contradictor *although* indicates that this blank must be filled with a negative word whose meaning contrasts with that of the word in Blank (ii). Only *scoffed at* (disparaged, mocked) makes sense in context, indicating that psychologists once looked down on the idea that fiction could provide a window into human behavior. (C) is thus the answer to Blank (i).

4. A, F

If the idea of art as a positive force is a recent one, then philosophers of prior eras must have viewed art as a force that created or contributed to unrest. Even though that idea is negative, Blank (i) must be filled with a neutral or positive word indicating the close relationship between art and chaos. *Distaste* is negative and can be eliminated. *Penchant* (liking or preference) is positive, but it does not make sense to say that art has a preference for unrest – only a living thing can have preferences. That leaves *catalyst*, which fits: philosophers believed art was dangerous because it facilitated unrest. (A) is thus the answer to Blank (i).

Blank (ii) must be filled with a word referring to a state that could be avoided if art was properly channeled (managed). Logically, the correct word must be negative and mean something similar to unrest. *Contamination* and *exclusion* are negative but have nothing to do with conflict, whereas *discord* refers to unrest. (F) is thus the answer to Blank (ii).

5. C, D, G

The phrase *confirmation bias* is the most important piece of information the question provides. It refers to the tendency to accept information consistent with what one already thinks, and to discard information that goes against one's existing beliefs.

For Blank (i), the key word is *subset*. If people only recall a subset of evidence, then they are by definition not remembering everything, i.e. they are remembering *selectively*. (C) is thus the answer to Blank (i).

In the context of confirmation bias, people would logically remember only the subset of evidence that supported their assumptions. Blank (ii) must therefore be filled with a word meaning something like supports. *Defies* and *mitigates* (lessens) do not fit, but *bolsters* means supports or strengthens, making (D) the answer to Blank (ii).

If confirmation bias leads people to reject information that is inconsistent with their assumptions, then Blank (iii) must be filled with a phrase that is consistent with the idea of existing beliefs. Confirmation bias would not lead people to reject what they *want to understand* because the whole point is that they think they already understand. Likewise, it would not cause them to *struggle to convey* anything – they are rejecting information that is coming at them, not trying to convey information to others. *Expect to see*, however, is consistent with the idea of reinforcing established assumptions: people who hold a particular belief are more likely to accept evidence that supports their expectations. (G) is thus the answer to Blank (iii).

6. B, F, G

The sentence in which Blank (i) appears does not provide any information about the definition of the word in the blank, so you need to look to the following sentence for a clue. The statement *In reality, these microorganisms have existed for millennia* indicates that it is inaccurate to describe viruses as "emerging." In other words, the term is incorrect. It is not, however, self-contradictory – it is possible for new viruses to be created, so such thing as an emerging virus can exist. Besides, the sentence focuses on the fact of the term's wrongness, not its contradictory nature. *Paradox* is therefore incorrect. Likewise, the sentence gives no indication that the term is used as a justification (*pretext*) for anything. *Misnomer* simply describes something whose name is inaccurate, making (B) the answer to Blank (i).

Blank (ii) must be filled with a word consistent with the ideas of overpopulation and of ancient viruses coming into contact with people. Logically, human *encroachment* onto lands where viruses have traditionally dwelled would result in the emergence of those viruses. In contrast, human habitation's *insistence* or *fixation* on existing viruses would not produce that effect. (F) is thus the answer to Blank (ii).

Blank (iii) must be filled with a word indicating the result of people's encroachment onto viruses' territory. The passage has already indicated that those viruses "emerge," so the correct answer must be consistent with that idea. Saying that something is forced *into the open* is another way of saying that it is exposed, making (G) the answer to Blank (iii).

7. B, C

If food manufacturers are afraid to convey *the impression that the foods are suspect*, then they must strongly want to avoid informing customers that their products have been genetically engineered. The blank must therefore be filled with negative words conveying that desire to avoid revealing the truth. *Eager, fortunate,* and *wont* (accustomed) are all positive, and *compelled* does not make sense. Although *reluctant* and *loath* are not exact synonyms, they create the same meaning when plugged into the sentence: food manufacturers want to avoid labeling their food as genetically modified. [B] and [C] are thus correct.

8. A, D

The sentence contrasts the *two-dimensional world of maps*, with their *sharp lines* used to mark clear boundaries between countries, and the blank. Logically, the blank must be filled with words indicating that boundaries are *less* sharp, or less clearly demarcated, than they appear on maps. *Impregnable* (impenetrable), *salient* (conspicuous), *elaborate*, or *defensive* all do not describe borders that are the opposite of sharp. In contrast, *fluid* and *porous* both describe borders that are flexible and that allow people to pass easily from one country to the other. [A] and [D] are thus correct.

9. D, F

The sentence indicates that Kyoto has more than 2,000 temples and shrines but only 17 World Heritage sites – a very small proportion. The blank must therefore be filled with words denoting something small or insignificant. *Substantive* means exactly the opposite of the required words; *discrete* (separate) and *cumulative* do not fit at all. *Reductive* is generally related to the idea of smallness, but the sentence gives no indication that the number of World Heritage sites has declined. In addition, this word carries a connotation of oversimplification that does not fit the sentence. That leaves *negligible* and *trivial*, which can both be used to describe a very small or insignificant quantity. [D] and [F] are thus correct.

10. E, F

The sentence makes clear that the ancient Greeks held Orpheus in extremely high regard, so the blank should logically be filled with strongly positive words meaning something like worship. *Imbued* (permeated with) does not make sense, and *excoriated* has the opposite definition of the one required. Both *depicted* and *contemplated* could plausibly fit in the blank, the former more so than the latter, but neither of these words has a close synonym among the other choices. Only *extolled* (strongly praised) and *venerated* have similar meanings and are consistent with the clues in the sentence. [E] and [F] are thus correct.

11. B, D

This sentence contains multiple negations, so make sure to keep the logic straight. In this context, *unqualified* means unequivocal or absolute, and *disparaging* means insulting. The statement that the praise was entirely _____ by any disparaging commentary therefore indicates that the praise was completely positive, without any negative elements. Logically, then, the blank must be filled with a word indicating that negative commentary was absent from the praise, or that the praise was not tempered by negative commentary. Praise that was *dependent on, adapted to,* or *mitigated by* (reduced by) disparaging commentary would not be absolute praise. *Unequal to* simply does not make sense: the issue is that the critics' commentary did not contain any negative aspects. Equality or inequality is beside the point. Praise that was *devoid of* (lacking in) any negative comments would, however, be absolute praise, as would praise that was *unmarred by* (not ruined by) negative comments. Even though these words do not have precisely the same meaning, both reinforce the idea of absolute praise when plugged into the sentence. [B] and [D] are thus correct.

Set 4

1. Mies van der Rohe used the slogan "less is more" to characterize his philosophy, a paradox that is reflected in the _____ nature of the buildings he designed.

(A) minimalist
(B) deliberate
(C) appealing
(D) enduring
(E) innovative

2. There is no disputing matters of taste when it comes to the values of simplicity and complexity in works of art; however, in science, simplicity is not a matter of _____ but rather one of accuracy.

(A) context
(B) relevance
(C) formality
(D) originality
(E) perspective

3. Anxieties about exhaustion are not (i) _____ our age; those who imagine that life in the past was simpler, slower, and better are mistaken. In fact, the subject has (ii) _____ thinkers since classical antiquity.

Blank (i)	Blank (ii)
(A) compatible with	(D) preoccupied
(B) alien to	(E) gratified
(C) peculiar to	(F) placated

4. Traffic engineers are (i) _____ characters: we are rarely (ii) _____ the influence that they wield over our daily lives, even as they determine how we move through many kinds of public spaces.

Blank (i)	Blank (ii)
(A) obscure	(D) coerced by
(B) illicit	(E) bemused by
(C) profligate	(F) cognizant of

5. Readers of Mark Twain's autobiography may occasionally find some of the more (i) _____ references to nineteenth century scandals (ii) _____, but taken in its entirety, the work is seldom less than (iii) _____.

Blank (i)	Blank (ii)	Blank (iii)
(A) ludicrous	(D) pathetic	(G) belligerent
(B) impenetrable	(E) stultifying	(H) enervating
(C) obstreperous	(F) inspiring	(J) captivating

6. Unless purposefully (i) _____, numbers cannot lie; they can only be used to misrepresent the public statements and ranking systems we take seriously. Statistical data do not (ii) _____ outright falsehoods so much as semantic manipulation: numbers drive the (iii) _____ of words.

Blank (i)	Blank (ii)	Blank (iii)
(A) recanted	(D) allow for	(G) contortion
(B) doctored	(E) yield to	(H) creation
(C) interrogated	(F) derive from	(J) usefulness

7. Proponents of the Arts and Crafts movement claimed that the style's simple but refined designs would lead to a more _____ experience of industrial consumerism, making individuals more rational and society more harmonious.

[A] cosmopolitan
[B] whimsical
[C] edifying
[D] germane
[E] elevated
[F] voluble

8. Discovery of cancer-ridden animals in nature is happenstance, so comparing the rate of cancers in wild animals to the rate of cancers in humans cannot be done with any degree of _____.

   [A] consistency
   [B] reliability
   [C] conviction
   [D] security
   [E] caution
   [F] accuracy

9. In a _____ state at the time of its rediscovery in 1911, the once-powerful city of Machu Picchu has now been partially restored to its historic grandeur.

   [A] vacuous
   [B] decrepit
   [C] redolent
   [D] deplorable
   [E] treacherous
   [F] lurid

10. The discovery of the Shoemaker-Levy 9 comet was _____ event, the comet's namesakes having inadvertently identified the body while searching for near-Earth objects.

   [A] a fortuitous
   [B] an acrimonious
   [C] a specious
   [D] a fleeting
   [E] an infelicitous
   [F] a serendipitous

11. Inspired in part by the theories of psychologist Jean Piaget, who saw children's development as a series of discrete stages marked by periods of transition, Thomas Kuhn posited two kinds of scientific change: incremental developments that occur in the course of "normal science," and scientific revolutions that _____ these more stable periods.

   [A] articulate
   [B] corrupt
   [C] elucidate
   [D] punctuate
   [E] pinpoint
   [F] interrupt

Explanations: Set 4

1. A

The statement *less is more* indicates that van der Rohe embraced an uncluttered building style, and the blank must be filled with a word consistent with that fact. *Deliberate, enduring, appealing,* and *innovative* are all adjectives that could be used to describe an architectural style, but none of these options fits the clue. *Minimalist* would logically characterize a style based on doing less, making (A) correct.

2. E

The contradictor *however* indicates that the sentence is setting up a contrast between art and science. The first half of the sentence asserts that personal preference determines whether people like simplicity in works of art. Logically, then, the second half of the sentence must convey the opposite: that in scientific matters, a liking for simplicity is not a matter of personal preference but of objective fact. The blank must therefore be filled with a word consistent with the idea of personal preference, i.e. *perspective. Relevance, formality,* and *originality* do not fit, but be careful with *context*: the focus is on the subjective nature of preference in art vs. the objective nature of preference in science, not on the importance of background circumstances. (E) is thus correct.

3. C, D

The statement that people who *imagine that life in the past was simpler, slower, and better are mistaken* suggests that *anxieties about exhaustion* are not a recent phenomenon. Logically, Blank (i) should be filled with a word meaning unique or exclusive. It makes no sense to say that anxieties about exhaustion are *not* compatible with our age – the entire point of the passage is that people are incorrect in thinking that these concerns did not exist before today. *Alien to* (foreign to) implies exactly the opposite of the required definition. In addition to meaning odd, *peculiar* can also mean unique. That meaning fits perfectly, making (C) the answer to Blank (i).

Blank (ii) must be filled with a word indicating that concerns about exhaustion have existed since antiquity. *Gratified* does not make sense because worrying about exhaustion is not a particularly pleasing or fulfilling activity. *Placated* (calmed) likewise does not make sense. In contrast, *preoccupied* correctly implies that the problem of exhaustion is a topic of longstanding concern. (D) is thus the answer to Blank (ii).

4. A, F

The sentence contains two parts: the first part describes a quality of traffic engineers, while the second part describes that an effect of that quality on the perception of traffic engineers.

There is more information about Blank (ii), so start with it. The key phrase *even as* indicates a contradiction between the fact that traffic engineers *determine how we move through many kinds of public spaces* and our lack of awareness of that reality. Blank (ii) asks for something that we *rarely* are. Based on the information provided, we are rarely *aware* that traffic engineers shape our reality. *Bemused* (puzzled) clearly does not fit, but be careful with *coerced*. The sentence suggests that our behavior *is* coerced by traffic engineers, but again, the negation *rarely* makes this word inconsistent with what the sentence is asking for. In contrast, *cognizant of* means aware of and fits perfectly, making (F) the answer to Blank (ii).

Now back up. Blank (i) must be filled with a word describing a trait of people who wield influence without others knowing. *Illicit* is too strong here – there is nothing to suggest that traffic engineers' behavior is illegal – and *profligate* (wasteful) does not fit at all. *Obscure* correctly conveys the shadowy nature of traffic engineers' influence, making (A) the answer to Blank (i).

5. B, E, J

The sentence provides little information about the definitions of any of the blanks, so you must rely primarily on the relationships between the ideas to answer this question.

Blank (ii) must be filled with a word indicating how readers of Twain's autobiography would react to the type of scandals described by the word in Blank (i). The reference to *nineteenth century scandals* does provide a subtle clue here. It is reasonable to assume that those scandals hold little significance for the modern reader, who would likely react negatively to reading about them – most likely with either puzzlement or boredom. The only two answers consistent with that meaning are (B) and (E). Readers would likely find *impenetrable* (incomprehensible) references to nineteenth century scandals *stultifying* (incredibly boring). References that were *ludicrous* (ridiculous) would not produce reactions consistent with any of the options for Blank (ii), and it does not even make sense to describe references as *obstreperous* (loud, noisy).

For Blank (iii), the contradictor *but* sets up a contrast between the boring character of certain historical references and Twain's autobiography as a whole. Note the negation here: *seldom less than* means usually or typically, so Blank (iii) must be filled with a word describing what the work *is*. *Belligerent* (aggressive) does not make sense at all, and *enervating* (exhausting, draining energy) means exactly the opposite of the required word. Only *captivating* fits as the opposite of *stultifying*, making (J) the answer to Blank (iii). The sentence is essentially saying that even though Twain's autobiography has some uninteresting parts, it's really pretty interesting on the whole.

6. B, D, G

The statement that *numbers cannot lie* unless something is done to them implies that Blank (i) should be filled with a word indicating how numbers could be made to lie – something like *falsified*. *Interrogated* clearly does not fit, and *recanted* simply means taken back; it does not imply falsification. In contrast, numbers that were *doctored* (manipulated) would convey false information, making (B) the answer to Blank (i).

Consider Blanks (ii) and (iii) in context of the first sentence. Basically, numbers tell the truth unless people deliberately mess with them; however, when people do mess with them, they can be used to convey inaccurate information to the public. Blank (ii) should therefore be filled with a relatively neutral word meaning something like convey. It does not make sense to say that statistical data *yield to* (give in or give way to) outright falsehoods, and *derive from* gets the relationship backwards. Falsehoods result from twisted data, not the other way around. Only *allow for* creates a logical meaning: provided they are not flat-out made up, statistics alone do not permit lies.

For Blank (iii), consider the entire first part of the sentence: even if statistics themselves cannot lie, they can be selectively interpreted in a way that twists their meaning (*semantic manipulation*). The information after the colon describes some effect of numbers on words. Given the context of the previous sentence, Blank (iii) must logically be filled with a word meaning something like manipulation. The only option consistent with that idea is *contortion* (twisting), making (G) the answer to Blank (iii).

7. C, E

The key phrase *making individuals more rational and society more harmonious* indicates that proponents of the Arts and Crafts movement believed that their style of choice had an extremely positive effect, one that lifted people up and made them experience industrial consumerism on a higher level. The blank must be filled with words consistent with that idea. *Cosmopolitan* (worldly) could plausibly fit in the blank, but this word lacks a close synonym among the other choices. *Whimsical* (fanciful in a spontaneous way) has a positive connotation, but this type of experience would not make people more rational or society more harmonious. *Germane* (relevant) and *voluble* (talkative) do not make sense at all. That leaves *edifying* (enlightening) and *elevated*, both of which would accurately describe a more rational and harmonious society. [C] and [E] are thus correct.

8. B, F

The fact that the discovery of cancer-ridden animals in the wild is the result of *happenstance* (chance) implies that it is very difficult to compare disease rates among animals to those among humans. The sentence, however, contains a negation: it asks for what *cannot* be true of the comparison. Logically, then, the blank must be filled with a positive word that, when negated, conveys the difficulty of comparing human and animal disease rates. *Security* and *caution* do not fit at all. *Consistency* make sense – if the discovery of diseased animals in the wild occurs by chance, then it would be very difficult to consistently compare animal vs. human cancer rates. However, there is no close synonym for this word. The lack of data would also make it difficult for scientists to have any *convictions* (strong beliefs), but this word too lacks a close synonym. The only words that create the same meaning when plugged into the sentence are *reliability* and *accuracy*. Both indicate that any conclusions drawn from data obtained by chance would be entirely suspect. [B] and [F] are thus correct.

9. B, D

The statement that *Machu Picchu has <u>now</u> been partially restored to its historic grandeur* implies that the Machu Picchu's grandeur was no longer apparent at the time the city was discovered. Logically, the blank should be filled with a negative word meaning something like run-down. *Vacuous* means empty, but in the sense of uninspired or unoriginal; this adjective cannot really be applied to a physical location. *Redolent* (reminiscent) and *lurid* (sensationalistic) do not fit at all. It is reasonable to assume that a severely run-down city would be *treacherous* (dangerous), but this word lacks a close synonym among the other choices. *Decrepit* does in fact mean run-down, making [B] the first correct answer. Although *deplorable* (terrible, lamentable) is not an exact synonym, it likewise conveys the meaning that Machu Picchu had fallen into a state of disrepair prior to its rediscovery. [D] is thus the second correct answer.

10. A, F

The key word is *inadvertently*, which indicates that the discoverers of Shoemaker-Levy 9 discovered the comet by accident. The blank must therefore be filled with words meaning something like unexpectedly or unintentionally. The only two answers consistent with this idea are *fortuitous* and *serendipitous*, both of which describe chance occurrences. The discovery process might have been *fleeting* (brief) or *infelicitous* (unfortunate), but there is nothing in the sentence to support either interpretation. The remaining answers do not make any sense in context. [A] and [F] are thus correct.

11. D, F

The sentence indicates that Kuhn was *inspired* by Piaget, so you can assume that Kuhn conceived of scientific change in a way similar to the manner in which Piaget conceived of children's development. How did Piaget view children's development? *As a series of discrete (distinct) stages marked by periods of transition.* Logically, then, the description of what Kuhn posited must have a similar structure. *Incremental developments* correspond to *discrete stages*, and *periods of transition* correspond to *scientific revolutions*. The blank must be filled with words describing the relationship between the periods of transition and the revolutions. *Elucidate* (clarify) does not make sense and can be eliminated. *Corrupt* might seem like a reasonable choice, but this revolutions usually overthrow or *disrupt*, not corrupt, and this word also lacks a close synonym among the other choices. *Articulate* and *pinpoint* have similar meanings, but revolutions do not normally explain periods of calm. *Punctuate* and *interrupt* both logically indicate that revolutions are events that create breaks, or ruptures, with the periods of stability that precede them. [D] and [F] are thus correct.

Set 5

1. A renowned scientist, surveyor, almanac author, and farmer, Benjamin Banneker was also _____, having received little formal education in spite of his many accomplishments.

(A) a novice
(B) a dabbler
(C) an apprentice
(D) a recruit
(E) an autodidact

2. DNA evidence is not necessarily _____: it can be compromised by contamination from extraneous DNA anywhere along the chain from the crime scene to the laboratory where the sample is sequenced.

(A) specious
(B) infallible
(C) superfluous
(D) ambiguous
(E) immaterial

3. Scientists who receive too many (i) _____ often develop an arrogance that prevents them from perceiving the kinds of (ii) _____ solutions that led to their original success.

Blank (i)	Blank (ii)
(A) platitudes	(D) novel
(B) diatribes	(E) duplicitous
(C) accolades	(F) arduous

4. Any present-tense version of the world is (i)_____; what we currently consider true is not only (ii)_____ but also subject to change at any moment.

Blank (i)	Blank (ii)
(A) precarious	(D) unprecedented
(B) ongoing	(E) provisional
(C) immutable	(F) redundant

5. Experts in a subject are more likely to recognize that other people will disagree with them, and they are more able to accurately present (i)_____ points of view. Novices (ii)_____ themselves by being unable to fathom any position (iii)_____.

Blank (i)	Blank (ii)	Blank (iii)
(A) relevant	(D) humble	(G) on the whole
(B) conflicting	(E) embarrass	(H) beside their own
(C) fashionable	(F) betray	(J) without reservation

6. King Louis XIV of France (1638-1715) demanded that his courtiers behave in a (i)_____ manner: he rewarded the ones who were most (ii)_____ in their praise of him and punished those who failed to show the proper amount of (iii)_____.

Blank (i)	Blank (ii)	Blank (iii)
(A) mercurial	(D) effusive	(G) veracity
(B) sycophantic	(E) laconic	(H) candor
(C) garrulous	(F) pugnacious	(J) obsequiousness

7. Sometimes, unattractive or unpleasant landmarks should be preserved precisely because they _____ terrible decisions; the best parts of history can withstand the bad.

[A] epitomize
[B] sustain
[C] embody
[D] override
[E] illuminate
[F] announce

8. The power of certain investigative techniques such as hair analysis has been vastly overblown; the FBI admits that its analysts made _____ statements in more than 90 percent of the microscopic hair-comparison cases reviewed.

[A] spurious
[B] tentative
[C] erroneous
[D] pessimistic
[E] alarming
[F] condescending

9. Many observers have attempted to detect tension between Angela Merkel and her main rival, Peer Steinbrück, but their public relationship has remained _____.

[A] ponderous
[B] inscrutable
[C] cordial
[D] aloof
[E] amicable
[F] chilly

10. Mountain weather is infamously _____, with light drizzles quickly transforming into torrential downpours and cloudless skies abruptly giving way to heavy snows.

[A] implacable
[B] frivolous
[C] fickle
[D] capricious
[E] intemperate
[F] harrowing

11. Ed Ruscha's artwork is strongly influenced by the movie industry: his Mountain Series evokes a film studio logo, and "Large Trademark with Eight Spotlights" (1962) is _____ a movie screen.

[A] befitting to
[B] redolent of
[C] depicted on
[D] confined to
[E] detached from
[F] reminiscent of

Explanations: Set 5

1. E

The statement that Banneker *received little formal education* implies that he acquired sufficient knowledge to be renowned in a variety of prestigious fields through untraditional means. *Novice* (beginner) does not make sense. *Dabbler* implies a lack of seriousness – if this word described Banneker, he would not have become renowned. *Recruit* and *apprentice* both describe people who are taught formally by others – exactly the opposite of Banneker. An *autodidact* is a person who is self-taught, and this word provides a logical explanation for how someone who lacked formal education could became so accomplished in so many fields. (E) is thus correct.

2. B

The fact that DNA *can be compromised by contamination* indicates that it is not necessarily 100% reliable as a form of evidence. In other words, it is flawed. The blank, however, must be filled with a positive word describing what DNA evidence is *not* - the correct answer must therefore mean something like flawless. *Specious* (fake, false) means exactly the opposite of the required word. *Superfluous* (excessive, unnecessary) and *immaterial* (irrelevant) do not fit the required definition either. The only answer that makes sense is *infallible* (IN-, not + FALL-, error), which refers to something that is never wrong. *Not* never wrong = sometimes wrong. (B) is thus correct.

3. C, D

Blank (i) must be filled with a word describing something that would cause scientists to become arrogant. Neither *platitudes* (clichés) nor *diatribes* (angry rants) would be likely to result in scientists becoming arrogant, but a scientist who received too many *accolades* (awards) could logically develop that quality. (C) is thus the answer to Blank (i).

Blank (ii) must be filled with a word indicating a type of discovery that scientists were earlier able to make, but that arrogance would prevent them from making in the future. Logically, this word should be positive. *Duplicitous* (deceitful) and *arduous* (laborious, requiring a lot of effort) are negative and can be eliminated. *Novel* (new, innovative), is both positive and a good descriptor for a type of discovery that arrogance would prevent scientists from noticing. People who are excessively confident in their own abilities tend to become less curious and open to new ways of thinking. (D) is thus the answer to Blank (ii).

4. A, E

The beginning of the sentence provides no direct information about the definition of the word in Blank (i); you must read to the end for a clue. The semicolon indicates that the second half of the sentence will expand on or explain the first half. Logically, then, Blank (i) must be filled with a word consistent with the statement that *what we currently consider true [is]...subject to change at any moment*. Don't be fooled by *ongoing*. Although this word is consistent with the idea of the present tense, it does not describe something that is perpetually subject to change. *Immutable* (unchangeable; IM-, not + MUT-, change) means exactly the opposite of the required word. *Precarious* (fragile) accurately describes a world that can change at any moment, making (A) the answer to Blank (i).

For Blank (ii), the construction *not only…but also* implies that this blank should also be filled with a word consistent with the idea of a constantly changing world. Neither *unprecedented* (occurring for the first time) nor *redundant* (repetitive) describes such a world. *Provisional* means subject to change and is thus a perfect fit for the blank, making (E) the answer to Blank (ii).

5. B, F, H

The first sentence indicates that experts are better able *to recognize that other people will disagree with them*, so logically, the first blank must be filled with a word related to points of view they would disagree with. There is no reason experts would disagree with *relevant* or *fashionable* points of view. Although they might disagree with the latter, they could just as well agree with them. In contrast, *conflicting* points of view are by definition ones with which experts would disagree. [B] is thus the answer to Blank (i).

Blank (iii) is a bit more straightforward than Blank (ii), so you may find it easier to start with. Novices (beginners) are the opposite of experts, so we can infer that they behave in a contrasting way. Logically, if experts can *accurately present conflicting points of view*, then novices must do the opposite – that is, they can only present their own point of view. In other words, they cannot *fathom* (conceive of) *any position beside their own*. [H] is thus the answer to Blank (iii).

Blank (ii) must be filled with a word describing something novices do to themselves. These people would not necessarily *humble* or *embarrass* themselves by being unable to fathom other viewpoints; either of those things could be true, but the sentence provides no direct information about the consequences of novices' lack of understanding. Although *betray* might strike you as an unlikely answer, the word is used in the more neutral sense of *reveal* or *give oneself away* here. That definition creates a logical meaning: novices reveal themselves as novice by being unable to imagine viewpoints that differ from their own. [F] is thus the answer to Blank (ii).

6. B, D, J

For Blank (i), consider the fact that the sentence is describing the behavior of a king. Logically, a king would want his courtiers to behave in a deferential manner toward him, or at least hold him in very high regard. *Mercurial* (changeable) does not describe a particularly desirable quality in a courtier. *Garrulous* (talkative, outgoing) wouldn't necessarily be considered either good or bad. A *sycophantic* (extremely flattering) courtier, however, would be a very logical thing for a king to want. (B) is thus the answer to Blank (i).

Blank (ii) must be filled with a word describing the type of praise a sycophantic courtier would offer. Neither *laconic* (not talkative) nor *pugnacious* (violent, aggressive) is consistent with the idea of flattery, but *effusive* (unreservedly enthusiastic) praise is exactly what a sycophantic courtier might offer. (D) is thus the answer to Blank (ii).

Blank (iii) must be filled with a word referring to a quality whose lack would cause a courtier to be punished. As established, Louis XIV only valued those who flattered him, so the correct word must again be consistent with the idea of flattery. (Note that the negation *failed* indicates the need for a positive word.) *Veracity* (truth) and *candor* (directness) are positive, but a courtier who was honest or forthright might say things to a king that were not in fact flattering. In contrast, courtiers who failed to demonstrate sufficient *obsequiousness* (servile, fawning deference) toward a vain king would logically be punished. (J) is thus the answer to Blank (iii).

7. A, C

The blank must be filled with words indicating the relationship between *unattractive or unpleasant landmarks* and *terrible decisions*. Those two ideas go together, so the correct answers must be positive and convey that connection. The preservation of ugly landmarks would not *override* terrible decisions. They also would not *announce* terrible decisions – logically, the landmarks would be the result of terrible decisions rather than a way to advertise the fact that such decisions were about to occur. Unattractive landmarks could feasibly *sustain* or *illuminate* (shed light on) bad decisions, but neither of these words has a close synonym among the other choices. In contrast, *embody* and *epitomize* are synonyms that create a logical meaning when plugged into the sentence: unattractive landmarks are the physical representation of bad ideas and should thus be preserved as warnings or counterexamples that make the qualities of better-designed structures more apparent. [A] and [C] are thus correct.

8. A, C

The assertion that *the power of certain investigative techniques has been vastly overblown* implies that those techniques are far less effective than is normally thought. The blank must therefore be filled with negative words indicating that the FBI analysts made incorrect statements. The only answers consistent with that idea are *erroneous* and *spurious*, both of which mean false. Although the remaining words are negative, they are all inconsistent with the clue provided by the sentence. [A] and [C] are thus correct.

9. C, E

The contradictor *but* sets up a contrast between the two halves of the sentence. The first half indicates that observers have tried to find evidence suggesting that Merkel and Steinbrück don't get along, so the second half must convey the idea that their public relationship reveals no evidence of tension. *Ponderous* (weighty, serious) does not make sense at all and can be eliminated. *Aloof* (standoffish) and *chilly* have similar meanings, but these words would support the idea that Merkel and Steinbrück's relationship was tense, not contradict it. If the relationship were *inscrutable* (enigmatic), the public would not be able to detect tension in it, but although this word fits, it lacks a close synonym among the other choices. On the other hand, both *cordial* and *amicable* describe a relationship devoid of obvious tension in public. [C] and [E] are thus correct.

10. C, D

The description of light drizzles *quickly* turning into downpours and cloudless skies *abruptly* being replaced by snowfall indicate that mountain weather is extremely unstable. The blank must therefore be filled with words indicating instability. *Implacable* (relentless) does not quite fit this definition, and although both *intemperate* (extreme) and *harrowing* (frightening) could describe torrential downpours and heavy snows, these words do not convey the idea that the weather is highly changeable. A person who is *frivolous* might possess that quality, but this word indicates a lack of seriousness and carries a connotation of superficiality, and is not an appropriate descriptor for the weather. In contrast *fickle* and *capricious* are both used to describe something that is highly changeable, making [C] and [D] correct.

11. B, F

The structure of this sentence is key, with the colon serving as a signal that the second half explains or elaborates on the first half. As a result, the information after the colon must convey an idea similar to the one conveyed before the colon. In addition, the sentence contains two major key words. First, *influenced* indicates that the works of Ruscha described here reflect the movie industry in some way. In addition, because the two items in the second part of the sentence are structured parallel to one another, the blank must be filled with words conveying the same idea as *evokes*. *Detached from* clearly indicates the opposite, and *confined to* does not make sense at all. *Depicted on* could plausibly describe how "Large Trademark with Eight Spotlights" was presented; alternately, the painting could be reasonably described as *befitting to* a movie screen. The problem is that both words lack a close synonym among the other choices. Only *reminiscent* and *redolent* have similar meanings and convey the idea of evoking something (the image of a movie screen). [B] and [F] are thus correct.

Set 6

1. When average temperatures increase very slowly, it becomes difficult to notice the difference in baseline standards for normalcy because the shift is all but _____.

(A) evident
(B) comprehensive
(C) indiscernible
(D) deceptive
(E) irrelevant

2. In contrast to Spinoza, Hume believed that no knowledge of the world could be as certain as the truths of mathematics. All of our understanding depends on experience, making knowledge _____, not absolute.

(A) unabridged
(B) authentic
(C) omnipotent
(D) contingent
(E) invincible

3. In some fictional dystopias, such as that portrayed in Margaret Atwood's novel *The Handmaid's Tale*, the family has been abolished as a social unit because it is considered a potential source of (i) _____, and continuing efforts are made to (ii)_____.

Blank (i)	Blank (ii)
(A) evasion	(D) resolve its contradictions
(B) contemplation	(E) prevent its resurgence
(C) sedition	(F) expose its shortcomings

4. To date, cancer research has led to some treatments that cure certain cancers and some treatments that do not cure cancer but that put the disease in (i) _____. While the malady is (ii) _____, patients can experience a high quality of life for an extended period.

Blank (i)	Blank (ii)
(A) ascent	(D) recalcitrant
(B) circulation	(E) rampant
(C) abeyance	(F) quiescent

5. It is hard for us to comprehend how totally Western consciousness was transformed during the seventeenth and eighteenth centuries, precisely because we live in its (i) _____. Only a few generations preceding ours, every fixed point that had (ii) _____ the world for thousands of years began to (iii) _____.

Blank (i)	Blank (ii)	Blank (iii)
(A) service	(D) oriented	(G) wobble
(B) aftermath	(E) pierced	(H) taper
(C) domain	(F) circumvented	(J) resist

6. In his book *The Poverty Industry*, David Hatcher makes clear that governors from across the political spectrum are equally (i) _____ when it comes to schemes designed to profit from the poor. In other words, the misappropriation of funds intended for some of society's most (ii) _____ members is not a (iii) _____ problem.

Blank (i)	Blank (ii)	Blank (iii)
(A) culpable	(D) diffident	(G) pressing
(B) dismayed	(E) gregarious	(H) trivial
(C) prudent	(F) impecunious	(J) partisan

7. Noise from sonar can deafen sea creatures, but evidence suggests that whales are able to _____ some of the damage by internally blocking their ears.

[A] avoid
[B] undo
[C] exclude
[D] reduce
[E] exempt
[F] alleviate

8. The brain _____ 90 percent of the approximately 30 images it receives of every object, retaining only enough visual information to form a coherent whole.

   [A] conserves
   [B] expunges
   [C] scrutinizes
   [D] evaluates
   [E] regulates
   [F] winnows

9. Isamu Noguchi's sculptures are influenced by _____ styles and national traditions, including ones from the United States, Japan, France, Mexico, and China.

   [A] eclectic
   [B] indigenous
   [C] scintillating
   [D] heterogeneous
   [E] intricate
   [F] arcane

10. Contrary to popular belief, hens raised in "cage free" environments do not inhabit _____ settings, pecking for bugs in large green fields; rather, they are housed in crowded "aviaries" in enormous barns.

   [A] luxurious
   [B] cramped
   [C] lofty
   [D] cultivated
   [E] rustic
   [F] bucolic

11. At first _____, the senator gradually became more loquacious as the interview progressed.

   [A] exuberant
   [B] irascible
   [C] laconic
   [D] voluble
   [E] taciturn
   [F] eloquent

Explanations: Set 6

1. C

The sentence states that increases in temperature are *difficult to notice* when they occur slowly, and the blank must be filled with a word indicating why that fact is true. Logically, the correct answer should mean something like extremely subtle or imperceptible (Remember that *all but* means essentially.) *Evident* and *comprehensive* clearly do not fit that definition and can be eliminated. Be careful with *deceptive* and *irrelevant*. Although the change is hard to notice, *deceptive* would imply that the shift in temperature is not actually a shift – that something else is occurring – and there is absolutely no evidence for that interpretation. Likewise, even though the shift is small, there is nothing to suggest that it is *irrelevant*. Besides, the blank must convey the idea that the temperature increase is hard to notice, not that it is either important or unimportant. That leaves *indiscernible*, which is a synonym for *imperceptible* and fits perfectly. (C) is thus correct.

2. D

If you find the philosophical allusions confusing, focus on the information right around the blank. The phrase *not absolute* indicates that the word in the blank must mean the opposite of *absolute*. For a bit more context, consider the statement that *all of our understanding depends on experience*. Basically, the sentence is saying that people's knowledge of the world is subjective, that there are no fixed formulas for understanding it. The blank must be filled with a word reflecting that fact. *Unabridged* would describe the complete version of an artistic work such as a novel – it makes no sense in this context. People's experiences may indeed be *authentic*, but this word is not the direct opposite of *absolute*. Knowledge that was *omnipotent* (all-powerful: OMNI-, all + POT-, power) would indeed be absolute, making this word the opposite of the correct answer. *Invincible* (unbeatable) has a similar problem. *Contingent* means dependent on the circumstances, and this word logically conveys the idea that knowledge is subjective and dependent on personal experience. (D) is thus correct.

3. C, E

Consider the context for the blanks: the passage is describing *fictional dystopias* – nightmare societies – where the family *has been abolished as a social unit*. Why would a dystopian society abolish families? Most probably because it viewed them as some sort of threat. It is therefore reasonable to assume that Blank (i) should be filled with a negative word indicating a threat or rebellion. *Evasion* (avoidance) is negative, but this word does not necessarily describe an act that a dystopian society would go so far as to abolish the family in order to prevent. The same is true of *contemplation*. *Sedition* (rebellion) is a much more direct example of an activity that a dystopian society would want to clamp down on, making (C) the answer to Blank (i).

If families pose a threat in a dystopian society and have consequently been abolished, then logically, steps must be taken to ensure that they do not crop up again. In other words, it is necessary to *prevent their resurgence*. Neither of the other answers makes any sense in context. (E) is thus the answer to Blank (ii).

4. C, F

The sentence in which Blank (i) appears describes two different outcomes of cancer treatment. The first type of treatment is clearly successful (it can *cure certain cancers*), and it is implied that the second is also successful (*patients can experience a high quality of life for an extended period*), even if it is not an actual cure. Logically, then, Blank (i) must refer to a state in which a disease is no longer active – a word similar to *remission* is called for. *Ascent* implies an increase or strengthening, and *circulation* implies activity. Both words thus convey the opposite of the definition required here. Only *abeyance* (cessation, hiatus) correctly describes the effects of a treatment that can hold an illness at bay for an extended period. (C) is thus the answer to Blank (i).

Blank (ii) must be filled with a word describing an inactive disease. *Recalcitrant* (extremely stubborn) does not fit at all, and *rampant* means exactly the opposite of the required word. *Quiescent* means quiet or inactive, and accurately describes a disease in remission. (F) is thus the answer to Blank (ii).

5. B, D, G

Even if you're not totally sure what type of word belongs in Blank (i), think carefully about what the sentence is most probably saying. Logically, why would it be hard for us to comprehend how totally western consciousness changed in the seventeenth and eighteenth centuries? Because we weren't around to witness those changes. The answer to Blank (i) must therefore be consistent with the fact that we are living much later; the only answer that corresponds directly to that reality is *aftermath*. (B) is thus the answer to Blank (i).

For Blanks (ii) and (iii), remember that the previous sentence alludes to the total transformation of western *consciousness* – in other words, a mental revolution occurred. Logically, then, *points* (ideas or mentalities) that had been stable, and that had structured (*oriented*) society for centuries, no longer stayed fixed but rather began to shift (*wobble*). No other pair of words conveys this meaning as clearly. (D) is thus the answer to Blank (ii), and (G) is the answer to Blank (iii).

6. A, F, J

The first sentence provides no explicit information about the definition of Blank (i) – we do not know what sort of attitude politicians have toward schemes designed to profit from the poor. Logically, such schemes would be negative, but these are politicians featured in a book entitled *The Poverty Industry*, so it isn't safe to assume that the politicians would condemn these schemes. As a result, you must keep reading and/or start with one of the later blanks.

Blank (ii) must be filled with a word characterizing the type of citizen affected by the misappropriation of funds. Again, the book title provides an important clue. *Diffident* (shy, standoffish) and *gregarious* (outgoing) are both unrelated to poverty, but *impecunious* (poor) is consistent with the idea of a poverty industry. (F) is thus the answer to Blank (ii).

The phrase *from across the political spectrum* is key for Blank (iii). Be careful, though: the question asks for what sort of problem the poverty industry is *not*. If the problem involves members of both Left and Right, then it is by definition not restricted to one party, i.e. it is not *partisan*. That the problem could be construed as either *pressing* or *trivial* depending on one's perspective is irrelevant; neither word fits the clue. (J) is thus the answer to Blank (iii).

Now back up to Blank (i). If governors from across the political spectrum are involved in making money off of poor constituents, then they are all responsible, i.e. *culpable*. Although other people may be *dismayed* by this situation, the sentence provides no indication that the governors feel that way. There is likewise no suggestion that the governors are *prudent* (practical) in their exploitation of poverty. (A) is thus the answer to Blank (i).

7. D, F

The fact that whales are able to block their ears to sonar suggests that they are able to protect themselves against the deafening noise. The blank must be filled with words conveying that fact. Damage is not something that can be *excluded* or *exempted* (something can only be exempted *from* damage), eliminating those answers. It is also unlikely that blocking their ears would allow whales to *undo* damage that had already occurred; they could only prevent the damage from occurring in the first place. Be very careful with [A]: *avoid* fits perfectly, but this word lacks a close synonym among the other choices. Only *alleviate* and *reduce* have the same meaning and convey a logical result of whales' ability to block out deafening noise. [D] and [F] are thus correct.

8. B, F

The information after the comma is key: if the brain retains *only enough visual information to form a coherent whole* [of an object], then it must be getting rid of the rest of the information it takes in. The blank must therefore be filled with words meaning something like *discards*. *Conserves* means exactly the opposite and can be eliminated. The brain might *scrutinize*, *evaluate*, or *regulate* information, but those words do not make sense in this context. Although *expunges* (erases) and *winnows* (separates out) are not exact synonyms, they both convey the idea that the brain eliminates most of the visual information it receives about an object, leaving only what is necessary for perception. [B] and [F] are thus correct.

9. A, D

The list of countries whose styles and traditions influenced Noguchi's sculptures provides an important clue because it suggests that Noguchi had many different influences. It is therefore reasonable to assume that the blank should be filled with words indicating diversity or variety. *Eclectic* means diverse, making [A] a good fit for the blank. Despite the clue, it would also make sense to say that Noguchi was influenced by the *indigenous* (native) styles and traditions of the various countries; however, this word lacks a close synonym among the other choices. *Scintillating* (glittering), *intricate*, and *arcane* are all words that could plausibly be used to fill the blank as well, but all of them have very different meanings. That leaves *heterogeneous* as a synonym for *eclectic*, making [D] the second answer. Note that you can make an educated guess about this word's meaning based on the prefix. HETERO- means different, and difference is consistent with the idea of diversity.

10. E, F

The sentence sets up a contrast between the type of environment so-called "cage free" hens are commonly believed to inhabit, and the unpleasant reality of their actual lodgings. The blank must be filled with words indicating what the hens' settings are NOT, so the correct answers must be positive. In addition, the phrase *large green fields* provides an important clue, suggesting that the words in the blank must mean something like natural. *Cramped* describes the reality of the hens' environment – exactly the opposite of what is required. Likewise, *cultivated* is the opposite of natural, eliminating this answer as well. While large green fields might be *luxurious* or *lofty* to hens, neither of these words is an exact fit, and both lack a close synonym among the other choices. In contrast, *rustic* and *bucolic* both describe a countrified environment, making them much more logical descriptors for an environment filled with large green fields. [E] and [F] are thus correct.

11. C, E

The phrase *gradually became* is used to set up an implicit contrast between the senator's behavior at the beginning vs. the end of the interview. If the senator was *loquacious* (talkative) at the end, then she or he must have been short on words at the beginning. The only two words to convey that meaning are *laconic* and *taciturn*, both of which describe someone who is not inclined to talk a lot. *Voluble* is a synonym for *loquacious*, and *exuberant* (outgoing) conveys a similar idea. *Irascible* (irritable) and *eloquent* do not make sense at all. [C] and [E] are thus correct.

Set 7

1. Research suggests that people tend to be more creative if they feel that they have been socially rejected, even if no actual rejection has taken place. Sometimes _____ is more powerful than reality.

(A) novelty
(B) perception
(C) curiosity
(D) intention
(E) hope

2. The biographer often adopts _____ tone, discussing incidents for their moral lessons rather than simply describing their historical significance.

(A) a didactic
(B) a supercilious
(C) an offhanded
(D) a breezy
(E) a skeptical

3. Ancient documents imply that Darius the Great (i) _____ the heir to the Persian kingdom by force and seized the throne for himself, suggesting that his rise to power was most likely (ii) _____.

Blank (i)	Blank (ii)
(A) solicited	(D) illicit
(B) suspended	(E) calculated
(C) deposed	(F) factitious

4. All of the screens in consumers' lives – whether on televisions, smartphones or computers – can be (i) _____. They do not, however, completely (ii) _____ what is happening around someone the way virtual reality headsets do.

Blank (i)	Blank (ii)
(A) absorbing	(D) transmit
(B) cacophonous	(E) occlude
(C) finicky	(F) elucidate

5. In Renaissance Europe, private studies, or *studioli*, were (i) _____ of display as much as (ii) _____ for intellectual labor. Inventories and other historical texts list (iii) _____ array of items kept in these rooms: books, of course, but also gems, chess boards, musical instruments, small sculptures, ancient coins.

Blank (i)	Blank (ii)	Blank (iii)
(A) tomes	(D) sectors	(G) an incredulous
(B) venues	(E) repositories	(H) a prolific
(C) stewards	(F) apparatuses	(J) a multifarious

6. One reason that groups can display no more insight than a single individual is the (i) _____ of common knowledge. Even when people make independent judgments, they may be working from the same set of assumptions. Information that is known to all is considered (ii) _____, giving it more significance than it deserves and (iii) _____ diverse sources of knowledge.

Blank (i)	Blank (ii)	Blank (iii)
(A) hegemony	(D) deliberately	(G) drowning out
(B) instability	(E) haphazardly	(H) calling up
(C) adaptability	(F) repeatedly	(J) sorting out

7. Many coastal nations claim exclusive economic zones stretching two hundred nautical miles from their shores, with dozens of overlapping claims causing constant _____ between countries.

[A] migration
[B] tension
[C] confrontation
[D] rivalry
[E] equality
[F] friction

8. In the past, scientific progress was often _____, but recent technological advances have permitted researchers to make many significant breakthroughs in only a short period of time.

   [A] halting
   [B] surprising
   [C] unsubstantiated
   [D] incremental
   [E] explosive
   [F] unanticipated

9. Valued for their delicate flavor, shrimp are surprisingly _____ creatures that have a high tolerance for the toxins found in polluted waters.

   [A] intrepid
   [B] hardy
   [C] timid
   [D] voracious
   [E] robust
   [F] determined

10. The novel undoubtedly contains some _____ elements, yet it is at the same time so full of idiosyncrasies that it defies any attempt at categorization.

    [A] pedestrian
    [B] obtrusive
    [C] hackneyed
    [D] provincial
    [E] sanguine
    [F] recondite

11. Dickinson grew increasingly _____ of social gatherings as she aged and, in her later years, remained virtually confined to Homestead, as her Amherst, Massachusetts, home was known.

    [A] petrified
    [B] resentful
    [C] chary
    [D] defiant
    [E] accepting
    [F] leery

Explanations: Set 7

1. B

The key piece of information is that people *tend to be more creative if they feel they have been socially rejected*. Basically, the outcome (increased creativity) is driven more by their emotions than by what is actually happening (they haven't necessarily been socially rejected). In other words, their *perception is more powerful than reality. Novelty, curiosity, intention,* and *hope* all do not convey that idea, making (B) the answer.

2. A

The blank must be filled with a word describing the type of tone often adopted by the biographer. The key phrase *moral lessons* provides the most important clue, indicating that the tone is pedagogical – that is, designed to teach. The only word to correspond to that definition is *didactic. Supercilious* (condescending), *offhanded* and *breezy* (casual), and *skeptical* all clearly do not fit. (A) is thus the only possible answer.

3. C, D

Blank (i) must be filled with a word indicating something that Darius the Great did *by force*. The fact that he *seized the throne for himself* suggests that the correct word will mean something like overthrow. It would not make sense to say that Darius *solicited* the heir to the Persian throne, and *suspended* indicates only a temporary interruption that is inconsistent with the idea of overthrowing. It would, however, be logical to say that Darius *deposed* the expected ruler. Although this word can be used in a legal context to refer to the act of requiring a witness to testify, it can also be used as a synonym for *overthrew*. [C] is thus the answer to Blank (i).

Blank (ii) must be filled with a word that is again consistent with the idea of taking the throne by force. *Factitious* (false) does not quite fit because Darius did in fact rise to power (he would not be known as Darius the Great otherwise), even if his method for doing so was questionable. Be careful with *calculated*: although it may be the case that Darius deliberately and carefully plotted to overthrow the heir to the Persian throne, it is also possible that he decided to do so spontaneously – the sentence provides no information about either possibility. In contrast, the fact that Darius seized the throne by force directly implies that his rise to power was probably illegal, i.e. *illicit*. [D] is thus the answer to Blank (ii).

4. A, E

The first sentence provides no direct information about the meaning of the word in Blank (i) – depending on the context, any of the answers could fit. It is thus necessary to look at the following sentence for clues. The contradictor *however* indicates that a contrast is being set up between screens and virtual reality headsets, but the fact that those two pieces of technology are relatively similar also suggests that the word in Blank (ii) will be a stronger form of the word in Blank (i). What is the difference between a screen and a virtual reality headset? The former is something a viewer merely looks at, whereas the latter covers viewers' faces completely, blocking out their surroundings. For Blank (ii), the only option that accurately conveys the obstructive nature of virtual reality headsets is *occlude* (block), making [E] the answer to Blank (ii).

Now back up to Blank (i). The correct word must indicate that screens do not literally block out all of a person's surroundings, but that they have a generally similar effect. *Finicky* (picky) does not make sense at all. Screens that were *cacophonous* (loud and noisy) would certainly make people unaware of their surroundings, but this word is not by definition a milder version of *occlude*. In contrast, *absorbing* makes sense as a descriptor of objects that do not physically block out the world in the same way virtual reality headsets do, but that similarly cause people to become unaware of their surroundings.

5. B, E, J

Blanks (i) and (ii) must be filled with words indicating what the private studies served as. Although the sentence indicates two opposing uses (*display* vs. *intellectual labor*), it is reasonable to assume that the words in the blanks must mean something rather neutral such as place or location. For Blank (i), the most direct match for that definition is *venues*, making [B] the answer. *Tomes* are books. Even if a room contains many books, it cannot actually be one. *Stewards* refers to people who act as agents or representatives, which also does not fit the context.

For Blank (ii), *sectors* refers to divisions, either physical or economic, and does not fit. Likewise, *apparatuses* are machines, and the correct word must refer to what is essentially an office. The list of various objects contained in the *studioli* does, however, fit the description of a *repository* – a place where things are stored. [E] is thus the answer to Blank (ii).

The list of objects provides the most important clue for Blank (iii). It indicates that the *studioli* contained a highly varied range of objects (*books, gems, ancient coins*), so the blank must be filled with a word meaning something like diverse. Don't get tricked by *incredulous* – this word means disbelieving, not incredible. *Prolific* means productive and does not make sense in context. *Multifarious* is a synonym for diverse, making (J) the answer to Blank (iii). Note that even if you do not know the definition of this word, you can make an educated guess from the prefix MULTI-, many.

6. A, F, G

If you're not sure about what sort of word belongs in Blank (i), look to the following sentence for clarification. The fact that people who make separate judgments may be working from the same assumptions suggests that groups may be no more insightful than individuals because both are influenced by the same beliefs and are thus likely to draw the same conclusions. That similarity suggests that the power of common knowledge is very strong indeed. Blank (i) must be therefore be filled with a word indicating that strength. *Instability* and *adaptability* do not fit that definition, but *hegemony* (predominant influence) is a match, making [A] the answer to Blank (i).

For Blank (ii), the statement that *information that is known to all [is given] more significance than it deserves* indicates a disproportionate influence. Information that was considered *haphazardly* (randomly) would not have that type of influence, nor would information that was considered *deliberately*. Information considered *repeatedly* would, however, be likely to have an outsized impact, making [F] the answer to Blank (ii).

For Blank (iii), if groups consider common knowledge more heavily than other types of information, than *diverse sources of knowledge* are by definition given shorter shrift. The blank must therefore be filled with a word indicating that this type of knowledge is in some way overlooked or discounted. Neither *calling up* or *sorting out* is consistent with that idea, but *drowning out* describes a way in which less common/popular types of knowledge are discounted. [G] is thus the answer to Blank (iii).

7. B, F

If countries make *dozens of overlapping claims* within nautical zones, then it is reasonable to assume that the result is constant disagreement. The blank must be filled with words indicating that fact. *Migration* and *equality* clearly do not fit and can be eliminated. *Confrontation* and *rivalry* both describe a type of relationship that could arise between countries with many conflicting claims, but neither word contains a close synonym among the other choices. *Tension* and *friction* describe similarly logical consequences of overlapping claims and have similar meanings, making [B] and [F] correct.

8. A, D

The contradictor *but* indicates a contrast between the two halves of the sentence. The second half indicates that technology has allowed researchers to make many discoveries quickly, so logically, the first half must convey the opposite – that progress in the past was slow and/or inefficient. *Surprising* and *unanticipated* are synonyms but do not describe slow progress. It may have been more difficult for scientists to prove their theories in the past, but there is nothing in the sentence to indicate that scientific progress was *unsubstantiated* (unproven). *Explosive* is likewise unsupported. Only *halting* and *incremental* both convey the idea that scientific progress was once slow and that it occurred on a smaller scale than it does today.

9. B, E

The fact that shrimp are *surprisingly* _____ suggests that they possess a quality that contrasts with their *delicate flavor*. The blank must therefore be filled with words meaning the opposite of delicate. *Timid* (shy) would be consistent with the idea of delicacy, so this word is the opposite of what is required. *Intrepid*, *voracious* (insatiable, devouring), and *determined* could all fit, but each of these words lacks a close synonym among the other answer choices. *Hardy* or *robust* are synonyms describing a creature that is the opposite of delicate, making [B] and [E] correct.

10. A, C

The contradictor *yet* signals a contrast between the two halves of the sentence. The second half indicates that the novel is extremely *idiosyncratic* (quirky, original), so logically, the first half must convey the idea that some of the elements it contains are unoriginal. A novel cannot be *obtrusive* (interfering, nosy), and *sanguine* (cheerful) and *recondite* (esoteric) do not fit as the opposite of *idiosyncratic*. *Provincial* (narrow-minded) could plausibly fit, even if it isn't an exact match, but this word lacks a close synonym among the other choices. *Pedestrian* and *hackneyed* both mean unoriginal and fit perfectly, making [A] and [C] correct.

11. C, F

The fact that Dickinson eventually *remained virtually confined to her...home* implies that she grew increasingly less fond of social gatherings. The blank must therefore be filled with negative words indicating dislike or aversion. *Accepting* conveys exactly the opposite of the required definition and can be eliminated immediately. *Resentful* is negative, but the sentence does not indicate that Dickinson had any reason to be jealous of or indignant about social gatherings, as this word would imply. *Petrified* would be an excellent match, but it lacks a close synonym among the other choices. *Defiant* is not a perfect match – people cannot really go against social gatherings the same way they go against social conventions – but could plausibly fit; however, it also lacks a close synonym. Only *chary* and *leery* (wary, skeptical) imply the type of moderate dislike that could eventually harden into outright reclusiveness. [C] and [F] are thus correct.

Set 8

1. Much like particle physics, modern medicine has become far too subtle and complex to offer _____; with so many different kinds of therapies available, it is often impossible to say which one will be most effective.

(A) reassurance
(B) consolation
(C) efficacy
(D) certainty
(E) relief

2. The Symbolists believed that the purpose of art was to convey absolute truths that could only be described indirectly, a conviction reflected in their _____ style of writing.

(A) histrionic
(B) ingenious
(C) forthright
(D) brisk
(E) elliptical

3. Children who investigate the world through "make believe" are seldom accused of (i) _____, whereas adults who experiment with the liberties of masquerade are inevitably charged with (ii) _____.

Blank (i)	Blank (ii)
(A) plundering	(D) exploitation
(B) beguiling	(E) duplicity
(C) dissembling	(F) impeachment

4. When Scandinavians settled Greenland in the tenth century, the southern part of the island was relatively (i) _____; however, as climate conditions (ii) _____, and the ground developed a thick covering of ice, the country's name became an ironic misnomer.

Blank (i)	Blank (ii)
(A) temperate	(D) evaporated
(B) egalitarian	(E) materialized
(C) barren	(F) deteriorated

5. Bureaucracies are good at enforcing rules but not necessarily at defining the (i) _____ that inspire them. This opens a space for the emergence of charismatic leaders who redefine those goals, sometimes (ii) _____ the political system in the process. Charisma is utterly (iii) _____; power casts its own irrational spell.

Blank (i)	Blank (ii)	Blank (iii)
(A) regulations	(D) validating	(G) malevolent
(B) purposes	(E) transforming	(H) vapid
(C) hierarchies	(F) defending	(J) enchanting

6. To lack interest in ideas about being and meaning is (i) _____ because these are the fundamental concepts that structure our experience of the world. People who claim not to care about metaphysics really mean that their received ideas about such matters are so (ii) _____ that they have (iii) _____ from consciousness.

Blank (i)	Blank (ii)	Blank (iii)
(A) inevitable	(D) precise	(G) hailed
(B) undeniable	(E) amorphous	(H) vanished
(C) impossible	(F) fixed	(J) emerged

7. Hildegard of Bingen was among the most _____ writers and composers of the Middle Ages, producing hundreds of songs, letters, and treatises.

[A] prolific
[B] prominent
[C] infamous
[D] pretentious
[E] productive
[F] majestic

8. Although the language of *The Declaration of Independence* is remarkably
   _____, the florid eighteenth century handwriting can be difficult for modern
   readers to decipher.

   [A] succinct
   [B] clear
   [C] powerful
   [D] lucid
   [E] stark
   [F] poignant

9. Phthalates, a class of chemicals used as solvents and fixatives, are virtually
   ubiquitous in the environment, found in _____ array of everyday products,
   from food containers to shampoos and perfumes.

   [A] a subtle
   [B] an imaginative
   [C] a selective
   [D] a boggling
   [E] a motley
   [F] a staggering

10. When Ernest Hemingway confessed to having rewritten the ending of *A Farewell
    to Arms* thirty-nine times, he set a precedent for _____ that few writers
    since have come close to matching.

    [A] perseverance
    [B] scrupulousness
    [C] eloquence
    [D] punctiliousness
    [E] expressiveness
    [F] verbosity

11. Because novelist Milan Kundera considers his characters' external appearances
    _____ his stories, he often provides only perfunctory descriptions of their
    looks.

    [A] distinct from
    [B] peripheral to
    [C] contingent on
    [D] integral to
    [E] ancillary to
    [F] imbued with

Explanations: Set 8

1. D

The sentence indicates that modern medicine has become *too subtle and complex*, and that the many available therapies make it impossible to determine the effectiveness of any particular one. The blank must describe the result of that situation. Be very careful with *reassurance*: although it may be difficult to choose between the numerous treatment options, that does not automatically imply that none of them will reassure patients. The same is true for *consolation*. The sentence indicates that it is difficult to determine which therapy is *most effective*, implying that there are multiple effective options. It is therefore contradictory to suggest that medicine is incapable of offering *efficacy* (effectiveness) or *relief*. The overwhelming number of options available and the impossibility of telling which one is best do, however, make it difficult to decide anything with *certainty*. (D) is thus correct.

2. E

The fact that the Symbolists believed *absolute truths could only be described <u>indirectly</u>* suggests that their writing style was equally indirect, and the blank must be filled with a word indicating that fact. Writing that was *histrionic* (hysterical), *ingenious* (clever), or *brisk* would not necessarily be indirect. *Forthright* writing would be direct, so this word implies exactly the opposite of the meaning that the blank requires. An *elliptical* (cryptic, obscure) writing style would by definition be indirect, so (E) is correct.

3. C, E

The contradictor *whereas* indicates that the sentence is setting up a contrast between the reaction to children who play "make believe" and *adults who experiment with the liberties of masquerade* – that is, adults who pretend to be something other than what they are. The key words *accused* and *charged* imply a negative reaction, and the parallel structure of the sentence (*children who do x are accused of...adults who do y are charged with...*) suggests that the words in both blanks have similar meanings consistent with the idea of pretending to be something one is not. The only two words to fit those criteria are *dissembling* and *duplicity*, making (C) the answer to Blank (i) and (E) the answer to Blank (ii).

4. A, F

The first half of the sentence provides no clear information about the type of word that belongs in Blank (i), so you must focus on the information after the semicolon. The statement that the ground developed a covering of thick ice implies that the ice was not present when Greenland was first settled. Blank (i) must therefore be filled with a word indicating a more moderate climate. An *egalitarian* country would not necessarily have a moderate or an immoderate climate – this word refers to a type of social equality, not a climatic one. It is true that southern Greenland may have been *barren* during the tenth century, but again, this word has nothing to do with the climate. Only *temperate* accurately describes a place with a moderate climate, making (A) the answer to Blank (i).

Given that context, the fact that southern Greenland was later covered in ice indicates that the climate became much worse. Blank (ii) should therefore be filled with a negative word conveying that fact. *Evaporated* is negative, but a climate itself cannot evaporate. It would be accurate to say that negative climate conditions *materialized* (appeared), but it does not make any sense to say that climate conditions themselves materialized – they were there all along, just in a more favorable form. In contrast, *deteriorated* clearly describes the worsening climate conditions that resulted in Greenland's ceasing to be green and turned the country's name into a *misnomer* (inaccurate name). (F) is thus the answer to Blank (ii).

5. B, E, J

The key word *inspire* suggests that Blank (i) should be filled with a word meaning something like reasons – it is logical to assume that rules would be invented to serve a particular function. That assumption is further reinforced by the reference to *those goals* in the following sentence. *Regulations* are rules, but the correct answer must refer to what is behind the rules, not the rules themselves. Likewise, *hierarchies* is a concept often associated with bureaucracy, but this word does not describe the impetus for inventing a rule. *Purposes* is a much more direct fit, as well as a synonym for goals. (B) is thus the answer to Blank (i).

The phrase in which Blank (ii) appears serves to modify the previous phrase, so this blank must be filled with a word reinforcing the idea that charismatic leaders redefine goals. Neither *validating* (proving true) nor *defending* implies redefinition, but *transforming* is a logical way to describe what would happen to a political system whose rules were redefined by a charismatic leader. (E) is thus the answer to Blank (ii).

For Blank (iii), focus on the information after the semicolon. If *power casts its own irrational spell*, then this blank must be filled with a word consistent with that idea. *Vapid* (empty, banal) does not fit at all. Now be careful: this type of power may indeed be *malevolent*, but the information after the semicolon is not overtly negative, and this word is not an exact fit for the idea of casting a spell (there are good spells and bad spells, after all). In contrast, *enchanting* is a much more precise fit – by definition, a spell is something that is enchanting, so this word is a perfect match for the clue. (J) is thus the answer to Blank (iii).

6. C, F, H

The statement that being and meaning are *the fundamental concepts that structure our experience of the world* implies that they are very important concepts indeed. Lacking interest in them would thus be either very odd or extremely difficult. *Undeniable* does not create that implication when plugged into the sentence. Be very careful with the remaining answers and the double negatives, however. The fact that being and meaning are fundamental concepts that structure our experience suggests that having an interest in them is inevitable. Lacking an interest implies exactly the opposite – namely, that people have no reason to be interested in these big questions about existence. *Impossible* is consistent with the idea that people cannot lack interest in questions about being and meaning – that is, people are, by default, interested in those questions. (A) is thus the answer to Blank (i).

The construction *so...that* in the second sentence indicates that Blank (iii) must be filled with a word indicating the logical outcome of the situation described in Blank (ii). The most logical pair is *fixed...vanished*. It implies that people who claim not to think about metaphysical issues (being and meaning) do so because they are firm (i.e. *fixed*) in their beliefs about the world and therefore have no reason to think about the big questions of existence. That is another way of saying that those issues have *vanished* from their consciousness. Beliefs that were *amorphous* (lacking in form, unclear) or *precise* would not lead to any of the outcomes indicated in Blank (iii). (F) is thus the answer to Blank (ii), and (H) is the answer to Blank (iii).

7. A, E

The key phrase *hundreds of songs, letters, and treatises* indicates that Hildegard of Bingen was very busy and presumably well known. Logically, then, the blank must be filled with positive words consistent with that idea. *Infamous* and *pretentious* are both negative, and although *majestic* is positive, the sentence does not suggest Bingen behaved like royalty. The remaining three words all make sense in context, but *prolific* and *productive* both connote the act of creation, whereas *prominent* merely means famous. [A] and [E] are thus correct.

8. B, D

The sentence sets up a contrast between the appearance of the handwriting in which *The Declaration of Independence* was composed (*florid, difficult for modern readers to decipher*) and the language itself. Logically, then, the blank must be filled with words indicating that the language of the *Declaration* is easy to decipher. Basically, it's clear, i.e., *lucid*. *Succinct* (short, to-the-point) could plausibly fit, but this word lacks a close synonym among the other choices. The same is true for *stark* (unadorned). The remaining choices do not make sense in context. [B] and [D] are thus correct.

9. D, F

The key phrases *virtually ubiquitous* (everywhere) and *from food containers to shampoos and perfumes* suggest that phthalates are found in an extraordinarily wide range of products. The blank must be filled with words consistent with that idea. *Subtle, imaginative,* and *selective* all do not make sense. *Motley* (eclectic) is a good fit, but this word lacks a close synonym among the other choices. Only *boggling* and *staggering* have similar meanings and convey the enormity of the range of products in which these chemicals are found. [D] and [F] are thus correct.

10. B, D

The blank must be filled with words indicating what sort of precedent Hemingway set for the writers who came after him. The fact that Hemingway *rewrote the ending of* <u>A Farewell to Arms</u> *thirty-nine times* suggests that he was an extraordinarily hard worker, one who was obsessed with getting things just right and who would be a very difficult act for just about anyone to follow. The correct words must be positive, however, because they describe a quality of Hemingway's detail-oriented approach to rewriting. *Verbosity* (wordiness) does not make sense. We only know that Hemingway rewrote the ending to his novel many times – we do not know anything about the actual style of that writing, or about whether he used a lot of words. (In fact, Hemingway was famous for his spare, stripped-down style.) *Perseverance* is an excellent fit, but this word lacks a close synonym among the other choices. Be careful with *eloquence* and *expressiveness*. Again, the sentence only tells us that Hemingway worked very hard rewriting the ending; these words both describe a characteristic of the writing itself, and the sentence says nothing about that. *Scrupulousness* and *punctiliousness* both refer to meticulousness and accurately describe the quasi-obsessive approach of an author who would rewrite the same section of a book nearly forty times. [B] and [D] are thus correct.

11. B, E

Unless you can identify *peripheral* and *ancillary* as the only pair of synonyms in this set of answer choices, you must know the meaning of *perfunctory* (brief) in order to answer this question. The sentence indicates that Kundera provides only *perfunctory* descriptions of his characters' looks as a result of his attitude toward the relationship between his stories and the characters' appearances. Logically, then, Kundera must not consider those looks particularly important, and the blank must be filled with negative words indicating that fact. *Integral* is positive, and *contingent* and *imbued* do not make any sense. The former would imply that Kundera's characters' appearances depend on his stories, the latter that they are filled with his stories. *Distinct* is similarly illogical – the physical appearance of fictional characters cannot be separate from their stories. An author who considered his characters' looks *peripheral* or *ancillary* (secondary, unimportant) to his stories, however, would logically offer only brief descriptions of them. [B] and [E] are thus correct.

Set 9

1. The sun that revolves around the Earth is unusual in its solitude; most of the other stars in the sun's neighborhood have a stellar _____.

(A) equal
(B) companion
(C) duplicate
(D) culmination
(E) replica

2. Although heavy storms often buffet the island with heavy rains and high winds, they are usually fleeting, _____ after about an hour.

(A) dissipating
(B) intensifying
(C) originating
(D) radiating
(E) coalescing

3. Even when new vaccines are devised, they cannot necessarily be produced at the right scale and the right time. Drug development is slow and (i) _____ by the economic concerns of the pharmaceutical industry. If a new drug has only (ii) _____market, it is unlikely to ever be sold.

Blank (i)	Blank (ii)
(A) reinforced	(D) an accessible
(B) constrained	(E) a modest
(C) sustained	(F) a discernible

4. When theories grow too convoluted, scientists reach for Ockham's Razor, the principle of (i) _____, which posits that simpler explanations are usually correct, as long as they are (ii) _____what can be observed.

Blank (i)	Blank (ii)
(A) parsimony	(D) negated by
(B) autonomy	(E) compatible with
(C) refutation	(F) distinguished from

5. Modern biologists point to the near universality of the genetic code as strongly favoring the hypothesis of universal common ancestry over the hypothesis of multiple ancestors. The shared code would be a surprising (i) _____ if different groups of organisms arose from different (ii) _____. It is much more probable that all current life can be traced back to a single (iii) _____.

Blank (i)	Blank (ii)	Blank (iii)
(A) coincidence	(D) forebears	(G) point of origin
(B) permutation	(E) predilections	(H) impetus for change
(C) expression	(F) prototypes	(J) source of influence

6. Linguistic symbols enable us to track features of the world that we would otherwise (i) _____, and structured sentences allow us to develop new, more abstract modes of reasoning. With a pen or laptop, we can construct extended patterns of thought that we could never (ii) _____ with our brains alone. In writing, we are not simply recording our mental processes but doing the actual work of (iii) _____.

Blank (i)	Blank (ii)	Blank (iii)
(A) perceive	(D) concede	(G) inculcation
(B) overlook	(E) divulge	(H) rebuttal
(C) explore	(F) formulate	(J) rumination

7. Supporters of the new law are requesting that it be implemented as slowly as possible in order to give those affected the necessary time to _____.

[A] prepare
[B] adjust
[C] settle
[D] disperse
[E] organize
[F] adapt

8. The director earned a reputation for _____ behavior as a result of his tendency to reflexively berate any actor who dared to question his instructions.

[A] reclusive
[B] inscrutable
[C] tyrannical
[D] heretical
[E] impetuous
[F] despotic

9. While social hierarchies do exist among bonobo chimpanzees, rank plays a less _____ role in their societies than it does in other primate societies.

[A] salient
[B] generic
[C] malleable
[D] conspicuous
[E] flexible
[F] disruptive

10. Lonesome George, the last surviving Pinta tortoise, became an icon for conservation-minded tourists, thousands of whom _____ for a glimpse of him at his home in the Galapagos islands each year.

[A] yearned
[B] angled
[C] vouched
[D] rummaged
[E] vied
[F] atoned

11. Contemporary historians of science have a tendency to _____ the originality of the so-called scientific revolution and to stress that the discoveries of the early modern period evolved as a natural outgrowth of medieval experiments in alchemy.

[A] deprecate
[B] expurgate
[C] downplay
[D] efface
[E] postulate
[F] lionize

Explanations: Set 9

1. B

The statement that the Earth's sun is unusual because it is solitary implies that other stars in the Earth's neighborhood are not solitary – that is, they are accompanied by another star, i.e., a *companion*. *Culmination* makes no sense whatsoever. *Equal, duplicate,* and *replica* all imply that stars appearing together are similar or identical, but the sentence gives no indication that that is the case; it only states that stars do not typically appear alone. (B) is thus correct.

2. A

The key word is *fleeting* (short-lived), which implies that the storms must die down or go away shortly after they begin. *Intensifying, radiating,* and *coalescing* imply exactly the opposite, and *originating* does not make sense because the word in the blank must describe what happens to storms after they have been going on for about an hour. Only *dissipating* (evaporating, petering out) is consistent with the idea of a fleeting storm. (A) is thus correct.

3. B, E

Although the first sentence does not contain a blank, it does provide important information. Essentially, it states that vaccines don't necessarily get distributed where and when they are needed, even if they can be produced. Given that, it is reasonable to assume that Blank (i) should be filled with a negative word indicating that drug development is dependent on the economy in some way. *Reinforced* and *sustained* are both positive, but *constrained* implies that drug development is limited by the economy – a meaning consistent with the fact that new vaccines don't always end up where they are required. (B) is thus the answer to Blank (i).

Blank (ii) must be filled with a word describing the type of market that would render a drug *unlikely to be sold*. If economic concerns are paramount, then drugs probably wouldn't be sold if they were unprofitable – that is, if there was only a small market for them. An *accessible* or a *discernible* (identifiable) market would not necessarily be small, but a *modest* market would by definition be a limited one. (E) is thus the answer to Blank (ii).

4. A, E

The statement that scientists turn away from *convoluted* (excessively complex) theories and toward *simpler* ones suggests that Blank (i) should be filled with a word similar to simplicity. Neither *autonomy* nor *refutation* is consistent with that idea; however, *parsimony*, which means stinginess, implies a whittling away of everything non-essential. (A) is thus the answer to Blank (i). (In fact, Ockham's Razor is often referred to as the parsimony principle.)

Given the scientific context, it is reasonable to assume that Blank (ii) must be filled with a word indicating that theories must be consistent with observable reality in order to be considered correct. *Negated by* and *distinguished from* both imply the opposite, but *compatible with* describes a logical relationship between scientific theories and *what can be observed*. (E) is thus the answer to Blank (ii).

5. A, D, G

Although the first sentence does not contain any blanks, it sets up the statements that follow and provides crucial information for determining what sorts of words belong in the blanks. The first sentence indicates that the genetic code serves as evidence for the theory that all life arose from the same organism rather than from different groups of organisms. The implication is that it would be rather remarkable if different groups of organisms just happened to produce so many creatures with the same genetic code. In other words, it would be an extraordinary *coincidence* if different groups of organisms with the same genetic code arose from different ancestors, i.e. *forebears*. Don't be fooled by the prefix PRE- in *predilections*; this word refers to a preference or liking for. A *prototype* can only refer to a new model of an inanimate object, not a living creature. (A) is thus the answer to Blank (i), and (D) is the answer to Blank (ii).

For Blank (iii), the first sentence again provides an important clue; in fact the third sentence simply restates it. If the existence of the genetic code supports the idea that all life arose from a common ancestor, then Blank (iii) must be filled with a phrase consistent with that idea. It does not make sense to refer to an *impetus for change*. Although the ancestor in question evolved, the focus is on the organism itself, not on the change. Be careful with (J): the ancestor wasn't really a *source of influence* – it was simply the living being with the genetic code that got passed down to all its descendants. *Point of origin* is a much more direct match, indicating that the ancestor in question was the one from which all other creatures derived. (G) is thus the answer to Blank (iii).

6. B, F, J

The word *otherwise* in the first sentence indicates a contrast between the ability to *track features of the world* – that is, to pay attention to over time – and the word in Blank (i). Logically, then, this blank must be filled with a word meaning something like *miss*. *Perceive* and *explore* both imply the opposite, but *overlook* fits. People who were unable to track features of the world would by definition overlook those features. (B) is thus the answer to Blank (i).

For Blank (ii), the repetition *can...could* indicates that the sentence is setting up a parallel between what the brain *can construct* and what the brain *could never* _____. As a result of this structural similarity, the blank must be filled with a word similar to *construct*. Neither *concede* (give in) or *divulge* (reveal) makes sense, but *formulate* fits as a general synonym for *construct*. (F) is thus the answer to Blank (ii).

For Blank (iii), the sentence sets up an opposition between *simply recording our mental processes* and what the brain actually does. The word *simply* implies that in comparison to recording mental processes, what the brain does is more complex. The blank must therefore be filled with a word indicating higher level or deeper thinking. *Inculcation* implies rote repetition rather than complex thought, and although *rebuttal* (refutation) can involve more complex skills, it does not carry the same connotation of deep thought as *rumination* does. (J) is thus the answer to Blank (iii).

7. B, F

Logically, supporters of the law would request that it be implemented slowly in order to give the people it affects time to get used to it. *Prepare* might seem like a good choice, but preparation is something that would be done before the law was implemented, not while it was being implemented. Besides, this word lacks a close synonym among the other choices. *Organize* might also seem plausible, but in the context of a discussion of laws, organizing is something that people typically do in order to protest, and there is nothing in the sentence to imply that people are actively opposed to the law. *Settle* and *disperse* do not make sense at all. Only *adjust* and *adapt* logically describe what implementing a law slowly would give those affected a chance to do. [B] and [F] are thus correct.

8. C, F

The key phrase *as a result* indicates that the blank describes something the director was considered because of his tendency to *reflexively berate* (automatically insult) actors who dared to question him. Logically, the blank should be filled with words meaning something like nasty or harsh. *Reclusive, inscrutable* (mysterious), *heretical* (going against accepted doctrine), and *impetuous* (spontaneous) do not make sense at all. *Despotic* and *tyrannical* both describe a person who behaves in an autocratic manner and cannot tolerate being questioned. [C] and [F] are thus correct.

9. A, D

The contradictor *while* indicates that the two parts of the sentence will express contrasting ideas. The first part indicates that bonobo chimpanzees have social hierarchies (ranking systems), with the construction *while social hierarchies do exist* signaling a concession. Essentially, this part of the sentence is acknowledging that bonobo societies do contain this feature while also implying that it is not particularly important. As a result, it can be inferred that social hierarchies are less important than they are in other primate societies. The blank must therefore be filled with a word similar to important. *Generic* and *disruptive* do not make sense at all. Although *malleable* and *flexible* have very similar meanings, neither of these words is consistent with the idea of importance. In contrast, saying that social hierarchies play a less *salient* or *conspicuous* role in bonobo society than in other primate societies correctly conveys the idea that social rank is comparatively less important among bonobo chimpanzees.

10. B, E

The fact that lonesome George was an *icon for conservation-minded tourists* indicates that these individuals were extremely eager to get a glimpse of him. The blank must be filled with words conveying that enthusiasm. *Yearned* (longed for) makes perfect sense, but unfortunately this word lacks a close synonym among the other choices. In contrast, *angled* and *vied* both logically describe the actions of tourists who would have to maneuver around numerous competitors just to get a glimpse of the famous tortoise. None of the other options creates a logical meaning when plugged into the sentence. [B] and [E] are thus correct.

11. A, C

The blank must be filled with words indicating historians' attitude toward the scientific revolution. While a logical reaction would be to assume that such people would view the scientific revolution positively, the key phrase *so-called* and the rest of the sentence suggest otherwise. The emphasis historians of science place on the fact that early modern scientific discoveries *evolved as a natural outgrowth of medieval experiments in alchemy* suggests they do not consider the scientific revolution particularly revolutionary. The blank must therefore be filled with negative words conveying skepticism or criticism. *Lionize* (celebrate) is positive and can be eliminated. *Postulate* does not make sense since historians of science who postulated the originality of the scientific revolution would agree with the idea that the scientific revolution was truly original. *Expurgate* and *efface* are synonyms, but this pair does not make sense either: historians of science could not erase or eliminate the scientific revolution from history. A far more logical meaning is the one created by *deprecate* and *downplay*: essentially, historians of science avoid promoting the idea that the scientific revolution represented something radically new because it emerged naturally from earlier pseudo-scientific experiments. [A] and [C] are thus correct.

Set 10

1. In psychology experiments, people who can perform a task with great accuracy
    tend to express high levels of confidence. Unfortunately, the converse is not true:
    people with high levels of confidence are not necessarily more _____.

(A) diligent
(B) practical
(C) capable
(D) disdainful
(E) fervent

2. What Strasser calls the "supposedly unprecedented data-driven sciences" are in
    fact the heirs to a significant body of research. It is necessary to understand
    what came before in order to grasp what is actually _____.

(A) true
(B) absolute
(C) present
(D) innovative
(E) authentic

3. Modern life, which we tend to think of as an accelerating series of gains in
    knowledge, wealth, and power over nature, is (i) _____ a loss: the loss of
    contact with the past. Depending on one's point of view, this can be seen as
    either a disinheritance or (ii) _____.

Blank (i)	Blank (ii)
(A) adjacent to	(D) an emancipation
(B) predicated on	(E) a misconception
(C) attenuated by	(F) a concatenation

4. In the novels and many of the stories Shirley Jackson wrote in the mid-twentieth century, the polite banter of seemingly (i) _____ common folk develops into outright mockery and (ii) _____.

Blank (i)	Blank (ii)
(A) loquacious	(D) subterfuge
(B) nefarious	(E) reticence
(C) congenial	(F) indignation

5. Even if an idea is based on (i) _____, it still has the potential to conquer the world. Despite their factual (ii) _____, many creeds have gained enormous popularity and become unassailable (iii) _____.

Blank (i)	Blank (ii)	Blank (iii)
(A) a consequence	(D) complacency	(G) criteria
(B) an inevitability	(E) shortcomings	(H) procedure
(C) a fallacy	(F) underpinnings	(J) dogma

6. The factors that allowed cholera to take hold of newly industrializing cities – lack of faith in political governance and the rapid growth of the industrial economy – also (i) _____ to make selfishness pay off. Since the regulatory infrastructure necessary to (ii) _____ their excesses had yet to be built, private interests faced few penalties when their pursuit of riches and power (iii) _____ public health.

Blank (i)	Blank (ii)	Blank (iii)
(A) conspired	(D) restrain	(G) ameliorated
(B) neglected	(E) pursue	(H) undermined
(C) sought	(F) cultivate	(J) incited

7. The D'Oyly Carte opera company kept Gilbert and Sullivan's operettas in the public eye for over a century, leaving _____ legacy of production styles that continues to be emulated in new performances.

    [A] a complex
    [B] a devastating
    [C] a compelling
    [D] a lasting
    [E] a controversial
    [F] an enduring

8. Before the construction of the Berlin Wall, more than three million East Germans _____ emigration restrictions and crossed over the border into West Berlin.

   [A] defied
   [B] flouted
   [C] subdued
   [D] alleviated
   [E] debunked
   [F] unearthed

9. Although the book is ambitious in scope, it fails to offer a cohesive argument and instead presents a _____ collection of testimonies interspersed with the author's commentary.

   [A] diverse
   [B] cumulative
   [C] terse
   [D] motley
   [E] prurient
   [F] facetious

10. Voters who hoped that the new cabinet would prove more decisive than the previous one were disappointed to discover that it was just as _____, its promises just as vague.

   [A] equivocal
   [B] reactionary
   [C] evasive
   [D] militant
   [E] doctrinaire
   [F] influential

11. Unlike sheep, which are famously docile and complacent animals, kangaroos are known for their _____ and are poorly suited to life on a ranch.

   [A] belligerence
   [B] recalcitrance
   [C] pliancy
   [D] agility
   [E] reticence
   [F] intransigence

Explanations: Set 10

1. C

The sentence sets up an opposition between people who are more accurate and people who are more confident. There is a clear correlation between accuracy and confidence (people who are more accurate are more confident), but the sentence tells us that the correlation does not work the other way – that is, higher confidence levels do not necessarily signal higher ability. The blank must therefore be filled with a word referring to accuracy or competence. *Diligent*, *fervent*, and *practical* do not fit because the only issue here is whether someone is accurate, not whether they are hard-working, enthusiastic, or realistic. *Disdainful* does not make sense at all. *Capable* accurately conveys the idea of competence, making (C) correct.

2. D

The key phrase is *supposedly unprecedented*. The word *supposedly* implies that the data-driven sciences appear to be new but are not actually new. Why? Because a *significant body of research* came before them. The second sentence points out the importance of distinguishing between appearance and reality – that is, the prior research (*what came before*) must be understood in order to determine which aspects of the current data-driven sciences are actually new, i.e. *innovative*. Whether those aspects are *true*, *absolute*, *present*, or *authentic* is irrelevant; the sentence is only concerned with what was done in the past vs. what is being done now for the first time. (D) is thus correct.

3. B, D

The first sentence sets up an opposition between two aspects of modern life: gains in knowledge vs. loss of contact with the past. In addition, the reference to modern life as something *which we tend to think of as an accelerating series of gains* implies that loss of contact with the past is in fact an aspect of modernity. Blank (i) must therefore be filled with a positive word conveying the close relationship between gains and loss. *Attenuated by* (weakened by) is negative, and it does not make any sense to say that modern life is *adjacent to* (next to) a loss. That leaves *predicated on* (based on), which creates a logical meaning when plugged into the sentence: modern life is based on a loss of the past. (B) is thus answer to Blank (i).

For Blank (ii), the statement *depending on one's point of view* sets up an implicit opposition between *a disinheritance* (negative) and the blank, which must be filled with a positive word meaning roughly the opposite of *disinheritance*. *Misconception* is negative, and *concatenation* (linked chain of events) is neutral and contradicts the idea of losing contact with the past. That leaves *emancipation*, which is positive and creates a logical meaning when plugged into the sentence: losing contact with the past can be seen as a negative thing because it causes people to forget where they come from, or as a positive thing that liberates them from old or outdated ways of doing things. (D) is thus the answer to Blank (ii).

4. C, D

The key word *seemingly* implies that the common folks' *polite banter* hid something not so polite. Blank (i) must be filled with a positive word consistent with *polite*, whereas Blank (ii) must indicate the negative behavior lurking behind the polite façade. *Banter* does refer to chit-chat, but the word in Blank (i) is not related to that idea, so *loquacious* does not fit. Be careful with *nefarious* (cruel) as well: this word refers to what the common folk actually are, not what they appear to be. Only *congenial* (friendly, easy to get along with) is positive and consistent with the idea of politeness, making (C) the answer to Blank (i).

Blank (ii) must describe a negative behavior consistent with mockery. Neither *reticence* (shyness) nor *indignation* (outrage at being falsely accused of something) fits, but *subterfuge* (deception) is negative and logically refers to an act committed by people who only appear to be nice. (D) is thus the answer to Blank (ii).

5. C, E, J

The sentence states that *an idea based on _____ still* has the potential to conquer the world, implying that the idea is not a particularly good one. Logically, Blank (i) must be filled with a negative word describing a weak or problematic basis for the idea. *Consequence* and *inevitability* are both unrelated to that definition, but an idea that was based on a *fallacy* (falsehood) would indeed be a problematic one. (C) is thus the answer to Blank (i).

For Blank (ii), the sentence sets up a contrast between the idea's popularity and the blank, which should be filled with a negative word indicating weakness. An idea that had factual *underpinnings* would not be a particularly bad idea, eliminating (F). *Complacency* (self-satisfaction) is negative but does not make sense in context. To describe an idea as having factual *shortcomings* is to imply that it doesn't have much of a factual basis at all. (E) is thus the answer to Blank (ii).

Blank (iii) must be filled with a positive word describing something that has gained *enormous popularity*. The fact that this word is described as *unassailable* (indestructible) suggests that it is a very strong word. Neither *criteria* nor *procedure* describes something that is popular to the point of being immune to attacks, but *dogma* (doctrine) is a synonym for *creed* and fits that definition perfectly. (J) is thus the answer to Blank (iii).

6. A, D, H

The first sentence is long and structurally complex, but you can simplify it by crossing out the information between the dashes: *The factors that allowed cholera to take hold of newly industrializing cities...also (i) _____ to make selfishness pay off.* The word *also* is key, indicating that the information before and after it is parallel: *The factors that allowed cholera to do x also allowed it to do y.* As a result, Blank (i) must be filled with a word similar to *allowed*. *Neglected* is exactly the opposite, and it does not make sense to say that *factors sought to make selfishness pay off* – factors cannot seek to do anything. Although *conspires* typically refers to an action performed by people, it is idiomatically acceptable in this context. To say that factors conspired to do something is to imply that they came together to produce a particular result. (A) is thus the answer to Blank (i).

Blank (ii) must be filled with a word indicating something that could not yet be done to private interests (*their = private interests*) because of insufficient infrastructure. We know from the previous sentence that *selfishness paid off*, and from the sentence in question that *private interests faced few penalties*. Logically, then, the blank should be filled with a word similar to *controlled*. Private interests that could not be *pursued* or *cultivated* by regulatory infrastructure would not necessarily lead to a public health crisis (the first sentence indicates that *cholera took hold*), but if those interests could not be *restrained*, then such a crisis would be a predictable outcome. (D) is thus the answer to Blank (ii).

Blank (iii) must be filled with a word indicating the effect of unrestrained private interests on public health. We know that a cholera outbreak occurred, so the blank must be filled with a word indicating a negative effect. *Ameliorated* (made better) means exactly the opposite of the required word, and *incited* (inspired) does not make sense. In contrast, public health that was *undermined* would result in an outbreak of disease. (H) is thus the answer to Blank (iii).

7. D, F

The sentence states that the D'Oyly Carte's legacy of production styles *continues to be emulated in new performances*, indicating that it remains extremely influential. The blank must be filled with positive words consistent with that idea. *Devastating* and *controversial* are negative, and *complex* does not make sense. *Compelling* fits, but this word lacks a close synonym among the other choices. In contrast, a *lasting* or *enduring legacy* is one that would still have an effect today. [D] and [F] are thus correct.

8. A, B

The fact that over three million East Germans *crossed over the border into West Berlin* suggests that those people were ignoring or going against immigration restrictions. One can *subdue* an opponent in a fight, but this word does not make sense in a legal context. Likewise, *alleviating* refers to lessening something negative; it does not make sense to say that a person *alleviated* a restriction. One can only *debunk* (reveal the truth about) a lie or a myth, or *unearth* something that has been hidden. *Defied* and *flouted* are the only two words that correctly describe the actions of people who acted in a manner contrary to what the law allowed, making [A] and [B] correct.

9. A, D

The assertion that the book *fails to offer a cohesive argument* but rather *presents a _____ collection of testimonies* suggests that the book's content is fragmented or incoherent. The blank must be filled with words indicating that quality. The only two possible options are *diverse* and its synonym *motley*, which imply a varied grouping. A work that was *cumulative* would be coherent by definition, and *terse* (succinct), *prurient* (titillating), and *facetious* (sarcastic) are all qualities unrelated to coherence. [A] and [D] are thus correct.

10. A, C

The statement that voters *hoped that the new cabinet would prove more decisive* implies that the old cabinet was indecisive, and the construction *just as* _____ indicates that the new cabinet was similarly indecisive. In addition, the phrase *its promises just as vague* implies that the blank should be filled with words similar to *vague*. *Militant* and *doctrinaire* have similar meanings but have nothing to do with being vague or indecisive. *Reactionary* and *influential* both refer to qualities commonly associated with governments, but these too are unrelated to vagueness. Although *equivocal* (refusing to commit to a particular point of view) and *evasive* (avoiding direct statements) do not have precisely the same meaning, both logically describe a characteristic of a governing body that was indecisive and vague. [A] and [C] are thus correct.

11. B, F

The sentence sets up a straightforward contrast between *docile, complacent* sheep and kangaroos, which exhibit an opposing quality. If sheep are tame and easy to manage, then the blank must be filled with words indicating that kangaroos are difficult to handle. *Belligerence* (violence) is an extremely logical choice, but this word lacks a close synonym among the other choices. A *pliant* animal would be easy to manage, and an animal that was *reticent* (shy) or *agile* would not necessarily be easy or hard to manage. An animal that demonstrated *recalcitrance* or *intransigence* (extreme stubbornness) would, however, be very hard to manage and poorly suited to life outside the wild. [B] and [F] are thus correct.

Set 11

1. Once hunted to near extinction, bison populations have in recent decades experienced _____ as a result of both conservation efforts and commercial demand.

(A) an awakening
(B) a convalescence
(C) a recognition
(D) a counterattack
(E) a resurgence

2. After several of his reproductions of Colonial-era furniture were bought by _____ dealers who artificially aged the pieces and sold them as originals, the artist Wallace Nutting began burning his signature into his works.

(A) elitist
(B) independent
(C) fashionable
(D) exuberant
(E) unscrupulous

3. There can be no objective measure of a thinker's legacy, but few would (i) _____ the verdict that Habermas has achieved a place of enduring significance that (ii) _____ that of any of his contemporaries.

Blank (i)	Blank (ii)
(A) acknowledge	(D) sabotages
(B) contest	(E) transcends
(C) exploit	(F) clinches

4. American newspapers publish editorials on their front pages (i) _____ and only for topics of unusual importance; in other countries, however, the practice of featuring editorials alongside headlines is much more (ii) _____.

Blank (i)	Blank (ii)
(A) sporadically	(D) confounding
(B) punctually	(E) striking
(C) systematically	(F) prevalent

5. The seasonal ozone hole over Antarctica, a cause of concern since 1984, now appears to be (i) _____. Although the improvement is (ii) _____, it suggests that the Montreal Protocol — the 1987 treaty signed by almost every nation that phased out the use of chemicals known as chlorofluorocarbons, or CFCs — is having the (iii) _____.

Blank (i)	Blank (ii)	Blank (iii)
(A) escalating	(D) insignificant	(G) intended effect
(B) diminishing	(E) slight	(H) predictable difficulties
(C) slackening	(F) encouraging	(J) opposite influence

6. The Thirty Years War represented a transition from (i) _____ medieval disorder to the more organized modern system of nation states in which monarchs agreed to respect each others' territorial (ii) _____. Today, the Peace of Westphalia, which ended the war, is remembered primarily for (iii) _____ the system of autonomous states that has framed international relations in the centuries since.

Blank (i)	Blank (ii)	Blank (iii)
(A) fragmented	(D) benevolence	(G) casting aside
(B) overbearing	(E) sovereignty	(H) ushering in
(C) imperial	(F) equilibrium	(J) reverting to

7. Although the building has many admirers who admire its groundbreaking design, it also has a number of detractors who are far less _____ its appearance.

[A] apathetic toward
[B] disturbed by
[C] enthusiastic about
[D] intrigued by
[E] enamored of
[F] representative of

8. Japanese artist Okakura Kakuzo is credited with salvaging Nihonga, or painting done with traditional Japanese techniques, at a time when Western-style painting was threatening to _____ it.

[A] expose
[B] replace
[C] supplant
[D] invalidate
[E] portray
[F] exclude

9. Frederick Law Olmsted believed that a city's green space should be equally accessible to all its citizens, and his design of New York's Central Park embodied that _____ ideal.

   [A] democratic
   [B] perpetual
   [C] tranquil
   [D] halcyon
   [E] arcane
   [F] egalitarian

10. Though he occasionally experimented with more esoteric themes, the director invariably acquiesced to the demands of his audience and returned to a focus on _____ topics.

   [A] notorious
   [B] licit
   [C] abstruse
   [D] quotidian
   [E] mundane
   [F] subdued

11. Authenticating a centuries-old work of art is seldom _____ process: ego, personal tastes, and the desire to avoid error all inevitably influence the final judgment.

   [A] a transparent
   [B] a disinterested
   [C] a byzantine
   [D] an exacting
   [E] an authentic
   [F] a detached

Explanations: Set 11

1. E

The sentence sets up a contrast between the bison populations of the past – if bison were *hunted to near extinction*, we can assume that those populations declined significantly – and the bison populations of recent decades. The reference to *both conservation efforts and commercial demand* suggest that bison populations have improved in recent decades, and the blank must be filled with a word indicating that fact. It does not make sense to say that buffalo populations *awakened* since they were not previously asleep (or, if that word is understood figuratively, ignorant of something). *Convalescence* (recovery from illness) does not make sense since the focus is on improving populations; the sentence gives no indication that the bison were *ill*, just that they were hunted. To say that the bison *counterattacked* would be to imply that they lashed out against those who hunted them to near extinction, but the sentence gives no indication that the bison themselves are attacking people. The growth of conservation efforts would imply that the importance of the bison has gained *recognition*, but this word does not imply an actual increase in the number of bison. Only *resurgence* is clearly consistent with the idea of an animal population that is rebounding as a result of human intervention. (E) is thus correct.

2. E

The sentence states that the dealers *artificially aged [Nutting's] pieces and sold them as originals*, implying that they were dishonest. The blank describes a characteristic of the dealers and so should be filled with a word consistent with the idea of dishonesty or fraud. An individual who is *elitist* is merely a snob; this word carries no connotation of dishonesty. *Independent*, *fashionable*, and *exuberant* (enthusiastic) are all words that could be applied to furniture dealers under other circumstances, but these words do not fit the clue in the sentence. *Unscrupulous* means dishonest and clearly fits the description of dealers who tried to pass Nutting's reproductions off as originals.

3. B, E

The contradictor *but* and the key phrase *enduring significance* indicate that despite the lack of objective measure for evaluating a thinker's legacy, all signs suggest that Habermas is leaving an extremely important one. It does not make sense to say that *few would acknowledge* Habermas's position; the sentence indicates exactly the opposite. It is similarly illogical to say that *few would exploit* his legacy. Given Habermas' *enduring significance*, however, his legacy would be difficult to dispute, i.e. *contest*. (B) is thus the answer to Blank (i).

For Blank (ii), the phrase *enduring significance* is again key. If Habermas's legacy can be considered so important, then logically, he must be superior to his contemporaries. Blank (ii) should therefore be filled with a positive word conveying the idea of superiority. *Sabotages* is negative and can be eliminated. Although *clinches* is positive, it does not connote superiority. Only *transcends* indicates that Habermas has surpassed his contemporaries, an achievement that would help secure his legacy. (E) is thus the answer to Blank (ii).

4. A, F

For Blank (i), the key phrase *and only for topics of unusual importance* implies that editorials are published on the front pages of American newspapers infrequently. *Systematically* does not convey that meaning, and *punctually* would only imply that the editorials were published at the correct time. *Sporadically* (occasionally) is a much more direct fit for the idea of unusual importance, making (A) the answer to Blank (i).

For Blank (ii), the contradictor *however* indicates that the practice of publishing editorials on the front pages of newspapers is much common in other countries. The blank must therefore be filled with a word meaning something like common. *Confounding* (perplexing) does not make sense at all, and whether *the practice of featuring editorials alongside headlines is striking* is irrelevant. Only *prevalent* conveys the idea of a common practice, making (F) the answer to Blank (ii).

5. B, E, G

The first sentence sets up an implicit opposition between the fact that the ozone hole over Antarctica has been a cause for concern since 1984 and events that are occurring now. The implication is that the hole must be improving, or getting smaller, an assumption supported by the reference to *the improvement* in the following sentence. For Blank (i), *escalating* would imply that the problem was getting larger, so that answer can be eliminated. Likewise, it does not make sense to say that a hole *slackened* (went limp). A hole that was *diminishing*, however, would signal improvement in the context of the Montreal Protocol. (B) is thus the answer to Blank (i).

The contradictor *although* sets up a contrast between the nature of the improvement and the results of the Montreal Protocol. The fact that there is improvement at all suggests that the treaty phasing out CFCs is working, i.e. it is having the *intended effect*. However, the pairing of the contradictor *although* with the reference to *improvement* suggests that the improvement was not particularly large, i.e. *slight*. For Blank (ii), be careful with *insignificant*: if the improvement truly were insignificant, then nothing about the treaty's effectiveness could be inferred from it. (E) and (G) are thus the answers to Blanks (ii) and (iii).

6. A, E, H

For Blank (i), the sentence sets up a contrast between _____ *medieval disorder* and *the more organized modern system of nation states*, so the blank must be filled with a word meaning something like disorderly or chaotic. A system that was *fragmented* would by definition be disorderly, making (A) the answer to Blank (i). *Overbearing* does not fit at all. Although *imperial* (pertaining to empire) might have described some medieval states, this word is inconsistent with the clues in the sentence.

Blank (ii) must be filled with a word describing a characteristic of *an organized modern system of nation states*. Since the existence of such a system is based on clear and fixed borders, the word in the blank must be consistent with that idea. *Benevolence* (kindness) does not make sense, and *equilibrium* (state of balance) does not fit either. *Territorial sovereignty* refers to a situation in which the government of a state has sole power over a particular area. That arrangement is the basis for nation states, making (E) the answer to Blank (ii).

Blank (iii) must be filled with a phrase describing the effect of the Peace of Westphalia on the system of nation states that has predominated since the Peace occurred. The passage implies that the end of the Thirty Years War, which was ended by the Peace of Westphalia, marked the beginning of the nation-state system. Logically, then, the correct phrase must mean something like introduced or initiated. *Casting aside* implies exactly the opposite, and *reverting to* implies a return to a pre-existing system – that meaning cannot be right because the nation-state system did not exist before the Peace of Westphalia. That leaves *ushering in*, which correctly describes a system being introduced. (H) is thus the answer to Blank (iii).

7. C, E

The sentence sets up a contrast between the building's admirers, who obviously have a positive attitude toward it, and its detractors, who by definition must view it negatively. Watch out for the double negative, though: the detractors display far *less* of the quality in the blank, so even though the idea is negative, the correct words must be positive and mean something like happy. *Apathetic* (indifferent) and *disturbed* are negative, and it does not make any sense to say that a person is *representative of* a building. *Intrigued* could plausibly fit, but this word lacks a close synonym among the other choices. That leave *enthusiastic* and *enamored*, both of which denote extremely positive attitudes that detractors would lack.

8. B, C

The fact that *Western-style painting was threatening* to do something to Nihonga implies a negative action. In addition, the key word *salvaging* (saving) suggests that Nihonga was on the verge of disappearing. The blank must be filled with negative words consistent with that idea. *Portray* is not negative, so it can be eliminated. A painting style cannot be *invalidated*, so this answer can be crossed out as well. To say that Western-style painting was threatening to *expose* Nihonga would illogically imply that Nihonga was doing something wrong. Likewise, it does not make sense to say that Western-style painting was threating to *exclude* Nihonga (exclude it from what?). It makes far more sense to say that Kakuzo saved Nihonga from being *replaced*, i.e. *supplanted*, by Western-style painting. [B] and [C] are thus correct.

9. A, F

Don't get distracted by the mention of Central Park, a reference that could lead you to think the blank should be filled with words related to nature. *Tranquil* and *halcyon* (idyllic) have similar meanings and would be seem to be consistent with a discussion of a park, but in reality, the key statement is that Olmsted wanted Central Park to be *equally accessible to all...citizens*. The blank must therefore be filled with words expressing the idea of equality. Given the lack of historical context, there is nothing to indication that Olmsted's desire was either *perpetual* or *arcane*. It was, however, directly consistent with the *democratic* or *egalitarian* (EGAL-, equal) ideal of wanting to create civic space in which the entire populace would be free to gather. [A] and [F] are thus correct.

10. D, E

The contradictor *though* indicates that the two halves of the sentence are presenting contrasting ideas. The first half of the sentence states that the director *occasionally experimented with more esoteric themes* (that is, high-minded themes only understood by a very sophisticated audience), so logically, the second half of the sentence must convey that he *acquiesced* (gave in) *to the demands of his audience* by focusing on less esoteric themes, i.e. more common one. The blank must therefore be filled with words meaning something like common. *Abstruse* is a synonym for *esoteric*, so this word is exactly the opposite of what is required here. *Notorious, licit* (legal), and *subdued* all do not make sense. That leaves *quotidian* and *mundane* (commonplace, everyday), which correctly describe themes that are the opposite of esoteric and that would please audiences. [D] and [E] are thus correct.

11. B, F

The information after the colon serves to clarify the meaning of the blank, which must describe the process of authenticating a centuries-old work of art. The fact that *ego, personal tastes, and the desire to avoid error* all play a role suggests that the authentication process is highly personal and subjective. The question, however, asks you to identify something that the authentication process *seldom* is. Logically, then, the blank must be filled with words meaning the opposite of subjective. Given them many influences indicated by the sentence, the authentication process hardly seems *transparent*, but this word does not have a close synonym among the other choices. *Disinterested* and *detached* are synonyms that fit as the opposite of subjective. (Note that *disinterested* means objective, not lacking interest.) The other answers do not fit the clue provided by the sentence. [B] and [F] are thus correct.

Set 12

1. Part of Joseph Epstein's traditional appeal as a writer has been his willingness to say precisely what he thinks, even at the risk of _____ his friends and acquaintances.

| (A) duping |
| (B) antagonizing |
| (C) vindicating |
| (D) deceiving |
| (E) exculpating |

2. The implications of secularism are often misconstrued. For the most part, early modern Europeans were profoundly religious. It was rather that the boundary between the religious and the secular became more _____ than before.

| (A) flexible |
| (B) preposterous |
| (C) haphazard |
| (D) distinct |
| (E) porous |

3. Of the more than 50,000 dietary supplements currently on the market, no more than a few are scientifically proven to be (i) _____. The popularity of the rest serves as a (ii) _____ to the power of self-delusion.

Blank (i)	Blank (ii)
(A) assiduous	(D) testament
(B) deleterious	(E) corrective
(C) efficacious	(F) rebuttal

4. Over the last half century, people have (i) _____ the existing array of antibiotics in such a reckless fashion that it is difficult to know where to place blame. Physicians are just as guilty of overprescribing these medications – even to (ii) _____ hypochondriacs – as patients are of demanding the drugs too often.

Blank (i)	Blank (ii)
(A) staved off	(D) admonish
(B) attended to	(E) counsel
(C) indulged in	(F) mollify

5. Revolutionary new paradigms generally do not accommodate old ones, (i) _____ their principles and approaches. Rather, they destroy the old ways of thinking or doing, (ii) _____ their ranks of those who remain (iii) _____.

Blank (i)	Blank (ii)	Blank (iii)
(A) scrutinizing	(D) purging	(G) faithful
(B) subsuming	(E) cautioning	(H) diligent
(C) inundating	(F) convincing	(J) lucid

6. The tendency to endorse a particular kind of reading as good inevitably fosters assumptions about what good reading entails. For example, "devouring" a book implies a certain (i) _____ – it idealizes the fast-paced reading experience. It also (ii) _____ a certain kind of writing. If a book grips us the way a Hollywood thriller does, it's doing its "job." Any work that elicits a more (iii) _____ reading experience is cast as defective.

Blank (i)	Blank (ii)	Blank (iii)
(A) pragmatism	(D) elucidates	(G) furtive
(B) spontaneity	(E) critiques	(H) decorous
(C) tempo	(F) promotes	(J) contemplative

7. By breeding dogs to suit their tastes, the Victorians _____ created
    genetically isolated canine populations, little knowing how useful the animals'
    descendants might be to future scientists.

    [A] deliberately
    [B] consistently
    [C] unintentionally
    [D] ostensibly
    [E] predominantly
    [F] inadvertently

8. Growing from several hundred residents in 1830 to nearly two million only eighty
    years later, Chicago epitomized the remarkable _____ of urbanization in
    the United States during the nineteenth century.

    [A] vigor
    [B] strain
    [C] brunt
    [D] velocity
    [E] decadence
    [F] swiftness

9. While technological prowess has increased immensely over the last half century,
    the principles of innovation have remained largely _____.

    [A] static
    [B] constant
    [C] ineffable
    [D] nebulous
    [E] inhibited
    [F] desultory

10. Opposition to the creation of a park based on Modernist principles has been
    limited; nevertheless, the criticism leveled against city officials is striking for the
    level of its _____.

    [A] rancor
    [B] veracity
    [C] retaliation
    [D] stridency
    [E] tension
    [F] perspicuity

11. The second century mapmaker Ptolemy was prone to the biggest and most insidious cartographic _____: when information was lacking, he simply made it up.

    [A] manifestation
    [B] ambiguity
    [C] vice
    [D] transgression
    [E] apprehensiveness
    [F] investigation

Explanations: Set 12

1. B

The sentence contains two key pieces of information: first, the statement that Epstein has *willingness to say precisely what he thinks* implies that he is perhaps blunt to the point of rudeness; and second, the phrase *even at the risk of* indicates that Epstein's bluntness has a potentially negative effect on his friends and acquaintances. Logically, they might get mad at him for being so frank. The blank must be filled with a negative word conveying that idea. *Vindicating* (proving right) and *exculpating* (freeing from guilt) are positive and can thus be eliminated. *Duping* and *deceiving* are synonyms, which in the context of a Text Completion is effectively guaranteed to signal two wrong answers – if only one word can be right, then two words with the same meaning must be wrong. Here, both are incorrect because there is nothing to indicate that Epstein was misleading people in any way. That leaves *antagonizing* (making angry, offending), which logically describes what a person who does not attempt to restrain his opinions might do to others. (B) is thus correct.

2. D

The first two sentences of the passage serve to clarify a common misconception about the rise of secularism: it did not make early modern Europeans less religious, as people tend to assume, but rather affected the line between secular and religious in some way. To answer this question, think about the definition of *secularism* – that is, the idea of separation between church and state. The process of secularization resulted in a society in which clear boundaries existed between sacred and secular, as opposed to one in which religion influenced every aspect of daily life. Given that context, the blank must be filled with a word indicating that although Europeans remained extremely religious, they distinguished more clearly between religious activities and non-religious activities. The only word to convey that the boundary grew clearer or sharper is *distinct*. *Flexible*, *haphazard*, and *porous* imply exactly the opposite. *Preposterous* makes no sense because the sentence gives no indication that the boundary between religious and secular was irrational or ridiculous to begin with. (D) is thus correct.

3. C, D

The sentence contrasts *scientifically proven to be* _____ (good) with *the power of self-delusion* (bad), so Blank (i) must be filled with a positive word. *Deleterious* is negative, so this answer can be eliminated. *Assiduous* is positive, but it is illogical to describe dietary supplements as hard-working. In contrast, *efficacious* (effective) is a word that could logically describe nutritional supplements, so (C) is the answer to Blank (i).

For Blank (ii), the sentence implies that most supplements (*the rest*) are popular as a result of self-delusion, so it is reasonable to assume that the word in the blank is positive. Supplements that offered a *rebuttal* to self-delusion would probably not be very popular. Although *corrective* (something designed to compensate for an error) is positive, it does not make sense to describe the popularity of a supplement in this way. It makes far more sense to describe the popularity of ineffective supplements as a *testament* to the power of self-delusion. In other words, the fact that people continue to consume tens of thousands of supplements whose effectiveness has not been proven supports (testifies to) the fact that people can fool themselves into thinking things are helpful when there is no evidence that that is the case.

4. C, F

The key word *reckless* and key phrase *where to place blame* suggest that people have been overusing or abusing antibiotics in recent decades. Blank (i) must be filled with a phrase consistent with that idea. *Staved off* (held off) implies the opposite, and *attended to* (focused on, took care of) does not really fit. In contrast, to say that people *indulged in the existing array of antibiotics* implies that people have taken advantage of the availability of these medications, or used them to excess. (C) is thus the answer to Blank (i).

Blank (ii) must be filled with a word describing why doctors would prescribe antibiotics to hypochondriacs. Logically, doctors would do so in order to support the illusion that these patients are actually ill. Such an act would not *counsel* such individuals, and it would certainly not *admonish* (scold) them – on the contrary, it would enable their fantasies. Prescribing antibiotics to hypochondriacs would, however, *mollify* (calm) these individuals by making them feel as if their ailments were being taken seriously. (F) is thus the answer to Blank (ii).

5. B, D, G

The phrase that includes Blank (i) serves to modify the statement before the comma, so the word in the blank must further describe or explain what *revolutionary new paradigms* (models) do <u>not</u> do to the *principles and approaches* of old paradigms. The sentence already tells us that the revolutionary paradigms do not *accommodate* the old paradigms, so the word in the blank must be consistent with the idea of accommodation. New paradigms would not accommodate old ones by *scrutinizing* them (examining them closely), and certainly not by *inundating* (flooding) them. In contrast, new paradigms that accommodated old ones would *subsume* (absorb) some of those old features. (B) is thus the answer to Blank (i). Basically, the sentence is saying that when new ways of thinking take over, they destroy the old ways completely and do not absorb any of the aspects of those old ways.

Blanks (ii) and (iii) must be filled with a word describing a consequence of these new paradigms' destruction of old ways of thinking. The word *remain* implies that the phrase is referring to individuals who continue to embrace the old models – in other words, those individuals who remain *faithful*. Logically, those individuals would no longer have a place and would be gotten rid of, i.e. *purged*. (D) is thus the answer to Blank (ii), and (G) is the answer to Blank (iii).

6. C, F, J

Although it does not contain any blanks, the first sentence provides crucial information because it sets up the information that follows. What idea does the first sentence convey? Essentially, that holding up a particular type of reading up as "good" reading creates assumptions about what it means to read well. Blank (i), however, depends on the information after the dash, which defines the word in the blank. The key phrase is *fast-paced*, which indicates that a key feature of *devouring a book* is reading it quickly. The only option to correspond to that idea is *tempo*, which means speed. *Pragmatism* (practicality) does not fit at all, but don't be fooled by *spontaneity*. Although acting spontaneously involves quick decisions, reading a book quickly is not the same thing as reading it impulsively. *Tempo* is a much more direct fit for the clue. (C) is thus the answer to Blank (i).

For Blank (ii), *it* refers to *the tendency*, all the way back at the beginning of the passage. That fact provides an important clue because it indicates that the structure of the third sentence must be parallel to that of the first sentence. (Note that the "interruption" of the second sentence makes the parallel structure more challenging than usual to pick up on.) The main verb in the first sentence is *fosters*, so the main verb in the third sentence – the word in Blank (ii) – must be filled with a positive word that is similar in meaning. The third sentence serves to reinforce the idea that considering a certain type of reading "good" creates further assumptions about reading that way. *Critiques* has a negative connotation, and *elucidates* (clarifies) is not similar to *fosters*. In the context of the passage, however, it makes sense to say that when "devouring" a book is considered positive, a certain type of fast-paced writing is *promoted* as a result. (F) is thus the answer to Blank (ii).

For Blank (iii), the key word is *defective*. If a fast-paced, cinematic type of reading is idealized, then the opposite type of reading must be looked down on. The blank must therefore be filled with a word meaning something like slow or serious. *Decorous* means polite, which does not have quite the right connotation, and *furtive* (secretive) does not make sense at all. *Contemplative* (thoughtful) logically describes writing that is the opposite of fast-paced and superficial, making (J) the answer to Blank (iii).

7. C, F

The key phrase *little knowing* indicates that the Victorians were unaware that their breeding dogs to suit their personal preferences would help future scientists. The blank must therefore be filled with a word indicating that the help provided by the Victorians was accidental. The only two words to convey that meaning are *unintentionally* and *inadvertently*. *Deliberately* is exactly the opposite of the required word, and *ostensibly* (supposedly) does not fit because the sentence indicates that the dogs' descendants were actually helpful to scientists. *Predominantly* does not make sense at all. And while the Victorians may have indeed bred genetically isolated canine populations *consistently*, that word is unrelated to the fact that they did so by accident. [C] and [F] are thus correct.

8. D, F

The sentence states that Chicago's population ballooned from several hundred to *nearly two million* between 1830 and 1910 – an extraordinary level of growth in only 80 years. The blank must therefore be filled with a positive word consistent with that fact. *Strain, brunt,* and *decadence* are all negative and can thus be eliminated. The type of growth described was certainly very vigorous (energetic), but *vigor* lacks a close synonym among the other choices. In contrast, *velocity* and *swiftness* are synonyms that accurately describe the remarkable speed with which Chicago's population grew.

9. A, B

The contradictor *while* sets up a contrast between the two parts of the sentence. The first part indicates that *technological prowess* (know-how) *has increased*, so the second part must convey the idea that *the principles of innovation* have not increased. Though not exact synonyms, *constant* and *static* are the only two words that create a logical meaning when plugged into the sentence — they imply that the principles of innovation have remained the same, a meaning that fits as the opposite of increasing. *Ineffable* (inexpressible) and *desultory* (haphazard) do not make sense at all. *Nebulous* (unclear) does not quite fit: the sentence is opposing change vs. stability, not clarity vs. lack of clarity. *Inhibited* also misses the mark: this word implies that the principles of innovation have remained hidden, or afraid to come out into the open — a not entirely logical meaning as well as one that does not fit the clues in the sentence. [A] and [B] are thus correct.

10. A, D

The blank describes a *striking level* of something related to criticism, so the correct words must refer to a very strong or negative type of criticism. *Veracity* (truth; VER-, true) and *perspicuity* (perceptiveness; PER-, through + SPEC-, see) are positive and can be eliminated. *Retaliation* is negative, but the sentence gives no indication that the people doing the criticizing are trying to get revenge on the city officials. *Tension* would be a reasonable match, if perhaps not too negative, but this word lacks a close synonym among the other choices. That leaves *rancor* and *stridency* which, although not exact synonyms, both convey the idea of extremely harsh criticism. [A] and [D] are thus correct.

11. C, D

The statement that *when information was lacking, [Ptolemny] simply made it up* implies that the blank should be filled with a word indicating that Ptolemy did something bad. That idea is reinforced by the key word *insidious*, which means sneaky or tricky. *Manifestation* and *investigation* are both neutral and do not make sense in context. *Apprehensiveness* (nervousness) is negative but likewise does not fit. *Ambiguity* would imply that Ptolemy made his maps unclear in some way, but the sentence does not indicate that they were unclear, just that they were wrong. *Transgression* and *vice* both refer to wrongdoing, and would logically describe the sneakiest error to which a mapmaker could fall prey. [C] and [D] are thus correct.

Set 13

1. The first phone booths were _____ craftsmanship; they were not simply convenient places to have a conversation but works of art in their own right.

| (A) paragons of |
| (B) references to |
| (C) forerunners of |
| (D) emissaries of |
| (E) precursors to |

2. Employee "wellness" programs, which sometimes tie financial incentives and penalties to losing weight, exercising, or lowering cholesterol or blood-sugar levels, have been accused of crossing the line between encouragement and _____.

| (A) expulsion |
| (B) obstruction |
| (C) coercion |
| (D) motivation |
| (E) confrontation |

3. Plants are nature's chemical wizards. When they find themselves in (i) _____ situations – feasted on by pests, ignored by pollinators – they cannot kick up their roots and relocate. Instead, they regulate the chemistry of their environments, perpetually (ii) _____ the ground and air, as well as their own tissues, with molecular cocktails intended to increase their chances of survival.

Blank (i)	Blank (ii)
(A) transitory	(D) embellishing
(B) hostile	(E) inflaming
(C) unforeseen	(F) suffusing

4. A key flaw in Chomsky's theories is that they posit young children are born with the (i) _____ capacity to form sentences using abstract grammatical rules. Much research now shows that young children begin acquiring language by learning simple grammatical patterns; then, gradually, they (ii) _____ the rules behind them.

Blank (i)	Blank (ii)
(A) innate	(D) disclose
(B) distinctive	(E) refine
(C) chronic	(F) intuit

5. For much of the history of science, observations that (i) _____ reigning belief systems were thrown out on theoretical grounds, no matter how well supported they were by (ii) _____ evidence – particularly when no alternative explanation could be convincingly (iii) _____.

Blank (i)	Blank (ii)	Blank (iii)
(A) buttressed	(D) synthetic	(G) discarded
(B) violated	(E) empirical	(H) articulated
(C) constructed	(F) hypothetical	(J) regulated

6. The new biography of the composer generally manages to avoid the critical squabbles that sometimes (i) _____ this genre of work, (ii) _____ references and accounts of (iii) _____ opinions to a few dozen pages of useful notes.

Blank (i)	Blank (ii)	Blank (iii)
(A) plague	(D) extending	(G) disquieting
(B) inflate	(E) administering	(H) pedantic
(C) irk	(F) relegating	(J) diverging

7. The air we breathe is not a fixed physical phenomenon, like gravity or magnetism, but rather a precise combination of gases whose balance can be _____ by human actions.

[A] disturbed
[B] understood
[C] concealed
[D] submerged
[E] upset
[F] propelled

8. Early experiences are not solely responsible for determining an individual's personality; the brain is sufficiently _____ that the neural pathways created in infancy and childhood can either be altered or reaffirmed by later experiences.

   [A] complex
   [B] plastic
   [C] evolved
   [D] sensitive
   [E] malleable
   [F] variegated

9. Finding a way to prevent or delay certain diseases has become a priority for researchers because decades of research on these ailments have resulted in only a few treatments, and even those become all but _____ after a few months.

   [A] salutary
   [B] prevalent
   [C] ineffectual
   [D] therapeutic
   [E] impractical
   [F] futile

10. Since the end of the last recession, consumers have grown increasingly confident about their financial _____, yet their knowledge of basic economic principles appears to be more tenuous than it was before.

    [A] station
    [B] acumen
    [C] candor
    [D] savvy
    [E] compunction
    [F] zeal

11. Although Emmy Noether's conceptual approach to algebra eventually proved to have many practical applications, it was at first controversial because many mathematicians then favored more _____ methods of investigation.

    [A] vivid
    [B] concrete
    [C] contemporary
    [D] streamlined
    [E] pragmatic
    [F] groundbreaking

Explanations: Set 13

1. A

The key phrase *works of art in their own right* indicates that the first phone booths embodied good craftsmanship. The blank must be filled with a word consistent with that idea – one that means something like embodiments. *References* and *emissaries* (messengers) are certainly not embodiments and do not make sense in context. *Forerunners* and *precursors* both refer to things that came before. These words do not fit either because the blank is referring to the first phone booths themselves, not what they influenced, and it does not make any sense to say that an object preceded craftsmanship. *Paragons* are perfect examples of something, and an edifice that was a perfect example of craftsmanship could logically be described as a work of art. (A) is thus correct.

2. C

The sentence contains two key pieces of information. First, employee "wellness programs" *sometimes tie financial incentives and penalties* to a variety of health-related activities; and second, such programs may *cross [a] line*. Both of these statements suggest that workers are left without a real choice about whether to take part. In other words, these programs manipulate their workers with the threat of financial repercussions if they do not participate – an act of *coercion*. *Motivation* is too close in meaning to *encouragement* and lacks its negative overtones. *Expulsion* is too strong – companies are not getting rid of employees who do not participate in wellness programs but rather threatening them with financial consequences. *Obstruction* does not make sense because companies are not preventing their employees from doing anything (just the opposite, in fact), and *confrontation* is likewise a poor fit because the sentence contains no reference to a standoff between employees and workers. (C) is thus correct.

3. B, F

The information between the dashes provides the most important clue for Blank (i). Being *feasted on by pests* and *ignored by pollinators* is a bad thing, so the blank must be filled with a negative word. *Transitory* (brief) does not make sense, and there is nothing to suggest that the situations described are *unforeseen*. Only *hostile* is consistent with the description of a plant under attack. (B) is thus the answer to Blank (i).

For Blank (ii), it is logical to assume that plants *regulate the chemistry of their environments* by filling the ground, air, etc. with the necessary molecular cocktails, so the correct word must be positive and mean something like filled. *Embellishing* (ornamenting) does not make any sense, and there is no reason that a plant under attack would *inflame* its surroundings or itself. *Suffusing* implies a spreading around of beneficial molecular cocktails, and this word logically describes what a threatened plant might do to ensure the proper environment for itself. (F) is thus the answer to Blank (ii).

4. A, F

The sentence first states that Blank (i) describes a *flaw* in Chomsky's linguistic theories, whereas the second sentence refers to what *research now shows*. As a result, the first sentence must convey an idea that contrasts with the idea in the second sentence. The second sentence indicates that *young children begin acquiring language by learning simple grammatical patterns.* If children must learn these patterns, then they cannot be born knowing them. In other words, they do not have the *innate* (inborn) capacity to use grammatical rules. (A) is thus the answer to Blank (i).

Given that context, Blank (ii) must be filled with a word conveying the idea that children eventually figure out the rules behind the simple grammatical patterns they have learned. The correct word must mean something like figure out or grasp. The issue is not whether children *disclose* (reveal) those rules; and even though children may *refine* their understanding of the rules, they do not actually *refine* the rules themselves. In contrast, *intuit* conveys the logical idea that after practicing simple grammatical patterns, children eventually develop a natural sense of how the rules of language work. (F) is thus the answer to Blank (ii).

5. B, E, H

Blank (i) must be filled with a word describing an action that would cause observations to be *thrown out on theoretical grounds,* even if they were well supported by evidence. Logically, the blank should be filled with a negative word describing observations that contradicted official doctrine. Observations that *buttressed* (supported) or *constructed* existing systems would not be problematic, but ones that *violated* those systems would pose a threat and cause the observations to be rejected. (B) is thus the answer to Blank (i).

The key phrase *no matter how well supported they were* implies that the word in Blank (ii) will describe a strong or valid type of evidence. Evidence that was *synthetic* (fake) or *hypothetical* would not be strong, but *empirical* (hard, factually-based) observations would be hard to refute. (E) is thus the answer to Blank (ii).

Blank (iii) must be filled with a neutral word meaning something like invented or stated.
The sentence is essentially saying that observations that didn't fit with accepted beliefs were thrown out for not making sense in theory, even if there was a lot of factual evidence for them; and furthermore, that this type of rejection was particularly likely to take place when the people in charge couldn't come up with better explanations. *Discarded* does not make sense, and neither does *regulated* – the alternative explanation would not need to be controlled, merely to be conjured up. *Articulated* (made clear) is the only option that fits, making (H) the answer to Blank (iii).

6. A, F, J

The reference to *critical squabbles* indicates that Blank (i) must be filled with a negative word with a meaning similar to detract from or ruin. Something that *inflated* a work would make it seem better than it was, an implication that clearly does not fit here. *Irk* is negative, but it would not make sense to say that a discussion of arguments among critics *annoyed* a book. *Plague* is a negative word that can be used figuratively to mean afflict. Here, it logically implies that many biographies of composers are weakened by intrusive references to critical debates about the composers' works. (A) is thus answer to Blank (i).

For Blank (ii), the fact that the biography in question manages to *avoid* critical squabbles indicates that it does not let them intrude too much in the main part of the text – that is, it shunts them off to *a few dozen pages of useful notes*. Blank (ii) must therefore be filled with a word indicating that references to critical debates are in some way limited or contained. *Extending* implies the opposite, and *administering* does not make sense. Only *relegating* (consigning to an inferior position) correctly implies that the discussion of critical debates is limited to a less important part of the text, making (F) the answer to Blank (ii).

Blank (iii) must be filled with a word describing the type of opinions that are relegated to the notes. Logically, this word must consistent with the idea of squabbles or debates. *Disquieting* (disturbing) does not fit. The opinions may in fact be *pedantic* (dull, scholarly), but the focus here is on the *squabbles*, which by definition involve *diverging* opinions. (J) is thus the answer to Blank (iii).

7. A, E

The sentence sets up an opposition between the *fixed* quality of phenomena such as gravity and magnetism, and the presumably *unfixed*, or changeable, quality of the air. It is therefore reasonable to assume that the balance of gases can be affected or altered by human actions, and the blank must be filled with words conveying that fact. The balance of gases in air may be *understood* as a result of human actions, but this word is inconsistent with the clue in the sentence. *Concealed, submerged,* and *propelled* do not make sense at all. Only *disturbed* and its synonym *upset* describe a logical effect of humans meddling with the composition of air. [A] and [E] are thus correct.

8. B, E

The key phrase is that *neural pathways created in infancy and childhood can either be altered or reaffirmed by later experiences*. In other words, the brain is capable of changing as a result of experience. The blank must therefore be filled with words referring to the capacity for change. The brain may be *complex, evolved,* and *variegated* (varied), but none of these words fits the clue in the sentence. A *sensitive* organ is one that could logically be altered by experience, but this word lacks a close synonym among the other choices. In contrast, *plastic* and *malleable* are both qualities indicating the ability to be altered or shaped. [B] and [E] are thus correct.

9. C, F

The sentence states that researchers consider *finding a way to prevent or delay certain diseases* a priority because *only a few treatments are available*. The continuer *and* indicates that the phrase containing the blank must support the idea that treatments are in short supply. Logically, it should convey the idea that existing treatments stop working after a few months. The blank must therefore be filled with negative words meaning something like ineffective. *Ineffectual* is a direct match for that idea, making [C] the first answer. *Salutary* (healthy) and *therapeutic* imply exactly the opposite of the required word, and treatments that did not work would not become *prevalent* either. *Impractical* is negative, and it would make sense for treatments with this quality to be stopped after a few months; however, this word lacks a close synonym among the other choices. *Futile* (worthless) is not exactly a synonym for *ineffectual*, but this pair represents the best option the question offers. The words produce the same essential meaning when plugged into the sentence: the therapies that do work quickly become useless and cease to offer hope. [C] and [F] are thus correct.

10. B, D

The contradictor *yet* indicates an opposition between what consumers think they know about finances (a lot), and their actual *tenuous* (weak) knowledge of basic economic principles. The blank must therefore be filled with positive words meaning something like knowledge or understanding. People who were confident about their financial *station* would be secure in their financial position, not in their knowledge of finances. *Candor* (directness, honesty) is not quite the same thing as knowledge – it is possible to have this quality while being ignorant. Although *zeal* (enthusiasm) is positive, this word does not refer to knowledge either. *Compunction* (guilt) is negative and does not fit at all. Only *acumen* and *savvy* are consistent with the idea of know-how, making [B] and [D] are correct.

11. B, E

The contradictor *although* and the fact that Emmy Noether's *conceptual approach to algebra* was met with *skepticism* sets up a contrast between Noether's approach and the type of investigations that were common at the time she conducted her research. The blank must be filled with words describing the approach favored by other mathematicians, so the correct answers must logically describe an approach that is the opposite of conceptual – something like hands-on. *Vivid* means the opposite of dull, and *streamlined* means the opposite of complicated, so these words do not fit. *Contemporary* and *groundbreaking* have similar meanings, but neither of these words means the opposite of conceptual. Only *concrete* and *pragmatic* (practical) convey they idea that Noether's contemporaries preferred methodologies based less on theory and more on application. [B] and [E] are thus correct.

Set 14

1. Howard Zinn's *A People's History of the United States* is considered
    _____ work because it was the first book to present American history
    through the eyes of the common people.

(A) a polemical
(B) an economical
(C) a comprehensive
(D) a mirthful
(E) a seminal

2. The classical Italian form of theatre known as *commedia dell'arte* is famous for
    its _____ acting style, which emphasizes exaggerated gestures and
    unrestrained shows of emotion.

(A) facetious
(B) demur
(C) histrionic
(D) officious
(E) surreptitious

3. Throughout his career, the diplomat has traveled the globe, relentlessly seeking
    solutions to the world's most challenging problems. His efforts have been daring
    and at times (i) _____ – in some instances, he has been no more
    successful than his predecessors in (ii) _____ lasting solutions to
    entrenched conflicts.

Blank (i)	Blank (ii)
(A) quixotic	(D) securing
(B) inane	(E) evading
(C) cryptic	(F) rationalizing

4. Because the candidates are considered to hold fringe positions by the mainstream media, they have received little (i) _____ and, consequently, voters have little idea of what they (ii) _____.

Blank (i)	Blank (ii)
(A) guidance	(D) rely on
(B) sympathy	(E) stand for
(C) scrutiny	(F) cling to

5. Risk sensitivity theory states that when choosing between stable and uncertain outcomes, organisms will behave cautiously when things are going well and act more (i) _____ when times are hard. This explains why people gamble more when they are losing money, or why birds will forage not knowing (ii) _____ rather than settle for a certain but (iii) _____ amount of food.

Blank (i)	Blank (ii)	Blank (iii)
(A) precipitously	(D) what they'll find	(G) insufficient
(B) defensively	(E) where they are	(H) indeterminate
(C) stoically	(F) how they'll cope	(J) extraneous

6. The enduring strength of the craft guilds and the restrictions they (i) _____ were among the reasons the Italian economy went into decline during the seventeenth century. One of the most (ii) _____ protected cartels was that of the glass-makers on the Venetian island of Murano; workers who (iii) _____ their fidelity to the guild and took their skills elsewhere faced severe penalties, including death.

Blank (i)	Blank (ii)	Blank (iii)
(A) controlled	(D) flimsily	(G) exhorted
(B) appointed	(E) jealously	(H) conjectured
(C) enforced	(F) erratically	(J) abrogated

7. Biologist Lynn Margulis's revolutionary theory of cell development was initially met with almost unanimous skepticism because it built upon ideas that had largely been _____.

   [A] discredited
   [B] eulogized
   [C] stifled
   [D] rejected
   [E] substantiated
   [F] circumvented

8. Many nineteenth century thinkers sought inspiration in nature, but John Muir went further, regarding woods and mountains with an admiration that bordered on _____.

   [A] urgency
   [B] awe
   [C] necessity
   [D] obsession
   [E] trepidation
   [F] reverence

9. With numbers of Great White sharks so low, even accidental catches can create _____ for the species which, as a top predator, has a disproportionately important role in managing the ocean's food chain.

   [A] distress
   [B] frustration
   [C] havoc
   [D] gridlock
   [E] mayhem
   [F] toil

10. The battleship Potemkin was made famous by its crew's _____ against commanding officers, a rebellion that later came to be viewed as an initial step towards the Russian Revolution of 1917.

   [A] insurrection
   [B] accusations
   [C] struggle
   [D] grievances
   [E] maneuvers
   [F] mutiny

11. When the author explores people's fears and desires, any conventional familiarity these subjects may have dissolves under his _____ narrative control and nuanced attention to language and psychology.

    [A] facile
    [B] adroit
    [C] wry
    [D] deft
    [E] animated
    [F] cagey

Explanations: Set 14

1. E

The key word *first* indicates that Zinn's book was groundbreaking for presenting American history through the eyes of the common people. The blank must therefore be filled with a word consistent with the idea of being groundbreaking or innovative. *Mirthful* (happy, amusing) does not fit at all. A book that offered such a perspective might have been considered *polemical* (controversial), but the sentence provides no information to support that idea. In addition, the sentence does not indicate how short or long the book was, so it is impossible to know whether it was *economical* (short, spare) or *comprehensive* (all-encompassing). Only *seminal* (SEM-, seed) refers to something that was the first of its kind, making (E) correct.

2. C

The key phrase *exaggerated gestures and unrestrained shows of emotion* indicates that *commedia dell'arte* was characterized by over-the-top acting, and the blank must be filled with a word conveying that fact. *Demur* describes a style that is understated, not overstated; *surreptitious* (secretive) has a similar implication. *Facetious* (sarcastic) does not make sense at all. Acting that was *officious* (pompous) might be somewhat exaggerated, but it would not necessarily be overly emotional. Only *histrionic* (hysterical) is consistent with both exaggeration and an excess of emotion, making (C) correct.

3. A, D

The statement after the dash in the second sentence serves to clarify what is meant by *daring and sometimes _____*. What do we learn? That the diplomat has sometimes *been no more successful than his predecessors*. As a result, Blank (i) must be filled with a word consistent with that lack of success. In addition, the pairing of the blank with the word *daring* suggests that the blank should be filled with a similar word. *Inane* (boring, unoriginal) is the opposite of daring, and *cryptic* (obscure) is inconsistent with the description as well. Only *quixotic* (bold to the point of being unrealistic about what one can accomplish) accurately describes a person who is inspired to take on challenges beyond what he can personally solve. (A) is thus the answer to Blank (i).

Blank (ii) must likewise be filled with a word indicating that the diplomat has not always been successful in finding solutions. Although the idea is negative, the negation *no more successful* implies that this word must be positive. *Evading* (avoiding) is negative, and *rationalize* does not fit because the focus is on the diplomat's failure to find workable solutions, not on his inability to justify them. It would be much more logical to say that a diplomat worked to *secure* (ensure) solutions to entrenched conflicts. (D) is thus the answer to Blank (ii).

4. C, E

The key transition *consequently* indicates that Blank (ii) must be filled with a word describing a logical result of the word in Blank (i). If the candidates in question *are considered to hold fringe positions by the mainstream media*, it stands to reason that they haven't gotten much coverage. The media is not responsible for providing *guidance*. Although it is unlikely that the media would have much *sympathy* for candidates holding fringe positions, there is no option for Blank (ii) that describes a logical outcome of the media lacking this quality. On the other hand, the media's job is to provide *scrutiny*, examining candidates' positions closely. If the media fails to provide this information, then voters will remain largely unaware of what candidates' platforms are, i.e. what the candidates *stand for*. Although *cling to* is similar in meaning, this phrase has far too emotional a connotation to be a good fit here. *Stand for* is a much better way of describing what political candidates believe in. (C) is thus the answer to Blank (i), and (E) is the answer to Blank (ii).

5. A, D, G

The first sentence sets up an opposition between organisms' behavior in good vs. bad times. The sentence states that organisms behave *cautiously* during good times, so we can infer that they will behave in a contrasting way during bad times. It would make sense for an organism that perceived itself as threatened to behave *defensively*, but this word is not the opposite of *cautiously*. The same is true for *stoically* (uncomplainingly). *Precipitously* (hastily, carelessly) is a much more direct match; it is also consistent with the kind of reckless behavior displayed by people who gamble more when they are behind. (A) is thus the answer to Blank (i).

Blanks (ii) and (iii) must be filled with a word/phrase illustrating a situation in which birds are inclined to behave precipitously – that is, a difficult situation. Logically, birds would take the risk of foraging for food rather than settle if they knew they were only guaranteed an *insufficient* amount. *Extraneous* implies that the birds would have too much food – exactly the opposite of what the sentence implies. (H) creates a contradictory meaning: *indeterminate* implies that the birds are uncertain how much food they would have if they didn't forage, but the sentence states that they know they would have a *certain* amount of food.

Why would foraging be a risk? Because the outcome is uncertain – the birds don't know *what they'll find*. (D) is thus the answer to Blank (ii), and (G) is the answer to Blank (iii).

6. C, E, J

The references to the craft guilds' *strength* and to *protected cartels* imply that the guilds had considerable leeway to impose restrictions on their members. Blank (i) must be filled with a word consistent with that idea. It does not make sense to say that the guilds *controlled* restrictions, and restrictions cannot be *appointed*. *Enforced* is a far better word to describe how the guilds used their restrictions to maintain power over their members. (C) is thus the answer to Blank (i).

Strong guilds (i.e. *cartels*) that enforced restrictions are ones that would protect themselves very strongly, so Blank (ii) must be filled with a word conveying that idea. *Flimsily* (weakly) and *erratically* (inconsistently) imply exactly the opposite, but *jealously* can be used colloquially to mean strong in the context of protection (literally, to protect something as if others were jealous of it). (E) is thus the answer to Blank (ii).

For Blank (iii), the fact that workers who *took their skills elsewhere* faced such severe punishment is key. This blank must be filled with a word referring to workers who violated their *fidelity* (faithfulness) to the glass-making guilds. *Exhorted* (pleaded with) does not fit this definition, nor does *conjectured* (hypothesized). Only *abrogated* (broke a contract) logically describes an action that would lead to serious punishment, making (J) the answer to Blank (iii).

7. A, D

Logically, Margulis's revolutionary theory must have been *met with almost unanimous skepticism* because it was based on weak ideas, or ideas that were no longer considered valid. The blank must therefore be filled with negative words meaning something like discarded or gotten rid of. *Substantiated* (proved) and *eulogized* (praised; EU-, happy) would imply exactly the opposite. *Circumvented* (gotten around) does not convey that the ideas Margulis's theory built on were no longer considered valid. *Stifled* could plausibly fit, although ideas that have this done to them are typically controversial or threatening in some way, and there is nothing in the sentence to support that interpretation. A more likely meaning is that the ideas were simply considered wrong. In any case, *stifled* lacks a close synonym among the other choices. *Discredited* and *rejected* both convey the logical idea that Margulis's colleagues initially refused to believe her theory because it was based on ideas that were no longer accepted.

8. B, F

The fact that John Muir *went further* than the nineteenth century thinkers who were inspired by nature, and that his *admiration bordered on* _____, suggests that the word in the blank is a more extreme form of *admiration* – something like *worship*. *Obsession* would make perfect sense, but unfortunately this word lacks a close synonym among the other choices. *Necessity* and *urgency* do not describe more extreme forms of admiration, and *trepidation* (fear, anxiety) does not make sense at all. That leaves *awe* and its synonym *reverence*, which correctly convey the idea that Muir admired nature to the point of being overwhelmed by it. [B] and [F] are thus correct.

9. C, E

If the Great White shark has *a disproportionately important role in managing the ocean's food chain*, and this species' population is already lower than what it should be, then it is reasonable to assume that the catching of even a single animal could have a very bad effect on the species as a whole. The blank should therefore be filled with a negative word consistent with the idea of a harmful effect. All of the choices are negative, however, so unfortunately there is no way to play positive/negative with this question. Start by eliminating the options that clearly do not make sense: *frustration* is not really a term that can be applied to sharks' feelings, and in any case, this word lacks a close synonym among the other choices. *Gridlock* typically refers to cars stuck during a traffic jam, although it can also be used to describe a political or legislative process that has come to a standstill. Either way, this word makes no sense here. *Toil* does not fit either – Great White sharks would have to work harder to obtain food if the species they preyed upon were disappearing, but their own disappearance would not have the same effect on the species <u>below</u> them in the food chain. *Distress* makes sense in context but lacks a close synonym among the other choices. That leaves *havoc* and *mayhem*, both of which refer to chaos and logically describe the result of a major disruption in the marine food chain. [C] and [E] are thus correct.

10. A, F

The information after the comma is key because it refers back to the blank and provides further information about it. The key word *rebellion* indicates that the blank must be filled with similar words. *Accusations* are not the same thing as outright rebellion, and *grievances* (complaints) and *maneuvers* do not quite fit the necessary definition either. *Struggle* would make sense in context, but this word does not have a close synonym among the other choices. *Insurrection* and *mutiny*, on the other hand, are direct synonyms that both refer to rebellion against authority – while they may involve struggle, these terms are closer to one another than *struggle* is to them. [A] and [F] are thus the best pair.

11. B, D

The fact that the author causes *conventional familiarity [to] dissolve* suggests that he is able to elevate overused subjects such as people's fears and desires to a level beyond cliché. The implication is that he must possess exceptional control over his narrative. As a result, the blank must be filled with positive words indicating that type of mastery. *Facile* (easy) has a connotation of superficiality, which does not fit in context. *Wry* implies that the author has a dryly humorous approach. There is nothing in the sentence to either support or contradict this meaning, but this word lacks a close synonym among the other choices and so cannot be correct. The same is true for *animated* (enthusiastic, energetic) and *cagey* (wary, cautious). That leave *adroit* and *deft*, both of which describe a high level of capability and are consistent with the idea of exceptional control. [B] and [D] are thus correct.

Set 15

1. Archaeologists unearthed many beautiful artifacts from the Roman villa during the twentieth century, but the process of _____ the structure had actually begun hundreds of years earlier.

(A) excavating
(B) withdrawing
(C) engulfing
(D) refurbishing
(E) obliterating

2. _____ at having received insufficient accolades for his contributions to the company, Tesla resigned from his job at Machine Works only six months after he arrived.

(A) Flustered
(B) Sheepish
(C) Coy
(D) Indignant
(E) Elated

3. Despite the astounding scientific advances of the past century, most of the universe remains (i) _____. Scientists estimate that around 95 percent of the cosmos is made up of substances such as dark energy, dark matter and dark radiation – things that we can only examine (ii) _____, through the forces they exert on our galaxies.

Blank (i)	Blank (ii)
(A) an outlier	(D) meticulously
(B) a conundrum	(E) indirectly
(C) a revelation	(F) occasionally

4. We often do not seem to know what we like or why we like what we do. Our preferences are (i) _____ unconscious biases and are easily swayed by social influences. Even experts are not infallible guides to their own (ii) _____.

Blank (i)	Blank (ii)
(A) immune to	(D) proclivities
(B) eliminated from	(E) anxieties
(C) riddled with	(F) curiosities

5. Just as Orwell wrote *1984* as (i) _____ rather than a prediction, Bradbury had a concerned eye on the present. *In Fahrenheit 451*, he envisaged an age when "firemen" would burn books because he was (ii) _____ contemporary censorship in America. His tales can be understood as cautionary, not (iii) _____.

Blank (i)	Blank (ii)	Blank (iii)
(A) a prognostication	(D) alarmed at	(G) clairvoyant
(B) an allegory	(E) consoled by	(H) satirical
(C) a caveat	(F) jubilant about	(J) euphemistic

6. It is easy to imagine our most cherished certainties appearing ridiculous to future generations, just as the cherished (i) _____ of our ancestors appear ridiculous to us. We should therefore strive to look upon our contemporary world as though it were the Victorian era, or the medieval period, or the Bronze Age — (ii) _____ the naïve confidence we place in our current version of reality and trying to detect how that version might be deeply and pervasively (iii) _____.

Blank (i)	Blank (ii)	Blank (iii)
(A) identities	(D) proffering	(G) profound
(B) convictions	(E) augmenting	(H) mistaken
(C) mysteries	(F) suspending	(J) timeless

7. Although there are numerous conflicting accounts of the pretzel's origin, culinary historians have reached _____, concluding that it was most likely invented by German monks.

   [A] a compromise
   [B] an agreement
   [C] an impasse
   [D] a decision
   [E] a consensus
   [F] an arrangement

8. In order to halt the demonstrations, which had already lasted for several weeks, government officials finally agreed to _____ a number of the protestors' demands.

   [A] turn against
   [B] cobble together
   [C] yield to
   [D] tamp down
   [E] pore over
   [F] comply with

9. Because migrant workers experience a variety of cultures and see the world from myriad cultural perspectives, they are often capable of identifying opportunities easily overlooked by their less _____ counterparts.

   [A] worldly
   [B] accomplished
   [C] astute
   [D] cosmopolitan
   [E] obstinate
   [F] condescending

10. Unlike some of its competitors, the automotive manufacturer has struggled to maintain its footing over the past several decades – a situation not helped by the company's erratic marketing strategy, which has left even long-time customers _____.

   [A] edified
   [B] contemptuous
   [C] nonplussed
   [D] flippant
   [E] disconcerted
   [F] vindictive

11. Many critics have disparaged the novels of Jody Picoult for being _____, apparently overlooking the fact that excessive sentimentality is precisely the quality that most appeals to many of Picoult's readers.

    [A] opaque
    [B] maudlin
    [C] vapid
    [D] mawkish
    [E] sanguine
    [F] interminable

Explanations: Set 15

1. A

The fact that *archaeologists* <u>*unearthed*</u> *many beautiful artifacts from the Roman villa* indicates that the sentence is discussing the process by which ancient ruins are dug up, and the blank must be filled with a word describing that process. The fact that individual artifacts were *unearthed* does not mean that the entire structure was *withdrawn* – besides, entire structures do not typically get removed. The sentence provides no indication that the villa itself was *engulfed* (flooded or taken over) by anything. Unearthing objects is not the same thing as *refurbishing* them, and archaeologists are not normally in the business of updating ancient homes. *Obliterating* (destroying completely) an ancient villa is certainly not something that archaeologists, or anyone who wanted to study the structure, would do. That leaves *excavating*, which refers to archaeologists' standard practice of digging up ancient structures in order to study their contents. (A) is thus correct.

2. D

Logically, Tesla would have resigned from his job because he was very upset at having received *insufficient accolades* (praise), so the blank must be filled with a negative word meaning something like angry. *Elated* (overjoyed) is extremely positive and can be eliminated. *Flustered* means unnerved or ruffled – it's negative, but not strong enough for this context. Someone who is *sheepish* feels embarrassed or foolish at having done something wrong, which is not at all the case here; and Tesla certainly did not resign because he was *coy* (shy). Failing to have his work recognized the way he wanted would, however, have made Tesla feel *indignant* – and it would make sense for someone who felt that he had been slighted, or that his dignity had been injured, to quit his job. (D) is thus correct.

3. B, E

The first sentence contrasts *astounding scientific advances* with Blank (i), implying that much of the universe is not yet well understood. It would only make sense to describe the universe as an *outlier* if it possessed characteristics that other universes lacked, but the sentence does not contain any type of comparison between universes. And if the universe is poorly understood, it hardly makes sense to describe it as a *revelation*. In contrast, a *conundrum* is a mystery, which logically describes a universe of which we cannot perceive 95%. (B) is thus the answer to Blank (i).

For Blank (ii), the fact that we can only examine dark energy, dark matter, and dark radiation *through the forces they exert on our galaxies* indicates that we cannot study these things directly – they can only be investigated through their secondary effects. In other words, these substances must be understood *indirectly*. (E) is thus the answer to Blank (ii).

4. C, D

Although the first sentence does not contain any blanks, it provides important information because it sets up a general scenario that is expanded on by the sentences that follow. What does it tell us? That people's preferences are mysterious even to people themselves. Given that context, the correct answer to Blank (i) must indicate that preferences are full of, or shaped by, *unconscious biases and are easily swayed by social influences* – factors that would explain why people's likings are so irrational. It does not make any sense to say that preferences are *eliminated from* or *immune to* unconscious biases. On the contrary, preferences are very much vulnerable to and influenced by these biases. *Riddled with* correctly implies that people's preferences are pervaded by prejudices and influenced by others' opinions, making (C) the answer to Blank (i).

For Blank (ii), the statement that *Even experts are not infallible guides to their own* _____ essentially means that people are not fully reliable judges of something. Given the passage's focus on preferences, this blank must be filled with a synonym for that word. *Anxieties* and *curiosities* do not refer to preferences, but *proclivities* does. (D) is thus the answer to Blank (ii).

5. C, D, G

The contradictor *rather than* indicates a contrast between *a prediction* and the word in the blank, eliminating *prognostication* (prediction). The reference to contemporary censorship provides an additional clue, suggesting that both Orwell and Bradbury were concerned with the present rather than the future. *Allegory* (story in which characters and events serve as symbols for ideas) is a word often associated with books, but it does not make sense in this context. A *caveat* (warning) is, however, something that would logically be made by an author worried about how current events might shape the future. (C) is thus the answer to Blank (i).

Blank (ii) must be filled with a word describing Bradbury's reaction to contemporary censorship. That's a negative thing, and the previous sentence has already alluded to the fact that Bradbury was concerned. The correct answer must therefore be a negative word consistent with the idea of concern. *Consoled* (soothed) is positive, and *jubilant* (rejoicing) is extremely positive, but *alarmed* conveys concern and describes an author's logical reaction to censorship. (D) is thus the answer to Blank (ii).

Blank (iii) is contrasted with *cautionary*, so the correct word must mean roughly the opposite. In addition, remember the context: the passage indicates that Bradbury's primary concern was *contemporary censorship*. Neither *satirical* nor *euphemistic* has anything to do with that idea; however, *clairvoyant* (able to see into the future) would logically describe a quality lacking in the novels of an author who was not literally attempting to predict the future. (G) is thus the answer to Blank (iii).

6. B, F, H

The first sentence sets up a parallel between how our ancestors' most cherished certainties appear to us, and how our most cherished _____ will appear to future generations. Logically, then, Blank (i) should be filled with a word similar to *certainties*. *Identities* and *mysteries* do not fit, but *convictions* is a synonym for certainties, making (B) the answer to Blank (i).

For Blanks (ii) and (iii), think about what the sentence is saying. Basically, we should try to observe our own time objectively, the same way we would view a historical period, in order to avoid falling prey to the idea that our own era has all the answers. Given that context, Blank (ii) should be filled with a negative word indicating a lack of confidence in current realities. *Proffering* and *augmenting* are both positive, but *suspending* confidence in current reality would allow people to view the present more objectively. (F) is thus the answer to Blank (ii).

Blank (iii) must be filled with a word describing what the current version of reality might be. Based on the previous information in the passage, we know that that version might be wrong, i.e. *mistaken*. *Profound* clearly does not fit, and *timeless* would imply that the present version of reality is true for all time – exactly the opposite of what the passage indicates. (H) is thus the answer to Blank (iii).

7. B, E

The contradictor *although* sets up a contrast between the *numerous conflicting accounts* and something that has been *reached* by historians. In addition, this factor has allowed historians to come to a conclusion about the pretzel's origins. Logically, the blank must be filled with words indicating the opposite of a conflict, i.e. *an agreement* or *a consensus*. There is nothing in the sentence to indicate that the historians' conclusion represented a *compromise*, and an *impasse* would imply that no conclusion was reached at all. *Decision* and *arrangement* might sound plausible, but neither of these words is the direct opposite of conflict in the way that *agreement* and *consensus* are; moreover, both words lack a close synonym among the other choices. [B] and [E] are thus correct.

8. C, F

If government officials wanted to <u>halt</u> *the demonstrations*, then it is reasonable to assume they sought to accommodate or listen to the protestors in some way. The blank must be filled with positive words consistent with that idea. *Turn against* and *tamp down* imply exactly the opposite – that the government officials sought to antagonize the protestors further. *Cobble together* does not make sense at all. *Pore over* does fit as something that government officials would do in order to better understand the protestors' position, but this phrase lacks a close synonym among the other choices. *Yield to* and *comply with* both convey that the government officials gave into the protestors' demands – a course of action that would logically cause the demonstrations to cease. [C] and [F] are thus correct.

9. A, D

Be careful with the negation in this sentence. The blank must be filled with words describing migrant workers' *counterparts*, who have <u>less</u> of a particular quality than migrant workers do. The sentence states earlier that migrant workers *experience a variety of cultures and see the world from myriad cultural perspectives*, so we can infer that they have a relatively sophisticated or nuanced understanding of how different cultures work. Based on the information in the sentence, we can also infer that their counterparts have a less sophisticated understanding of different cultures. As a result, the blank must be filled with positive words consistent with the idea of being well-traveled and understanding a variety of perspectives. *Obstinate* and *condescending* are negative and can thus be eliminated. *Accomplished* and *astute* (sharp, perceptive) are positive, but neither fits the required definition. Only *worldly* and *cosmopolitan* are synonyms that logically describe people who have lived in a variety of places and are comfortable with multiple perspectives. [A] and [D] are thus correct.

10. C, E

The sentence provides two key pieces of information: the automotive manufacturer has *struggled*, and its marketing strategy has been *erratic* (inconsistent). As a result, it is reasonable to assume that *even longtime customers* would be left with a negative attitude toward the company's marketing strategy. *Edified* (enlightened) is positive and can thus be eliminated. *Contemptuous* (strongly disdainful) and *vindictive* (out for revenge) are both very negative – perhaps a little too negative – but both of these words lack a close synonym among the other choices. *Flippant* (sarcastic, irreverent) does not make sense at all. The only pairs that fits is *nonplussed* and *disconcerted* (flustered, thrown off balance), which logically describes how even loyal customers would feel when presented with an incoherent marketing strategy. [C] and [E] are thus correct.

11. B, D

The statement that readers are drawn to Picoult's books because of their *excessive sentimentality* provides an important clue to the blank – it must be filled with words describing excessively sentimental books. *Opaque* (difficult to understand), *vapid* (trite, inane), *sanguine* (cheerful), and *interminable* (endless) all do not fit the required definition. Only *maudlin* and *mawkish* are synonyms that refer to excessive sentimentality, making [B] and [D] correct.

ABOUT THE AUTHOR

Erica Meltzer earned her B.A. from Wellesley College and spent more than a decade tutoring privately in Boston and New York City, as well as nationally and internationally via Skype. Her experience working with students from a wide range of educational backgrounds and virtually every score level, from the sixth percentile to the 99th, gave her unique insight into the types of stumbling blocks students often encounter when preparing for standardized reading and writing tests.

She was inspired to begin writing her own test-prep materials in 2007, after visiting a local bookstore in search of additional practice questions for a student. Unable to find material that replicated the contents of the exam with sufficient accuracy, she decided to write her own. What started as a handful of exercises jotted down on a piece of paper became the basis for her first book, *The Ultimate Guide to SAT® Grammar*, published in 2011. Since that time, she has authored guides for SAT reading and vocabulary, as well as verbal guides for the ACT®, GRE®, and GMAT®. Her books have sold more than 100,000 copies and are used around the world. She lives in New York City, and you can visit her online at www.thecriticalreader.com.

Made in the USA
Coppell, TX
28 January 2021